BEGINNING
WITH MY
STREETS

OTHER WORKS IN ENGLISH
BY CZESLAW MILOSZ

Bells in Winter
The Captive Mind
Collected Poems
Conversations with Czeslaw Milosz
(by Ewa Czarnecka and Aleksander Fiut)
Emperor of the Earth
Happy as a Dog's Tail: Poems by Anna Swir
The History of Polish Literature
The Issa Valley
The Land of Ulro
Native Realm
Nobel Lecture
Post-War Polish Poetry (anthology)
The Seizure of Power
The Separate Notebooks
Unattainable Earth
Visions from San Francisco Bay
With the Skin: Poems of Aleksander Wat
The Witness of Poetry

BEGINNING WITH MY STREETS

Baltic Reflections

Czeslaw Milosz

TRANSLATED BY
MADELINE G. LEVINE

I.B. TAURIS & CO. LTD
Publishers
London · New York

Published in 1992 by
I.B. Tauris & Co Ltd
45 Bloomsbury Square
London WC1A 2HY

Published by arrangement with Farrar, Straus & Giroux Inc.

A full CIP record for this book is available from the British Library.

ISBN 1-85043-602-9

Printed and bound in Great Britain by
WBC Ltd, Bridgend, South Wales

891. 85

TRANSLATOR'S NOTE

Two of the pieces in this collection have already been published in translation. They are "Dialogue about Wilno with Tomas Venclova," which first appeared in English in a translation by Maria Ostafin under the title "A Dialogue About Wilno: Czeslaw Milosz and Tomas Venclova" in *Cross Currents* 5 (1986): 143–72, and "Who is Gombrowicz?," in Lillian Vallee's translation, which was originally published in *Performing Arts Journal* 18 (vol. 4, no. 3, 1982) and has been reprinted as the introduction to Witold Gombrowicz, *Ferdydurke* (New York: Viking-Penguin, 1986). My own translations were completed independently and without reference to the previous English versions, but inevitably—either because the English choices were limited or because my memory is tenacious—they echo their predecessors in many instances.

I would like to thank Kathleen Ahern for her help in tracking down the published English versions of many of the works cited by Mr. Milosz.

Madeline G. Levine

CONTENTS

PREFACE

The word "geography" preserved till this century its aura of colorful atlases with the outlines of mysterious, little-known lands. As the planet grows small, fewer and fewer areas can lay claim to a bit of exoticism. I guess my vocation as a writer has consisted in behaving as a normal human being, even if my very place of birth had been enough, not so long ago, to mark me as a permanent stranger.

Thomas Jefferson, when writing a biography of his friend Brigadier General in the War of Independence Tadeusz Kościuszko, says he was born in the "Grand Duchy of Silliciania." Such a country has never existed, no more than the fabulous lands of Herodotus. Probably Jefferson just misspelled or illegibly wrote down the name of Lithuania. I myself, coming precisely from that Grand Duchy, have always had great difficulty in explaining the innumerable imbroglios resulting from the geography and history of that corner of Europe. Even for the Poles, though I write in Polish, I am somebody who comes from outside and whose tales deal with the unfamiliar. There are other spots testifying to the European puzzle; for instance, Transylvania, with its three languages, Hungarian, Rumanian, and German, or Finland, with Finnish and Swedish.

Perhaps one's country of origin is not so important in view of the progressing unification of the earth. After all, man is confronted everywhere with existential problems, and our bond of being born in the same time, thus being contemporaries, is already stronger than that of being born in the same country. An immigrant to America, I was confronted with a choice: either to leave behind what existed only in my memory and to find in what surrounded me material for my reflection or, without renouncing the present, to try to bring back the streets, landscapes, and people from my past. It seemed to me that my wealth consisted precisely in my knowledge of details, be they geographical or historical, that can be acquired only through a direct experience, not from books. Therefore, I chose the second solution, that of living simultaneously here and there, both in California and the city of Wilno, now Vilnius, of my childhood and youth, a city which only lately, with Lithuania's struggle for independence, has been made known to the Western world. And since I am primarily a poet, I have always believed I was a better writer in my mother tongue than in English or French acquired later, so I kept writing all my poems and the majority of my essays in Polish, not always even caring to translate them into other tongues. I do not regret my decision. To my surprise I have discovered that I can communicate with my American audiences through my poems in English translation and even that I have my rank among American poets. Also, some of my essays have found a favorable response from American literary critics.

This book is a selection of my essays taken mostly from my Polish-language volume of the same title. In a way, it may be considered a travel guide to a certain literary sensibility nourished by "another," less known Europe. As an introduction, I chose images of the streets in the old capital of the Grand Duchy of Lithuania. The dialogue that follows needs a few words of commentary. Tomas Venclova is an eminent poet of the Lithuanian language, once a dissident, now teaching at Yale. Not long ago we appeared together in the large hall at Jagiellonian University in Cracow, Poland, before some two thousand students, and spoke on the problem of nationalism as a possible obstacle to the harmonious coexistence of Poland and Lithuania, he taking a pro-Polish position; myself, a pro-Lithuanian one.

Another writer who figures in my book is Stanisław Vincenz, an émigré from Poland to France, author of sagas and tales about his native region in the Carpathian Mountains, where his family migrated in the seventeenth century from Provence, hence the name; Vincenz was also a scholar of Homer and Dante and a proponent of "Europe of fatherlands" (small provinces where one feels rooted, not states). My essay on the poetry of Aleksander Wat deals with the work of my late friend, whose poems I have translated into English (*With the Skin: Poems of Aleksander Wat*, translated by Czeslaw Milosz and Leonard Nathan, The Ecco Press, 1989) and with whom I tape-recorded his autobiography, *My Century: The Odyssey of a Polish Intellectual* (edited and translated by Richard Lourie, University of California Press, 1988, and Norton Paperbacks, 1990). Then I examine Witold Gombrowicz, who, it is true, has more devotees in France and Germany than in America; he is a major Polish writer of the last decades and his *Diary* (published in English by North-western University Press in Lillian Vallee's translation) is considered a classic.

My devotion to the Polish language and Polish letters has not excluded my interest in the Russian language, which I learned early in life, and in some Russian writers. As a matter of fact, I used to teach courses on Dostoevsky at Berkeley. I even scored a "first" in a domain overexplored by Dostoevsky scholars: I discovered borrowings from Swedenborg's *Heaven and Hell* in *Crime and Punishment*, and I include a dialogue on that subject. My years in California are also responsible for my meditation on its great poet, unjustly downgraded for a long time, Robinson Jeffers.

Playing with various themes on the border of literature, theology, and philosophy, I once took pleasure in putting together a small collection of miscellany, which I entitled *The Garden of Knowledge*. Essays from it trace my readings of many authors who belong to the common heritage of the Western world, including some little read today, like Thomas Traherne. Quotations from these writers serve as a springboard for remarks on the art of translation, time, reality, a classification of sins, and happiness. An interview rarely unveils the thought of the person interviewed, but as Rachel Berghash succeeded in achieving this through her questions, I decided our conversation should complete the chapter of miscellany.

Next, two persons are invoked not because of their literary merits but because of their gift of friendship. Together with another dear friend to whom I have not been able to pay the tribute he deserves, Constantin Jelenski, they were the main characters in *my* Paris, the first city of my exile and of my subsequent frequent visits. Zygmunt Hertz's biography is at the same time a brief survey of Polish fates during World War II and after. The partition of Poland between Hitler and Stalin in 1939 led to an exodus of many persons from the Nazi-occupied to the Soviet-occupied zone. Arrested there and deported to a gulag, Zygmunt Hertz managed to join the Polish army which was to be evacuated from the Soviet Union to the Middle East, soldiered in Italy, then settled in Paris, where he took part in an extraordinary publishing venture, *Kultura*, an émigré monthly published without interruption from 1947 until the present, and rightly honored now in Poland as a monumental achievement. A close friend of both his and mine, Józef Sadzik, did not correspond in any way to the image of the stiff Roman Catholic priest unfortunately so common among both religious and non-religious people. Openminded, generous, warm, he had his own little non-territorial

bohemian parish of artists, who were not asked about their denom-
ination and simply loved him. I owe my Polish translations of the
Bible primarily to his prompting and readiness to help.

My speech before the Swedish Academy ends the book, because
I say in it, I hope, something essential. In 1980, nobody expected a
strange turn of events at the end of the same decade and I am glad
my words have been vindicated. I have never been a political writer,
except during moments when to keep silent about certain things
would mean to assume an air of false innocence.

C.M.

Part 1

BEGINNING WITH MY STREETS

DICTIONARY OF WILNO STREETS

Why should that city, defenseless and pure as the wedding necklace of a forgotten tribe, keep offering itself to me?

Like blue and red-brown seeds beaded in Tuzigoot in the copper desert seven centuries ago.

Where ocher rubbed into stone still waits for the brow and cheekbone it would adorn, though for all that time there has been no one.

What evil in me, what pity, has made me deserve this offering?

It stands before me, ready, not even the smoke from one chimney is lacking, not one echo, when I step across the rivers that separate us.

Perhaps Anna and Dora Drużyno have called to me, three hundred miles inside Arizona, because except for me no one else knows that they ever lived.

They trot before me on Embankment Street, two gently born parakeets from Samogitia, and at night they unravel for me their spinster tresses of gray hair.

Here there is no earlier and no later; the seasons of the year and of the day are simultaneous.

At dawn shit-wagons leave town in long rows, and municipal employees at the gate collect the turnpike toll in leather bags.

Rattling their wheels, Courier and Speedy move against the current to Werki, and an oarsman shot down over England skiffs past, spread-eagled by his oars.

At St. Peter and Paul's the angels lower their thick eyelids in a smile over a nun who has indecent thoughts.

Bearded, in a wig, Mrs. Sora Klok sits at the counter, instructing her twelve shopgirls.

And all of German Street tosses into the air unfurled bolts of fabric, preparing itself for death and the conquest of Jerusalem.

Black and princely, an underground river knocks at cellars of the cathedral under the tomb of St. Casimir the Young and under the half-charred oak logs in the hearth.

Carrying her servant's-basket on her shoulder, Barbara, dressed in mourning, returns from the Lithuanian Mass at St. Nicholas to the Romers' house on Bakszta Street.

How it glitters! the snow on Three Crosses Hill and Bekiesz Hill, not to be melted by the breath of these brief lives.

And what do I know now, when I turn into Arsenal Street and open my eyes once more on a useless end of the world?

I was running, as the silks rustled, through room after room without stopping, for I believed in the existence of a last door.

But the shape of lips and an apple and a flower pinned to a dress were all that one was permitted to know and take away.

The Earth, neither compassionate nor evil, neither beautiful nor atrocious, persisted, innocent, open to pain and desire.

And the gift was useless, if, later on, in the flarings of distant nights, there was not less bitterness but more.

If I cannot so exhaust my life and their life that the bygone crying is transformed, at last, into a harmony.

Like a Noble Jan Dęboróg *in Straszun's secondhand bookshop, I am put to rest forever between two familiar names.*

The castle tower above the leafy tumulus grows small and there is still a hardly audible—is it Mozart's Requiem?*—music.*

In the immobile light I move my lips and perhaps I am even glad not to find the desired word. *

* "City Without a Name," Part 12. Translated by the author, Robert Hass, Robert Pinsky, and Renata Gorczynski.

ANTOKOL

First one passed the dock. Iron barriers along the sidewalk polished to a shine by the touch of hands; you could lean against them, or sit and watch. If I am to speak now about what one could see there, I should first explain that I am there simultaneously as a small boy and an adolescent and a young man, so that many years of watching are concentrated in a single moment. So, what one saw first of all was a boat preparing for departure or, rather, the public boarding by means of a gangplank, the pressing of fingers into ears as the whistle sounds once and then again, the untying of the ropes with Józiuk shouting at Antuk and Antuk at Józiuk; or, a boat approaching, still far away when the shimmering of its wheels is first discerned. The boats were named *Courier*, possibly *Express* (although I am not sure about that); later on there was a third one, *Speedy*, a wonderful boat with a real deck. A lot depended on which one you happened to take during school outings to Werki. They went upstream, to Werki and even farther, to Niemenczyn—never downstream. There was also a dock for the small boats painted with stripes of many colors along their sides, from the slightly elevated prow to the stern. The ferryman would seat five or six people and cross over to the other shore, to the Pióromont district, using a long oar, also painted, punting, unless the water, in spring or late autumn, was high. One also watched the "flats" floating by, long trains of floating timber, mainly pine, with a hut and a fire on the last raft, which also had an enormously long and heavy steering oar. The sawmills where the "flats" tied up, so that sometimes the Wilia would be completely covered by them, were somewhat farther downstream, past the Green Bridge, across from St. Jacob's.

I also knew larger boats—they were on the Niemen, not the Wilia—from my visits to Kaunas. Almost like illustrations in travel books, they had decks loaded with crates and barrels; sometimes there were cows and horses, too. They went to distant places, as far as Jurbork. To tell the truth, the one I used to take was not large, because it went up the Niemen for only part of its route, to the mouth of the Niewiaża, and then it sailed up the Niewiaża to the town of Bobty. The Niewiaża is quite deep but very narrow and tortuous; it is navigable to that point, but not farther upstream. For some reason, I thought of the local boats as something official, like the post office, and I was surprised that their crews spoke among themselves in exactly the same sort of Polish as the crews of the *Speedy* and the *Courier*.

One always walked past the dock on the way to Antokol; that is why I'm speaking of it now. Then the bridge or, rather, the bridge across the Wilenka where it flows into the Wilia. Antokol itself is, first of all, the boredom of a long, only partly built-up street, a muscular memory in the legs, about a space "in between": between the Wilia on the left and the hills on the right. Only the slopes of Castle Hill, in the angle formed by the Wilia and the Wilenka, were luxuriantly green, with the foliage of a deciduous forest. Three Crosses Hill and the other hills were sandy inclines sparsely dotted with pines. We often went climbing there, for the view and the solitude, but basically it was too windswept a place, and the somewhat more distant, hilly Antokol, beyond St. Peter and Paul's, was more interesting. I knew the Baroque statues of that church from photographs, and even from the postage stamps of Central Lithuania, but when I toured the interior I was disenchanted: a host of details obscured by whitewash, details so minuscule that they could be seen only with a magnifying glass. Beyond the church, deeply rutted, sandy roads wound through the forest; they had street names: Sunshine, Springtime, Forest, etc., with a few wooden houses concealed in the thickets, more like dachas than villas. In one of them lived Leopold Pac-Pomarnacki, my schoolmate and partner in my naturalist's passions: a phlegmatic elderly gentleman with a protruding belly, fourteen years of age. I was in awe of his collections of rare ornithological books and stuffed birds. An only child, the son of rather elderly parents, I think, he had his very own shotguns. An expedition with him to the country, to visit Nowicki, another schoolmate, whose face I remember but not his first name, remains in my memory as something exceptionally enigmatic, a tormenting darkness from which I am able to retrieve only one or another fragment that immediately disappears. It took place on All Souls' Day, somewhere on the southern boundary of the Rudnicka Wilderness, because it seems we got off the train at Stasiły, beyond Jaszuny. Frozen earth, sunsets and sunrises that mixed reds and blues, hoarfrost, a hamlet, fried bliny at dawn, conversations in Belorussian, hunting, and staying by ourselves in a house that was, I think, the residuary part of an estate. There were four of us, one a girl, a student at a Wilno *gymnasium* or technical school—her black eyes, pallor, throaty laugh (but I have no image of her face)—and although Pac and I were complete outsiders here, Nowicki and she kept getting into ominous erotic brawls that excluded me, a mere puppy, from their partnership. During that same school year, in early spring, she was found dead in Zakret, in the German military cemetery—it was suicide, poison or a revolver, but not connected with Nowicki.

Next to St. Peter and Paul's there were also some trails leading up to the ski slopes. An absolutely undeveloped highland, called Antokol Grove and Altaria on the city maps, extended all the way to the outskirts of Zarzecze and Belmont; the runs were mostly short and headlong. I skied like a cow, but for a brief period at the beginning of my university career and my ardent participation in the Vagabonds' Club, I did so stubbornly. It was the period of my friendship with Robespierre, who used to ski wearing a red flannel shirt, so for me the snow of the Antokol hills is fused with that shirt in a single image. But I remember the outskirts of Antokol, where the city ended and the highway to Niemenczyn began, because that is where as a child I observed the panic of the 1920 retreat.

Nevertheless, Antokol remains for me not so much streets which one walks on as a shore along which one sails: just beyond the bridge on the Wilenka were the rowing clubs, among them the AZS [Academic Sport Union], from whose landing we would push off in a kayak or canoe. The Wilia is a swift river and though we paddled energetically against the current, we could only glide quite slowly along the Antokol shore. Across from the AZS, on the opposite shore of the Wilia, was Pronaszko's Mickiewicz, a gigantic Cubist bloated figure, exiled there by the town fathers, who were probably right not to want to place it in the center of town among the old stones. There, too, all of a sudden, was the first sandy beach: Tuskulany. We were drawn to more distant places, so I was at that beach only once, while I was still a high-school student playing hooky. It happens that, for no obvious reason, particular hours in my life have been preserved with absolute clarity about their details, so I can see the naked people lying there beside me. One of them is a future electrical engineer and officer in the Royal Air Force: Staś. Many years later (it is painful to count them), in 1967, the two of us camped on the shores of big Eagle Lake in the California Sierras, and when we headed straight from our tent to the water the moment we woke up, or went kayaking along its wild forested shores, we didn't look the way we did in Tuskulany; yet it was difficult for me to grasp how our bodies had changed—only perhaps that his wedge-shaped, Russian tsar's beard had begun to turn gray.

In the names of the settlements along the Wilia one could discover amalgams of familiar and foreign words. Tuskulany, I assume, was named by enlightened readers of Latin literature, who perceived similarities between this region and Tusculum, the country retreat of wealthy Romans. Wołokumpie is less refined. Trynopol, actually only a white church on a bluff, a sign to oarsmen that they can relax because the most treacherous currents are behind them, makes one think of Trinitas and thus has a derivation similar to that of nearby Kalwaria. Charming forested Werki reminds one of German Werk, but according to legend the name is derived from crying eagle chicks—in Lithuanian, *verkti* means to cry.

The Wilia alongside Antokol and all the way to Werki was our city's *freeway*, a word I learned much later, substituting it for the dubiously Polish word *autostrada*. Although I would prefer to say *gościniec*—highroad. So, a highroad, down which the Wilno population would travel on a Sunday outing—the native population that had been living there for generations, which was neither gentry nor working-class but rather petit bourgeois and thus employed for the most part as artisans. On passenger ships or in small boats, in family groups: shirts, suspenders, taking turns at the oars, the women's colorful dresses, and a jar of pickles for a snack. Another popular amusement was the sauna. At the end of the week one could hear all sorts of idiosyncrasies of "local" speech there, which would have been a treasure for linguists, although I doubt that linguists ever frequent public saunas.

Upstream from Werki, and almost never frequented by people on excursions, the Wilia remained virtually untouched by "civilization." I have preserved it in my memory from the point where the Żejmiana emptied into it. Absolute silence, only the splashing of water against the hull, in the sunshine the brilliant whiteness of the steep sandy bluffs with holes drilled into them by cliff swallows, the dangling roots of the pines. Occasionally, a long string of floating log rafts with smoke rising from a stove. There is a particular majesty in the slow turning of these "flats" along the bend of a river. A steering oar in front, a steering oar in back, often plied by two people, a man and a woman, the long train of rafts gliding slowly into a new current. Occasionally a fishing boat would flash by in the other direction, toward the bank; sometimes there would be a naked lad in a kayak, who was probably spending his school vacation somewhere nearby, unaware of the devilish traps that History had already set for him.

In the summer the Wilia across from Antokol became shallow; sometimes it was possible to wander downstream for a couple of kilometers, swimming some of the time, but mostly touching the bottom. I associate the Wilia with Antokol because the sawmills beyond the Green Bridge signaled its end as a highroad. Farther on, the river headed for the closed Lithuanian border; besides which, it probably wasn't navigable, considering that in at least one spot it had whirlpools and rapids that were difficult to negotiate. The city's sewage, especially from the hospital in Zwierzyniec, made one loathe to swim in the river near Zwierzyniec and also near the opposite shore, by the Zakret forest. Excursions downriver exposed one to an arduous return trip against the current and therefore were rarely organized. We took the train to the settlements of the Students' Union in Legaciszki, which were right on the Lithuanian border.

ARSENAL STREET

This is a short street, stretching from the corner of Embankment Street, just beside the boat dock, to Cathedral Square. In the olden days, it seems, it was simply the continuation of Antokol Street, its extension. A handful of houses along a single sidewalk; in place of a second sidewalk, the iron curves of a low palisade enclosing a garden (at the rear of the cathedral) that was called the Calf Pen. The corner of Embankment Street was occupied by a large, rather ugly building, the Tyszkiewicz Palace, which was always locked; later on, I learned that it housed the Wróblewski Library; its function derived from the fact that it existed and I never asked myself why. A few years before the war it was taken over to house the Institute for the Study of Eastern Europe and then I often had occasion to go to this building. On the other hand, from the time I was in the lowest *gymnasium* classes I paid regular visits to the house in the middle of Arsenal Street, at number 6, because my relatives lived there, distant relatives, to be sure: the Pawlikowskis. The blood tie was with her, Cesia Pawlikowska, *née* Sławińska, I think; she insisted that I call her aunt. The man of the house, Przemysław Pawlikowski, was an ex-colonel of the tsarist army; on the walls hung photographs from Bessarabia, where they had lived for a long time and apparently once owned an estate. Tall, swarthy, lean, taciturn, he walked about in a patterned bathrobe, sat on the balcony staring at the green of the garden, or played patience. He also worked on his stamp albums, which tantalized me, because of course I was caught up in this mania, and he would give me rare specimens as a gift. Of their two sons, I have no recollection of the first, Danek, who committed suicide as a young man; the second, an engineer, went to Soviet Turkestan after the war to work there as a specialist (a "spets"), returned with a Russian wife, bought a car, and became one of the first taxi drivers in Wilno, an avant-garde profession—for who ever heard of a well-born man taking tips from a guest? His Russian wife wore Oriental *sharovary* at home and smoked cigarettes in a long cigarette holder. Wacek's sister, Marysia, worked in an office, and so that peaceful family collective (they all lived together) could serve as an illustration of the sociological changes that were taking place at the time. I met Marysia when I was a very young boy, because she stayed with my grandparents for a while in Szetejnie, in Kaunas Lithuania, and it was she who read *With Fire and Sword* to me on the oilcloth couch near the window in the dining room, where you had to curl up in a hollow and guard the spot you had warmed up, not letting your bare feet protrude onto the cold oilcloth beside you. Marysia, as I think the old folks told me, was somewhat "mannered"; for me, she was simply mysterious, introspective, pensive, swaying at the hips, tall; she wore a black velvet ribbon around her white neck. She belonged to the generation that came to maturity on the threshold of the First World War, which is why there were volumes of poetry and literary journals from that period in the house on Arsenal Street. If I had not examined the contents of those shelves, I would never have known, for example, that an almanac, *Żórawce*, was published in 1914 or 1915, filled with poetry and prose of late-period Young Poland. In general, my relatives, who were already grown-up young ladies, affected me somewhat erotically in my childhood, furnished me with an insight into an epoch that I could not remember; their style of living itself had preserved something from it. Today it strikes me as laughable to call those times, which then were only ten years in the past, another "epoch," for if those who were familiar with it seemed to me to have emerged from murky darkness, probably a general law was at work: for every generation the events, styles, and fashions that are just barely in the past are extremely distant. However, it is impossible to determine if that is always so and if, for example, the 1950s are another geological era for the young people today. Certainly, the First World War and the independence of Poland were a watershed for Marysia and her generation, but not as significant a one as I thought them to be.

Marysia lived an office life, which meant not only work but also friendships, picnics with colleagues, even office excursions abroad. During those years when I used to visit them, first as a *gymnasium* student, then as a university student, she was beginning to age and I would think about how it is that women become old maids. At 6 Arsenal Street I felt at home, and because it would have been hard to find a more central location in the city, sometimes I dropped in there simply to stretch out on the sofa. I wrote a couple of poems there that I like to this day. Also, I spent my last night in Wilno in that apartment, before my journey, which was more risky than I wanted to admit to myself, to Warsaw across the green border in 1940. This was shortly after the occupation of the city by Soviet troops, which was barely noticed by the family, because Uncle Pawlikowski was dying and their main worry was buying bottles of oxygen.

The Institute for the Study of Eastern Europe, housed in the rebuilt or added-on part of the large corner building, was modernity, lots of light, brightly painted walls, furniture made from light-colored woods. Usually I would wait patiently while Dorek Bujnicki attended to the students at his little window, after which we showed each other our poems and dreamed up literary pranks. There was a Lithuanian who also used to hang around there—Pranas Ancewicz. We were close friends and there was a time when we saw each other every day, because we both lived in the Student House on Bouffałowa Hill. Now that I've mentioned his name, I cannot refrain from remarking that I know of very few people who have been slandered the way that wise and good man was. And no one knows better than I that it was all bare-faced lies.

The Institute is for me the period just before my departure for Paris and immediately after my return, 1934 and 1935, a period of dramas and intoxications, also of travels. Perhaps, aside from strictly personal causes, one might detect in this some sort of short-lived opening up in the whole country, between the chaos of the economic crisis and the gathering darkness of the end of the thirties, a soaring, along with, to be sure, a presentiment of the approaching terror. I received a literary fellowship to Paris. Nika, a woman I had met in the Institute and had become friendly with, went to Moscow on a fellowship. The first book of poems by Boris Pasternak that I read, *Vtoroe rozhdenie* [*Second Birth*], was a gift from her. Just about that time Pasternak traveled abroad for the last time, to Paris, to the Congress in Defense of Culture, but he was in a tenuous position and was no longer being published.

The entrance to the Calf Pen was directly across from Arsenal Street. I had all sorts of experiences along the boulevard that led to Royal Street, but there are no sentimental memories associated with this garden. Open to passersby like a public square, it was not considered a congenial place for conversation or for holding hands, because the sight of all the nannies and the soldiers crowded together on its benches cast something of a pall on the splendid repetitiveness of such occupations. Probably my most detailed memories of the garden's recesses are from my childhood, from daytime games, when it was still neglected and practically empty.

BAKSZTA STREET

Never in my Wilno years did I stop to consider why this street bore this name. The word was vaguely associated with *baszta*, or tower, which is correct. Bakszta was a very old, dark, narrow street, with horrible ruts in the roadway, no wider than two or three meters in some spots, and with deep open gutters. As a child I was rather afraid to venture into it because it had a bad reputation: right after you turned onto Bakszta from Grand Street you passed a multistory building with white-painted windows—the hospital for venereal diseases. At the upper windows sat whores who were there for a compulsory cure, mocking the passersby and screaming ugly words. It is not because it was so widespread that prostitution in Wilno is worth paying attention to; this oldest of human professions shows no signs of disappearing anywhere, it just changes its form. In Wilno, prostitution maintained completely nineteenth-century forms or, rather, nineteenth-century-Russian forms, just as in Dostoevsky's novels. That is, the drinking bouts of officers and students in exclusively masculine company would end with trips "to the girls," to the numerous little brothels whose addresses were known by every cabby. On certain streets (especially those below Bakszta on the Wilenka River, such as Łotoczki Street, Safjaniki, etc.) creatures of the female sex would stand in front of the gates for hours, adapting to the rigors of the climate, so that in winter they wrapped themselves up in woolen scarves, wore thick felt boots or tall leather boots, and stamped their feet in the snow to keep warm. The reservoir for this working force, just as for servant girls, was the countryside or the wooden outskirts of the city, which were not too different from the village.

But, more than anything, Bakszta was Barbara. Here and there, especially from the direction of the hillsides and bluffs near the Wilenka, a pedestrian looking in through the gates would see large courtyards and gardens; one of these sprawling estates was the Romer House. If I am not mistaken, my first journey from Niewiaża to Wilno ended there, because we used horses, and the Romers' courtyard, outfitted with a stable and a carriage house, made a good stopping place. The journey was a long one, 120 kilometers, and its significance is not in the least diminished by the fact that later I learned to drive that same distance by car in an hour. That is why we stopped at the Romers'; I don't know what social ties there were between us. In any event, later, throughout my entire stay at the *gymnasium*, the Romer House was managed by Barbara, a major domo and a housekeeper. Barbara came from my part of the country, even somewhat deeper into Samogitia, from the environs of Krakinów, and she had once served as my grandfather's senior housekeeper; we preserved a certain intimacy on the basis of these ties, and Barbara frequently visited us on Foothills Street. Tall, erect, severe, thin-lipped, she looked like so many of those numerous dark-haired and dark-eyed Lithuanians. An old maid, a pious woman, and a fanatical Lithuanian—the older people in our household used to make fun of these traits of hers, but gently. In all of Wilno only one church, St. Nicholas's, held Lithuanian Masses (that is, sermons and singing in that language) and naturally Barbara went to Mass only at St. Nicholas's. Anyway, most of the faithful there were servants. I used to smile when, many years later, I would listen to my Viennese-Parisian friends' stories about Czech towns under the Habsburg monarchy. Naturally, German was spoken there, and Czech was considered the language of the household servants. I knew that only too well, except that in our eastern region Polish took the place of German.

From what I am saying about Barbara it is not easy to make any inferences about the strength of my emotional attachment. However, her image has accompanied me on my wanderings across a couple of continents. There must be a reason for someone surviving this firmly in our imagination. I remember Barbara's "lodgings" in Szetejnie, which were as severe as she was, and this undoubtedly long-dead person has remained for me one of the most important figures from my early childhood.

Since it was so close to the university, almost directly across from the corner of Grand and St. John's Streets, Bakszta played an important role in the students' lives, because that is where the Mensa was located. Not a dining room, not a cheap restaurant, not a cafeteria, not a canteen, not "a place of collective eating," but precisely: a *Mensa*. It was one of the Students' Union's chief undertakings; the free or reduced-priced dinner coupons served as a stake in the political struggles for power. A rather dingy, dark building, it apparently housed the seminarists' dormitory at one time; for many years it was the only dormitory in Wilno—before the second one, very modern, was built on Bouffałowa Hill. I never lived on Bakszta, but every now and then I ventured into its corridors, with their blackened and well-worn wooden floors, in order to visit my classmates. The smell of lye, naphtha, soapsuds, tobacco. A similar corridor, on the ground floor, led to the Mensa. I have only a hazy recollection of its tables, covered with stained tablecloths (or was it oilcloth?), but I can see very clearly the small cashier's table at the entrance where one bought tickets for individual dishes. Almost always they were sold by a little gnome with a withered face, wearing a fantastic floppy black bow instead of a tie: Gasiulis.* An "eternal student," an already legendary personality, because he was active in student organizations in prehistoric times, perhaps even in 1922 or 1923. In the Vagabonds' Club he was respected as an elder, as one of the founders; it was from his era that certain songs dated, quite obviously inspired by Kipling's *Jungle Book*, which was idolized at that time. ("On a high hill the baboons were dancing their wild dance.") Today I think that Gasiulis, like all the members of the Vagabonds' Club, was very much a *hippie*. Our wide black berets with colorful tassels made fun of the generally accepted head coverings. On the other hand, his black ascot came straight out of the bohemia of Young Poland, as did the cape of the popular city scoutmaster: skinny, sadfaced Puciata. Despite his pure Lithuanian surname, I don't think that Gasiulis knew Lithuanian. At one time he had wandered through various distant regions; perhaps he had even lived for a while in Cracow or Poznań—I could never find this out because the difference in generations precluded familiarity with such a celebrated, even if somewhat comic, figure.

FOUNDRY STREET

Foundry Street means walking downhill. Many a time, innumerable times, over the course of many years, because I usually lived in the newest part of the city, beyond Zawalna and Wileńska Streets, and it was Foundry Street that led from there to Napoleon Square and beyond, to the university or to bustling Grand Street. A triumphal descent, the ecstasy of physical exertion, the happiness of long, almost dancing steps, or absolute despair, or else, probably most often, that spiritual state when the young organism rejoices in its own way, despite the delusions of its tormented imagination. The descent began at the building on the corner of Wileńska, where the meeting

---

* Executed by the Soviet authorities for tearing down official posters.

halls of the Professional Unions and other similar institutions were located. A colorful array of notices was posted there, announcing lectures and boxing matches; fans of these performances, mainly young Jews, used to gather in groups on the sidewalk. A little farther down, on the right, but not as far as the corner of Tatar Street, were a couple of apartment houses with balconies that meant nothing to me until the moment when I began to spend my spring evenings on one of them with Stanisław Stomma, abandoning myself to intellectual disputes accompanied by rosy sunsets. It was 1929, I was a student in the eighth class at the *gymnasium*; Stomma, I think, was a second-year student in the law faculty and also an older brother in our lodge—the conspiratorial group "Pet." "Lodge" is an exaggeration, but I cannot think of our group or of the Vagabonds' Club, which I joined shortly afterward, other than as the peculiar creations of Wilno, the city of Freemasonry. Just as during the period of Wilno University's preeminence, prior to 1830, when many of our city's luminaries belonged to the Masonic lodges and rumors about this circulated freely, although I found out how numerous were the Masons among us only many years later. Unfortunately, the right-wing press erred in ascribing to Masonry a decisive influence on the course of historical events.

So, with Stomma on a balcony above a ravine of a street that descended toward tree-lined squares. We argued about Petrażycki, into whose theory of law and morality Stomma was being initiated by a young professor, a fanatic Petrażyckyist, a certain Lande. Having heard about Petrażycki, I, in turn, began reading some of his writings. We also argued about Henri de Massis's book, which was quite popular then—*La défense de l'Occident*. At the time I was devoting myself wholeheartedly to studying French in order to read French authors in the original. It was probably Stomma from whom I borrowed the Massis, and still, over thirty years later, in California, I appreciate his lending me that book. This does not mean that I was ever, then or now, attracted to the French nationalists, the heirs of the monarchy. One must admit, however, that they were the first to sound the alarm, alerting people to the presence of ergot, the black discoloration that had begun to contaminate thought and language. According to them, this disease would arise in Asia and spread to the European mentality through the intermediary of Germany in particular; after 1918, through Weimar Germany—Schopenhauerism, Hinduism, Buddhism, Spengler, Keyserling, etc. Massis and other defenders of the Cartesian trenches were unable to ward off the growing opaqueness of the French language under the influence of German philosophy, which, by the way, was not necessarily an import from the Orient. Who knows, perhaps my distaste for the "wisdom of the East" that is sweeping California can be explained by the fact that I read those early warnings when I was seventeen years old.

Past the corner of Tatar Street, on the right, there was the open space of a plaza; on the left, some small shops, unremembered, and a restaurant or cafeteria that opened during the second half of my time at the university, where one got good-tasting dinners for 60 groszy. The owner was a Warsaw Jew, the clientele was made up of students, but for the most part they were not the same students whom one saw in the Mensa. Here I met my Jewish classmates from the law faculty, who came mainly from Warsaw; Lithuanians and Belorussians also gathered here. I do not know why my memory has preserved only a few faces and names. One of them: my colleague Lerner.

A few more steps took one past the Church of the Bonifraters (the Brothers of the Order of St. John the Divine). It was the lowest church in Wilno, and the church itself, plus the monastery buildings, which were also low, formed a kind of miniature fortress on a small square that was full of trees—lindens, I think. The Brothers ran some sort of charitable enterprise; at one time, they had an institution for the mentally ill, which is why if someone talked nonsense, we would say that he was fit for the Brothers. The church had two little towers, but in keeping with the nature of the whole building, they were mere curves, just two breasts on the building. The interior was like a crypt or grotto decorated in Baroque style, with a small spring-fed well more or less in the center of its elongated rectangular space. Miraculous healing properties were ascribed to the water from this spring; although its fame did not extend even to other parts of the city, its reputation continued to be useful within the parish. What was special about the Church of the Bonifraters was the way it gave one a sense of security, of the homeliness of divine-human affairs, of an impregnable shelter from the world. Later—after Poland—I had occasion to visit Eastern Orthodox churches, which are like little chests made of gold, or cells of beeswax, where the warm radiance of the walls, the smell of incense, and the liturgical songs have a hypnotic effect. No doubt this fulfills a human need for an enclosed, delineated space, subject to its own laws and fenced off from that other, limitless space. That was why I loved the Brothers; particularly at Easter, when people visited the "tombs," it would not do to pass by that church. If in the other churches Christ's tomb, displayed with more or less ingenuity, vanished beneath the high vaulted ceilings, was diminished in comparison with the altar and the columns, in the Church of the Brothers of the Order of St. John the Divine it was the central place, because everything there was practically on the same level as the floor. I almost forgot to add that Foundry Street turned into the Street of the Bonifraters near that small square.

GERMAN STREET

Narrow and not too long, German Street was the most cosmopolitan of Wilno's streets, because the street that was supposed to be the main street was definitely not cosmopolitan. It was officially named St. George Boulevard at first, then Mickiewicz Boulevard; less officially, it was known as St. George Street, or Georgie for short. This thoroughfare, laid out with a straight edge and bordered by rows of apartment houses from the second half of the nineteenth century, did not elevate Wilno any higher than a provincial town, a Rennes or an Elizavetgrad, as I imagine it, where there must also have been a "boulevard" for the officers' and students' *gulianie*.* By contrast, German Street's cosmopolitan aspect was not diminished by its cobblestone roadway, which was repaved with bricks (as were all the important streets) only in the 1930s. As one approached German Street one left the underpopulated area behind and penetrated into a region of sudden density. Sidewalks, gates, doors, windows all sprouted multitudes of faces and seemed to bulge from the crowds. It seemed that on German Street every house concealed an infinite number of inhabitants who engaged in every possible trade. Beneath enormous painted signs, shop after shop fronted on the street, but the faces of lions, the pictures of stockings of monstrous proportions, of gloves and corsets, also advertised shops inside the courtyards, while the signs inside the gates gave information about dentists, seamstresses, hosiers, pleaters, shoemakers, and so forth. Trade also overflowed from the buildings into the roadway; it seethed around the pushcarts and the stalls erected at intervals in recesses along the sidewalks. Loaded carts, pulled by straining horses, thundered past. Touts circulated among the passersby; their job was to spot potential customers, praise their goods, and conduct those people they had managed to corral to a shop that often was located somewhere in a distant inner courtyard. I am positive that I never connected German

* *Gulianie*—Russian: rowdy "strolling," carousing.

Street with the illustrations in my French school texts that depicted nineteenth-century Paris; I arrived at that comparison slowly, only when I was already a resident of France. In the second half of our century, when it no longer exists, I have often thought about German Street, particularly when I wander about in the Marais district, staring at the signboards, especially since several of them practically beg to be remembered. For example, the one from the rue de Turenne on which to this day Monsieur Szatan recommends his tailoring establishment for men's suits.

German Street was exclusively Jewish, but it was significantly different from Warsaw's Nalewki, for example. More old-fashioned, more settled, it acted as the representative of a whole labyrinth of twisting, astonishingly narrow medieval alleys, and I never felt that hidden background in Warsaw. With its stones that bore the patina of time, Wilno's cosmopolitan fragments were probably closer to Paris than to Warsaw.

I visited German Street at various stages of my life, above all as a little boy accompanying Grandmother Milosz. We were living in an apartment house at 5 Foothills Street, so we would walk down Foothills to the corner of Sierakowski Street, then along Port Street to Wileńska. Sierakowski Street demands a digression. At that time one could still see veterans of the 1863 Uprising; they wore uniforms and cornered hats, which were navy blue with a raspberry-colored rim. They received a modest pension, and even the widows of these veterans were not excluded, although of course it only amounted to pennies. Grandmother Milosz also received such a pension. The street named after Sierakowski led to the Łukiszki district, to the square where the leader of the Uprising in Lithuania was hanged. My grandfather fought under Sierakowski in 1863, as his adjutant or officer for special commissions, I am not absolutely certain. In any event, he was a close collaborator and was saved, because in Serbiny, his family estate near Wędziagoła (north of Kaunas), he had as neighbors a village of Old Believers who liked him very much. The elders gathered and debated for an entire night over a by no means trivial problem: does a Christian have the right to swear a false oath in order to save a life? And they swore under oath that he had never left home throughout 1863.

From Foothills, across Sierakowski, then down Port Street to Wileńska and German Streets—always to Sora Kłok's store. The store was in the courtyard, but it didn't need signs or touts; it was famous in the city and had a faithful clientele. It was well known that buttons, linings, wadding, and similar items such as no other shop carried could always be found there. I was fascinated by Mrs. Sora Kłok herself—hideously ugly, fat, a faded redhead in a wig, with her goiter and her obviously shaved chin. She only commanded the troop of salesgirls; she was very imperious. From her store came the so-called tailor's supplements for my suits, which were either continually made over or sewn from homespun to leave room for growing. Shall I reveal the secret of habits I acquired in childhood? To this day a conditioned reflex takes over whenever I buy a suit: I'd better get it one size larger, because what if I should outgrow it?

After my boyhood years there is a big gap in my relations with German Street; I passed by there from time to time, and that's all. Only toward the end of my stay at the university did I begin to establish contact with it, attending guest performances of a Yiddish theater or visiting the little restaurants on its side streets with Pranas Ancewicz. The taste of chilled vodka and marvelous herring, but also the sensation of human warmth, dimly preserved in memory, guaranteed that I would always like Jewish restaurants. The jumble of side streets near German Street is worth mentioning, too, because that is where I sought out a rabbi in order to fulfill a certain errand. Namely, in 1933 or 1934 Oscar Milosz sent me three copies of his little book from Paris; he had published it privately in a very small number of copies. Considering its contents, it is not at all surprising that he did not intend this work for sale. *L'Apocalypse de St. Jean déchiffrée*—the book I'm talking about—prophesied catastrophes of cosmic dimensions that were supposed to strike humanity around the year 1944. It is possible, after all, that there were two pamphlets, not one—the other essay (either bound together with the first or separate) proposed the hypothesis that the most ancient fatherland of the Jews was located on the Iberian peninsula; and only there, and nowhere else, should one look for the biblical Eden. From this work, *Les origines ibériques du peuple juif*, it appeared that the Jews are, most likely, the oldest autochthonous people of Europe. So, one copy was for me, and the others I was supposed to give to the (in my opinion) two most appropriate individuals—one a Christian and the other a Jew, if possible one of the "illustrious rabbis." I selected Professor Marian Zdziechowski, because his pessimism about the future of Europe seemed to make him relatively open to gloomy prophecies. But I did not know Zdziechowski personally. As luck would have it, I approached him, stammering and blushing, on the steps of the university library, without having been properly introduced, and met with such an unresponsive welcome that it seems I didn't hand him the copy. Who the most famous rabbi

was and on what grounds I selected him, I do not recall. I gave the copy to his secretary. I shall never know if it was read and if the author's intention—to issue a warning—was fulfilled.

L'Apocalypse de St. Jean déchiffrée is a bibliophilic rarity, and my next adventure connected with this text took place many years after the death of Oscar Milosz, in 1952, in the vicinity of the rue Vaugirard, where I was living at the time. I had run into Henry Miller in a small restaurant; I was astounded when I heard that he had been searching for this text for a long time. I promised to get him a copy, which wasn't at all difficult, since the Collection Doucet collects Milosziana. I did not keep my promise and Miller excoriated me for that. Why didn't I keep it? It simply slipped my mind, but I suspect that the causes must have gone deeper than that and Miller rightly saw in it a reason to take offense. In my conversation with him I found his California catastrophism terribly distasteful: that's all we need, as if we don't have enough problems coping with the heritage of our European catastrophism. I detected intellectual chaos in what he said, and in his greediness for apocalyptic texts I saw a lust for sensationalism. So it cannot be ruled out that my resistance had a sacral character to it: I did not consider Miller to be one of the chosen to whom Oscar Milosz had once wanted to issue his warning.

WILEŃSKA

A street with a strange name, not homogeneous, changing form every dozen or so steps, ecumenical to boot, Catholic-Jewish. At its beginning (or end) at the Green Bridge, it was wide, lacking a distinctive consistency, for there were no more than a couple of apartment houses at the outlets of the various side streets; it constricted into a narrow throat beyond the intersection with St. George (or Mickiewicz) Boulevard. When I was a child, the foundations of an unfinished building sat there for a long time, until at last a huge edifice was erected, a department store owned by the Jabłkowski brothers, the first more or less "universal" store in Wilno, several stories high.

Not far from the Jabłkowskis', across from the Helios movie theater, was an amazing haberdashery, the likes of which I never saw anywhere else in the city. Its owners were not Jews but Poles from somewhere far away in Galicia, distinguished from ordinary people by their speech and their exaggerated politeness. The family: two women and a man, a family triangle, it seems. The man smelled of eau de cologne, his slightly curled hair was parted and combed smooth, his hands were white and puffy. They said, "I kiss your hand." And the shop did not remind one at all of what was normally meant by a "shop"; the gleaming parquet floor was polished so that there wasn't a speck of dust on it; the goods were in glass cases.

Next door to this shop was a small bookstore, where every year on the first of September I experienced strong emotions, jostling against the other pupils and buying my new schoolbooks. Without a doubt, one of the most powerful experiences is to only look and touch for a moment, without knowing what is hidden under the colorful dust jackets.

Across the street, as I said before, was the Helios movie theater, remembered along with various films seen there, among them Pudovkin's *Storm Over Asia*, which made a powerful impression on me. But this theater also has remained in my memory as a symbol that evokes a vague feeling of disgust and shame that has been pushed away to a level deeper than consciousness. Among Witold's many unsuccessful careers (before he died of tuberculosis at age thirty-six)—his service in the Borderland Defense Corps, for example, his participation in a Jewish fur-trading cooperative, etc.—there was also an attempt at founding a cabaret review. The premiere took place in the hall of the Helios, and I, a fourteen-year-old boy at the time, was unable to defend myself with rational judgment against the bawdy vulgarity of this show; hence the shame—because of Witold, who, like it or not, belonged to the family, and also because of my parents, who even laughed—remained undiminished, spreading like a greasy stain.

On the same side of the street, right behind the movie theater, Rutski's bookstore was to serve as a kind of counterweight much later on. The son of the dignified, dour Mr. Rutski was my colleague at the university and was married to Sitka Danecka; my relations with Sitka, before then, testify optimistically to the diversity of human relationships and the freedom from Form that is possible every now and then. We used to go on kayaking trips together, and we felt so comfortable with each other that we forgot about the difference in our sex. We were not, however, just "colleagues"; we were linked by a much warmer mutual heartfelt caring. Nonetheless, no Form compelled us into erotic intimacies; friendship was more precious.

Beyond Halpern's shop (I think that was his name), where there was dust, semi-darkness, a wealth of dyes, pencils, paper in many colors, notebooks, Wileńska Street, now even narrower, turned into a street of Christian harness makers, cobblers, tailors; there was even a Turkish bakery. From it, or perhaps from another, came my Gymnasium colleague Czebi-Ogły, who was a Muslim. Next, the façades of the buildings became subdivided into a multitude of little Jewish shops, and after a momentary rise in dignity across from the little square near the Church of St. Catherine (there was a beautiful old store there that carried hunting guns), Wileńska was dominated by impoverished trade all the way to the intersection of Trocka, Dominican, and German Streets.

From a courtyard on Wileńska, in its "artisan" section, one entered a lending library to which Grandmother Milosz had a subscription paid for out of her modest pension. I often turned up there, either delegated by her or to borrow books for myself, when I was twelve, thirteen. Mostly Zeromski, Rodziewiczówna, Szpyrkówna, that is to say, bad literature, and it seems to me that a tolerable intelligence in someone who received such training should not be underrated, with a few points added for the obstacles that he must have had to overcome. In all languages, *belles lettres* are predominantly kitsch and melodrama; however, the accidents of Polish history decreed that fiction had an exceptionally powerful effect on people's minds, as a language and as a sensibility, so that I suspect there is in the so-called Polish soul an exceptionally rich underpinning of kitsch. As for me—let's be frank: in the books that I borrowed from the library I was enchanted by such scenes as the death of the beautiful Helen in *Ashes*, who threw herself into a ravine, and perhaps even more so by the ending of a certain story that was translated from the French about the Chouans, or the counter-revolutionaries in the Vendée. The hero's head is sliced off on the guillotine, but that does not put an end to his highly emotional adventures. To this day I can remember the last sentence: "But his head, still rolling, whispered, · 'Amelie!' "

Berkeley, 1967

DIALOGUE ABOUT WILNO
WITH TOMAS VENCLOVA

Dear Tomas,

Two poets, one Lithuanian, the other Polish, grew to maturity in the same city. That should be reason enough for them to talk about their city, even to do so publicly. True, the city that I knew belonged to Poland and was called Wilno; my high school and the university used Polish. Your city was the capital of the Lithuanian SSR and was called Vilnius; you went through school and the university in a different epoch, after the Second World War. Nonetheless, it is the same city: its architecture, the landscape of the surrounding region, and its sky shaped us both. One cannot rule out certain, shall we say, telluric influences. Besides which, I suspect that cities have their own spirit or aura, and at times, as I walked the streets of Wilno, I seemed to have an almost sensual awareness of that aura.

Recently, one of my friends asked me why I return so insistently in my memories to Wilno and to Lithuania, as my poems and prose writings reveal. I replied that, in my opinion, this has nothing to do with an émigré's sentimentality, for I would not want to go back. What is at work here, no doubt, is a search for reality purified by the passage of time, as in Proust. But there is also another explanation. Wilno was where I passed my boyhood, thinking that my life would develop along quite ordinary lines; it was only later that everything in that life began to turn upside down. So Wilno became a reference mark for me—of possibility, the possibility of normalcy. But Wilno was also where I read the Polish Romantics and already had a hazy intimation of my own future abnormal fate, although in those days the wildest imagination could not have served up images of my individual, or the historic, future.

At this point, I would like to introduce a character who has no relation to Wilno even though he is important for all Europeans who come "from over there"—that is, from the borderlands of languages, religions, and cultures. Stanisław Vincenz came from the Czarnohora range of the Carpathian Mountains; his family settled there after emigrating from Provence in the seventeenth century. I met him in France, near Grenoble, in 1951, when my Wilno no longer existed. As an émigré, he was drawn to mountains; it was as if the Vincenz family's wanderings had come full circle. I was receptive to his teachings. Because, in addition to the written work he left, Vincenz was an itinerant sage, a talker, a teacher, virtually a *tzaddik* for people of various nationalities. He was opposed to the twentieth century although (or precisely because) in Vienna, before the First World War, he had written a doctoral dissertation on Hegel. For Vincenz, the most important thing was what Simone Weil called *enracinement*, and that is impossible without a fatherland. But a fatherland-state is too large, and when Vincenz dreamed of a "Europe of fatherlands" he had in mind small territorial units like his beloved Country of the Hutzuls, inhabited by Ukrainians, Jews, and Poles—a region made famous by the fact that it was where Baal Shem-Tov, the founder of Hasidism, once lived. At that time, when we held our first conversations, I was profoundly depressed; Vincenz helped me to rediscover the meaning of the word *fatherland*. Were it not for those conversations, I might not have written *The Issa Valley* several years later as a kind of self-therapy. And just as Vincenz remained rooted in his Carpathians throughout his life, I—or, at any rate, my imagination—have remained faithful to Lithuania.

I return to our peculiar city. Perhaps we will manage to discover some continuity despite the changes. We should probably also consider the university where we both studied, which is now celebrating its four hundredth anniversary. This is also a good opportunity to express our views on Polish-Lithuanian relations—bluntly, without diplomatic evasions.

Wilno cannot be excluded from the history of Polish culture, if only because of Mickiewicz, the Philomaths, Słowacki, and Piłsudski. I have often thought about a certain similarity between the Wilno of my youth and the Wilno of more than a century earlier, which, by the grace of Tsar Alexander I, had the best university in the empire. In those days it was a city of Freemasons; in fact, the crushing of the Philomaths coincides with Alexander's attack on Freemasonry throughout the empire. The Philomaths were connected with the Masons through Kontrym, the university librarian. I was aware of Masonic lodges in my own, newer Wilno, and the secret organization Pet, to which I was admitted as a high-school student, also had its own ties; politically, it was opposed to Endecja. I happened to meet my former professor—Stanisław Świaniewicz, one of our youngest law professors—not too long ago. He told me there were many Masonic lodges and that almost every professor belonged to one or another of them. The extent of Wilno's Masonic connections as he described it (he is an absolutely truthful man) astounded me. Whether or not some permanent inclinations of Wilno can be detected in this, I do not know. In any event, as early as high school I found my way into something like a "lodge"; I use this word not in its literal meaning, but only to designate the conspiracies of an elite to which one had to be admitted. And that elite was contemptuous of "right-thinking" people, of the entire mix: Polish nationalism, Sienkiewicz, the student fraternities with their special caps, etc. The Academic Vagabonds' Club, which I joined as soon as I matriculated at the university, was also that sort of a "lodge," as was also (somewhat later, during the great if short-lived swelling of the leftist wave in the early 1930s) the I.C., or Intellectuals' Club, a sort of cell that coordinated and planned activities and also organized discussions in the offices of the Union of Lawyers (actually, law students). I see in those "lodges" a legacy of Romanticism: the dream of mankind's salvation "from above" by those who "know better."

And what about the right, the champions of the slogan "God and Fatherland," of "one hundred percent Polishness"? The majority of Polish speakers belonged to the right. Linguistically, the old Wilno, the one from the time of the Philomaths, must have been more Polish than my Wilno; but I don't know if the surrounding countryside was Polish, as in my time, or Belorussian. Or perhaps the Lithuanian language (as we know, it was gradually displaced by Belorussian in that area) came closer to Wilno at that time. In the city itself, the nineteenth century, the century of Russian domination, left its mark; that is why I say that the old Wilno may well have been more Polish. After all, almost half the population of my Wilno were Jews, and a significant portion of them either adopted Russian or were responsive toward that language. That's why in my Wilno there were Russian *gymnasia* side by side with Polish *gymnasia*. There was also one Hebrew *gymnasium*, if I am not mistaken, and some Yiddish schools. (As you no doubt know, there was one Belorussian *gymnasium* and one Lithuanian, named after Witold the Great.) The Russian schools drew the children of the Jewish intelligentsia, who were devoted to Russian culture; after all, there were not many Russians in Wilno, just a few who had remained from tsarist times, plus a handful of émigrés. There were also some other Russian residues: the ugly architecture, peculiar to Russian garrison towns, that contrasted so sharply with the narrow lanes of old Wilno. The main street used to be called St. George's Boulevard, and when I was a schoolboy it was still called "Georgie" in colloquial speech. "Georgie" was a promenade, the place where officers and students went to stroll. Later on, people gradually became accustomed to its new name: Mickiewicz Street.

Wilno's specific characteristics become apparent when we compare it with other cities. The Psalmist calls Jerusalem a city "that is compact together," and to a certain extent this applies to Wilno, too, in stark contrast with cities built, like Warsaw, on a plain. Wilno's compactness reminds one of Cracow, but the layout of the two cities is different; after all, Wilno does not have a marketplace as the city center. I have a rather hazy childhood memory of Dorpat (or Tartu); perhaps I am wrong to think it shares some features with Wilno. And I have felt more "Wilno-ish" in Prague than in Warsaw. However, historic Wilno was destroyed by fire so many times that perhaps it is its location alone, at the confluence of two rivers and surrounded by hills, that lends the city its "compactness."

I had a very strong sense of Wilno as a provincial town, not a capital. And had all that territory, ethnically Lithuanian and Belorussian, been Polonized, it would have remained a provincial town. Consider France. The lands to the south of the Loire were not French. The people there spoke Oc, but after their subjugation in the thirteenth century under the pretext of a crusade against the Albigenses, they were gradually Frenchified. In the nineteenth century the entire countryside still spoke a patois, or Oc, but when I was in the Lot district several years ago I discovered that only people in the villages who were more than forty years old knew the language. During the war it was the language of the *maquis*—very useful, because city people (the French, in other words) could not understand it. Let us be brutally frank: if Poland had not lost its historic wager, it would have Polonized all the territory up to the Dnieper River, just as France spread its language all the way to the Mediterranean Sea. (After all, Dante once intended to write *The Divine Comedy* in the language of the poets; that is, in Oc!) And Wilno would have been a regional center like Carcassonne. But let us not get into historical "what ifs." In the twentieth century the Polish nationalists' program for the ethnically non-Polish lands was stupid, because Wilno and Lwów were enclaves, after all. I think that today it must be hard for young people to understand this characteristic of prewar Wilno as an enclave: neither Poland nor non-Poland, neither Lithuania nor non-Lithuania, neither a provincial town nor a capital, although it was more of a provincial town than anything else. And obviously Wilno, as I see it from a distance, was eccentric, a city of crazily commingled strata that overlapped each other, like Trieste or Chernowitz.

Growing up there was not the same as growing up in an ethnically homogeneous area; our sense of language as such was different. There was no folk idiom, either urban or rural, that was rooted specifically in Polish; the spoken language was "hereabouts"—a funny language that was probably closer to the spirit of Belorussian than Polish, although, to be sure, it did preserve many expressions that were common in sixteenth- and seventeenth-century Polish but had become obsolete in Poland proper. The boundary between "hereabouts" and the speech of the gentry (what Mickiewicz heard in his childhood and later, with his inner ear, in Paris) was fluid, of course, just like the boundary between the speech of the petty nobility and the manor, or the intelligentsia who were descended from the manor. But all this was really alien to the Polish peasant dialects. "Hereabouts" was the language of the Wilno proletariat; it was not at all like the speech of the common people in Warsaw, where, it seems, a certain peasant substratum was preserved. For me, a poet like Miron Białoszewski, for example, is exotic; I don't have those linguistic sources. I dare say our language was more sensitive to correctness and also to rhythmic expressiveness, which explains the fact that the clear Polish of the eighteenth-century poets, such as Krasicki or Trembecki, was perceived as "ours." It is difficult to analyze this. As for me, I would say that my language was influenced by my resistance to the lure of the East Slavic languages, above all to Russian, and by my search for a register in which I could compete with the East Slavic elements—at least in the area of rhythmic modulation. I do not know how resistance to Russian influences your Lithuanian. I do know that for me, as for everyone else whose ear is sensitive to Russian, surrendering to the strong beat of the Russian iamb is detrimental; the mainstream of Polish does not flow in that direction.

Wilno's provincialism. I found it very depressing and I yearned to break away into the world. So I shouldn't create a myth of a beloved, lost city, because I couldn't bear living there any longer, and when the Wojewoda, Bociański, demanded that Polish Radio in Wilno fire me as a politically suspect person, I accepted my resulting forced departure to Warsaw with relief. Because Wilno was a backwater: an incredibly narrow base, if you exclude the Jews who spoke and read Yiddish or Russian, and the people who were "hereabouts" and read nothing. What was left? A small intelligentsia of gentry origin who were, for the most part, fairly obtuse. This ties in with the question of nationality. Had we considered ourselves Lithuanians, Wilno would have been our capital and our center. A very difficult problem, as you know. A Finnish solution would have been logical. I am not familiar with the details; I don't know how the Swedish-speaking Finns worked this out, but it seems that Helsinki was their center, not Stockholm. In principle, we should have considered ourselves Polish-speaking Lithuanians and continued Mickiewicz's "Lithuania, my fatherland" in the new conditions, which would have meant creating a Polish-language Lithuanian literature parallel to a Lithuanian literature written in Lithuanian. But no one wanted that—neither the Lithuanians, who were bristlingly defensive toward Polish culture because it was "denationalizing," nor all those Polish-speakers, who thought of themselves simply as Poles and had contempt for the so-called Klausiuks—a nation of peasants. Individuals who thought otherwise were few and far between, although they were interesting, valuable, and energetic. In my Wilno, they were the so-called Localists, who dreamed of maintaining the traditions of the Grand Duchy of Lithuania as the only possible counterweight against Russia—that is, a federation of the nations that had once been part of the Grand Duchy. These circles coincided more or less with Wilno's Masonic circles. The history of this singular ideology should be written someday, but when I say it is interesting, even fascinating, I say it now, *ex post*, because as a young man filled with avant-garde yearnings and preoccupied with modern poetry, with French intellectual movements, etc., I paid precious little attention to what was right there in front of me. Anyway, it was an already defeated movement, the last echoes. It could not count on even a hint of sympathy from the Lithuanian side, because it presented itself as a continuation of the "Jagiellonian idea." Undoubtedly, in many of these descendants of yeomen, a dream of domination lurked behind the sentimental attachment to the idea of the Grand Duchy. Nonetheless, Ludwik Abramowicz and a couple of the other Localists were thoughtful people, sincerely opposed to Polish nationalism. They were the inheritors of a tradition of expansive thinking, the equals of the enlightened people of the old eighteenth-century republic. I don't think there was an equivalent grouping on the Lithuanian side; there, it seems, everything was the new nationalism, necessarily hypersensitive. One way or another, alone among the Polish-speaking inhabitants of Wilno, the Localists thought of

Wilno as a *capital*, not as a province. What I think now is that anyone who has this city's well-being at heart has to want it to be a capital, which automatically excludes any Polish claims to a "Polish Wilno."

Here I have to raise the problem of national treason. As you know, when feelings have been hurt it is easy to make such an accusation, and you have certainly experienced that yourself. The Localist idea was open to the accusation of "treason" from both sides, from Polish and from Lithuanian nationalists. A great many things came back to me when Adam Ważyk and I were in Montreal in 1967 at the *Rencontre Mondiale de Poésie* and found ourselves among the intellectual circles of Quebec, with their French fanaticism. And also several years later, when I participated in a poetry conference in Rotterdam at which I met many Flemish-speaking Belgians. They preferred to speak English instead of French; in fact, they knew English better than French. Before the war, during the year I spent in Paris as a student, my visits with Oscar Milosz in the Lithuanian legation smelled a little like "treason." To Poles, he was a "traitor," and I was able to observe how such enmity is transmitted, almost like an electric current, without any words. In such circumstances the collective has its mysterious ways of understanding each other. But Oscar Milosz's letters to Christian Gauss, which I discovered in the library of Princeton University and published in Paris in a separate volume, supply an answer to the question of how and why he declared himself a Lithuanian. When he took that step, in 1918, he knew nothing about the Lithuanian national movement; he was simply furious that the Poles did not want to recognize Lithuania's independence (he was probably referring to the nationalistic Poles who were followers of Dmowski and were diplomatically active during the Peace Conference). Subsequently, he worked for the Lithuanian cause in the international arena. Today, from a distance, one can see that his position on the question of Wilno was correct. Nevertheless, even though the Lithuanians respected him, they still treated him with suspicion, because he spoke Polish, not Lithuanian. In fact, he spoke French—which is why he could choose. If I were to declare myself a Lithuanian, what kind of Lithuanian would I be, since I write in Polish? This lack of trust was the reason for his voluntarily relinquishing a diplomatic career and settling for the modest post of counselor in the legation. Notice what long memories the Poles have—that's the other side of the equation. Not long ago, when Artur Międzyrzecki translated Oscar Milosz's novel *L'Amoureuse initiation* in Poland and began writing about Oscar's work, a letter to the editor was printed in *The Universal Weekly* in which the writer reminded everyone that Oscar Milosz had nothing in common with Polishness because he had renounced it.

In the Lithuanian émigré press there have been attacks on me for being a Pole, not a Lithuanian, even though I am a relative of Oscar Milosz. On the other hand, among Poles I have often run into the suspicion that there is something not quite right about my Polishness. And I must confess that there is a grain of truth in this, although as a child, in Russia, I used to declaim: "Who are you? A little Pole. What is your sign? The white eagle." In Russia, and in relation to Russians in general, I have always felt one hundred percent Polish, but that's easy. It's another thing entirely to come into contact with native ethnics, with Poles "from the Kingdom." My relations with Poland were painful, no less and perhaps even more so than were Gombrowicz's, but it would be an exaggeration to see in this a yearning for Lithuania when what was really decisive was my individual fate, my avoidance of total attachment to any human community— in other words, my own hump, my own deformity. But one must also see in this a conflict with the prewar Polish intelligentsia, for my mentality was much more international and cosmopolitan.

It is quite difficult to reconstruct all this today. Various influences were at work on me even in my school years, among them my reading of literary periodicals that were not so much journals of the Polish intelligentsia as of the Polish-Jewish intelligentsia; I am speaking of the periodicals published in Warsaw, such as *Wiadomości Literackie* (*The Literary News*). Perhaps that was the source of my early rebellion against Sienkiewicz and the Polish soul made manifest as *anima naturaliter endeciana*. Then, in my college years, there was the influence of Oscar Milosz, in whose political texts, which were published posthumously, you can find a very sober evaluation of the situation. In 1927 he wrote that Poland had reason to surround herself, through close alliances, with a bloc made up of the Baltic states, Finland, and Czechoslovakia, in order to create a counterweight against German pressures, but that in order to do this Poland would have to renounce her *messianisme national outrecuidant et chimérique*, which she would not be able to do, with the result that in about ten years there would be a catastrophe.

I must tell you about one more influence, and this will be a rather lengthy story. You are not my first Lithuanian friend. As a matter of fact, during my college years I was greatly influenced by a Lithuanian friend who was not from Wilno but, as people said then, from "Kowno Lithuania." How had he wound up among us? As you know, there were no diplomatic relations between Poland and Lithuania during my university years, from 1929 to 1934; the border was closed and both states kept playing tricks on each other: Poland by giving financial support to "Polishness" in Lithuania, and Lithuania by doing the same for "Lithuanianness" in the Wilno area. I met him in 1929 in a pro-seminar on the philosophy of law that was conducted by Assistant Professor Ms. Ejnik. Suddenly a strapping fellow with a mop of flaxen hair and wearing horn-rimmed glasses began to speak; it seemed as if he was trying to speak Polish but it was really Russian mixed with German. His name was Pranas Ancevičius, or Franciszek Ancewicz in Polish. This is his very sad story. He came from a poor peasant family; he had been admitted to the *gymnasium*, fell in love with Russian revolutionary literature (Gorky and others), and became a revolutionary. He took part in Plečkaitis's failed socialist coup in 1926 and had to flee Lithuania. He escaped to Vienna, where he lived in a workers' housing project named after Karl Marx and was helped by socialists. In general, Pranas, or Draugas, as I called him, would remain a radical socialist in the style of Viennese Marxism all his life, and therein lay his tragedy. For he was without a doubt a man who yearned for political activity but was fated to be an émigré. In Wilno, he was a marked man as far as the local Lithuanians were concerned, because they were loyal to the Kaunas government and that government considered him a political criminal. The Communist Lithuanians, on the other hand, nursed a special hatred for him, because he got under their skin with his knowledge of the way things were in the Soviet Union and for his habit of voicing his opinion without any constraints; so they employed their customary method of defamation, calling him a Polish agent, a provocateur, etc. They spread rumors that he had been bought, that he was in someone's pay; after all, where was the money for his studies coming from? But I lived on the same floor as Draugas in the Student House on Bouffałowa Hill, and I knew that his modest means (and Wilno was an unusually inexpensive city) came from America, from the, I assume, anti-clerical (he was a fanatical atheist) and left-wing Lithuanian press for which he wrote. When the money order was delayed, Draugas lived on credit. I was also witness to his lengthy, profound depressions, because his enormous talents were coupled with deep neuroses. My conversations with Pranas—note that they took place during my formative years—explain why it was that when I moved to Warsaw I knew ten times more about Communism than all my literary colleagues taken together, for Pranas followed everything that was happening on the other side of the eastern border. Obviously, my own perspective on Poland and on innately parochial, nationalist Polishness had to be different as a consequence of my training.

I don't want to exaggerate my political awakening. I was unsuited for any political commitment or action, for which I reproached myself, but I was never able to subdue my individualism and submit to organizational discipline. Pranas was the president of the ZNMS (the Union of Independent Socialist Youth) at the university, but I didn't join that organization; in other words, his friendship was one thing, but his revolutionary faith quite another.

Pranas received his doctorate in jurisprudence and began teaching at the Institute for the Study of Eastern Europe. This is as good an occasion as any to bring up a question that today seems quite mysterious: the inconsistency of Polish policy toward the Lithuanians, Belorussians, and Ukrainians. The fact of the matter is that, just as in America, various forces collided with each other in Poland, although in the thirties the right wing grew stronger every year, as did its program of "Polonization," which ranged from political means to the brutal cruel pacification of Ukrainian villages. In Wilno, Wojewoda Bociański was in charge of harassing the Lithuanians; this was already after Piłsudski's death. But at the same time the Institute for the Study of Eastern Europe came into existence; it was founded by entirely different forces which, to be sure, were already being pushed out by a fascistically insistent militant nationalism. Those forces could be described as liberal, with ties to Freemasonry, and loyal to Piłsudski's federalist dreams. They were not necessarily socialist or Masonic—for example, Świaniewicz was in the institute, as were many other professors from Stefan Batory University, and he was an ardent Catholic all his life. At one point the Wojewodship's administration began forcibly deporting Lithuanians, simply shoving them across the border into Lithuania; they also wanted to deport Pranas, but of course in Kaunas they would have thrown him in jail. It was the Institute people who protected him. Founding the Institute was a splendid idea; it might be different elsewhere, but in Poland people should have studied their neighbors, at least those people who were preparing for administrative and diplomatic service. Many years before that branch of learning developed in America, the Institute taught what is now called "Sovietology"; that is, there were courses in the economics, geography, and politics of the Soviet Union, and also the history and languages of our region: Lithuanian, Latvian, Estonian, Belorussian. It was characteristic that when Henryk Dembiński and Stefan Jędrychowski, ex-members of our *Żagary* group, were denounced in Wilno as Communists, and also somewhat later when they were defendants in a trial, the administrators of the Institute had no qualms about hiring them. The Institute's secretary was my colleague, the poet Teodor Bujnicki; Stanisław Baczyński (father of the future poet Krzysztof Baczyński) commuted from Warsaw to lecture there; he was very left-wing, rather typical of a certain mentality: a Piłsudskiite, a Legionnaire, a participant in the uprising in Silesia; a member of the Polish intelligentsia who went off to fight for an independent Poland in the name of its radical ideas. It seems to me that Pranas Ancevičius and Baczyński were particularly drawn to each other, and that it was Baczyński who convinced Pranas to move to Warsaw, away from the local administration's intimidation, and also helped him get a job (I no longer remember in which research institute or library). That happened just before the outbreak of war.

For me, during my student years, Wilno was whatever bordered Cathedral Square: on one side, the university; on the other, Rudnicki's café at the corner of Mickiewicz Street, and, next door to it, the Institute for the Study of Eastern Europe. There was a greater sense of continuity at our university than at other Polish universities, except for the Jagiellonian in Cracow. The period when it was shut down after the 1831 Uprising had somehow contracted, disappeared, and one lived within the aura of the Philomaths. Growing up in Wilno meant belonging to the twentieth century only to a limited extent, mainly via the cinema. Nowadays, I sometimes confuse the Academic Vagabonds' Club, particularly the Club of Senior Vagabonds, with the Society of 1820s, to which the young Mickiewicz's professors belonged. Even the Zealous Lithuanian lodge was still active, I believe, in my student years.

In comparison with Wilno, Warsaw was an ugly city, its central neighborhoods and a number of its outlying districts ulcerated by poverty (the Jewish poverty of cottage industries and small shops or the Polish, proletarian poverty). It couldn't begin to compare with civilized cities, such as beautiful Prague, but Warsaw was, nevertheless, the twentieth century. New arrivals from Warsaw, such as K. I. Gałczyński, saw Wilno as total exotica. But I was horrified by Warsaw. I spent a year studying law at Warsaw University and it was a bad experience. I failed my exams (with professors who couldn't begin to compare with my Wilno professors) and went back to Wilno.

To this day I am unable to answer the question: Why did I waste so many years studying law? Here is what happened: I began in

Polish language and literature, fled two weeks later, and from the moment I enrolled in law a stupid (Lithuanian?) obstinacy, the shame of abandoning what I had begun, forced me to suffer through until I received my diploma. Law offered a broad education at that time, like anthropology or sociology in America today; people who weren't sure what they wanted to do enrolled in law. The humanities demanded that you tell yourself: "Oh well, I'm going to be a schoolteacher." In one's youth one has such lofty, indefinite dreams; it's hard to be realistic and choose a modest career as schoolteacher. Were I making that choice today, knowing what I know now, I would choose neither Polonistics nor philosophy (I attended lectures and seminars in philosophy) but classical philology, and I would also study Hebrew and the Bible. It's just that at that time Latin and Greek were a traditional prescribed program, primarily the poets of antiquity. But I found the Greek tragedies, for example, which I had read in professional translations, incredibly boring. I had had my fill of Virgil in school. So philology as a whole meant utter boredom. Today, Latin and Greek (which I began studying in my sixties) mean something entirely different to me: admission into the world of Hellenism and the beginnings of Christianity. Had I found some wise person there who could have guided me, perhaps I would have slogged on through the boredom. There was one outstanding professor of Greek, Stefan Srebrny, and I should have studied with him. Had I studied Hebrew, too, I would have been among the very few well-educated men of letters. Nevertheless, in my opinion law was better in Wilno than at other Polish universities; that is to say, there was at least one outstanding course during each of the four years that it took to earn the diploma. These included the theory of law (Assistant Professor Ejnik), the political history of the Grand Duchy of Lithuania (Iwo Jaworski), criminal law (Bronisław Wróblewski, whose course was actually a disguised anthropology course), the history of the philosophy of law (Wiktor Sukiennicki). So I did receive a decent education in Wilno, both in high school and at the university, even though it could have been better. Let us note that after 1918 schooling had to be improvised all of a sudden; there was no lack of characters who found themselves in professorial positions by some accident. In any event, there wasn't a single incompetent professor in Wilno like the notorious Jarra in Warsaw, who ordered his students to prepare for their exams by memorizing his entire handbook on the theory of law (which was pure gibberish) and failed them if they answered "in their own words."

This is important to remember when we speak of Wilno: to a

significant degree, it was a Jewish city. But entirely different from Warsaw. The Jewish quarter in Wilno was a labyrinth of absolutely medieval, narrow little streets, the houses connected by arcades, the uneven pavements two or three meters wide. In Warsaw, there were the streets of hideous tenement houses from the nineteenth century. The Jewish poor in Wilno were less noticeable, which does not mean that they did not exist. But that doesn't explain how the cities differed. Wilno was a robust Jewish cultural center with traditions. I remind you that it was here, on a foundation of working-class, Yiddish-speaking Jews, that the Bund came into existence before the First World War. Its leaders, Alter and Ehrlich, were eventually shot by Stalin. Wilno had the Jewish Historical Institute, which was later moved to New York. I think Wilno made a particular contribution to the rebirth of Hebrew in Israel. Living as I did in such a city, I ought to have acquired some knowledge of all this, but custom placed an obstacle in my path. Jewish and non-Jewish Wilno lived separate lives. They spoke and wrote in different languages. As a student I had strong international leanings, but they were quite shallow. I knew nothing about the history of the Jews in Poland and Lithuania, about their religious thought, Jewish mysticism, Cabala. Only much later, in America, did I begin learning about them. This gives some indication of what the separation between the two communities was like. But why talk about other cities in prewar Poland when I, even though surrounded by such neighbors, was an ignoramus? No one in Poland, as far as I know, dared to propose that Hebrew should be taught in the schools as one of the "classical" languages, that the intellectual history of the Polish Jews should be studied, or even that the Old Testament should be read and discussed. Such a person would have been stoned. And though I am deeply offended and pained by Jewish hatred of Poles, despite their surprising forgiveness of Germans and Russians, I have to admit that petty anti-Semitism can get under the skin no less than crimes, because it is something one meets every day.

I hope that you will find material to reflect on in my letter. You and I both want Polish-Lithuanian relations to develop differently than they did in the past. The two nations have gone through terrible experiences; they have been defeated, humiliated, trampled upon. The new generations will talk to each other differently from the way people did in the prewar years. We must reckon with the power of inertia, however, and with the fact that in the ideological vacuum that has developed, nationalism—whether in Poland or in Lithuania—will keep returning to its well-worn tracks, since in every

country's history there are repetitive patterns. At the end of the
eighteenth century in Poland a division took place between the Reform camp and the Sarmatian camp, and that schism, in various
guises, has survived to this day, although in its unconscious, or semiconscious, state it eludes definition. It may be that Adam Michnik's
book *The Church, the Left, a Dialogue*, published in Paris by *Kultura*,
presages the end of this schism. After all, in our century, at least
until 1939, the mainstay of the Sarmatian mentality, which gave birth
to modern nationalism, was the Church. A new alliance is developing
now; the Church in Poland is concentrating enormous progressive
energies within itself, and in that system progress can only mean the
successful defense of man. But these are complicated changes that
cannot take place from one day to the next; they also do not by any
means predict the sudden disappearance of nationalistic inclinations,
prewar style, among a significant segment of the clergy.

During the years 1918–39, Lithuanians disliked everything in
Wilno that was dear to me: the Localists, federalist dreams, region-
alism, the liberal Masons who had once been followers of Piłsudski.
Apparently, they preferred to deal with the *anima naturaliter endeciana*, because at least then the enemy was clearly visible. Perhaps
they were right; I won't attempt to judge them. Nonetheless, it is
that line, not the Sarmatian line, that today offers hope of friendship
between the Poles and the Lithuanians. Finally, this is the political
heritage, from that line, of Jerzy Giedroyć, the editor of *Kultura* in
Paris, a journal with which I have been associated for many years.

Czesław Miłosz

Czesław,

I left Vilnius one and a half years ago and who knows if I will ever
return to that city; in any event, it won't happen in the near future.
One of my friends, also a recent émigré and a fairly ambitious So-
vietologist, insists that there may well be enormous changes in Eastern Europe literally in the next few years. If so, our emigration will
come to an end naturally. Although I tend to be an optimist, I don't
agree with his outlook; this business will undoubtedly drag on and
we must get used to this second life in the West. In a certain sense,
it reminds one of life after death. We meet people whom we had no
hope of meeting in this world, and are separated from old friends
more or less forever. Contacts with them take on a somewhat spiritualistic character. Old landscapes fade into the distance; in their

place, we see things that we used to have only the foggiest notion of. I am writing this in a hotel in Venice, several steps from San Marco. If someone had said to me five years ago that I would be engaged in a written conversation with you here, I would have replied that he had an incredibly wild imagination.

I still remember every back alley of Vilnius; I could walk through that city with my eyes closed, thinking about my own affairs, and still I would find everything there. Sometimes, in fact, I do that in my dreams. But it is receding from me irrevocably; I know it is changing, but I shall no longer participate in those changes. I am beginning to see the city in a simplified, generalized way—more historically, too, perhaps. I am not experiencing nostalgia. When I made the decision to emigrate, many people told me that nostalgia is a dreadful thing; I answered truthfully that I feel a terrible nostalgia for France, Italy, and so on—it couldn't be any more powerful. I am happy hearing the bells of Venice and knowing that in five minutes I can see San Giorgio Maggiore once more, perhaps the most beautiful façade in the world. I would not wish to return to present-day Vilnius; I really could not stand it there. I love that city, however, and now I am truly beginning to understand that it, too, is a part of Europe.

We do not know the same Vilnius; one might even say that they are two entirely different cities. An absolute transformation like that is not a common occurrence. I suspect that Warsaw, despite its having been totally destroyed, has changed less. It may be that the fate of Gdańsk or Wrocław is somewhat analogous to that of Vilnius (a much worse fate was suffered by Königsberg). There, too, the population changed, the language, the cultural models; furthermore, prewar Gdańsk had, shall we say, Polish hinterlands and a certain Polish substratum, just as the Vilnius that belonged to historic Lithuania rubbed shoulders with ethnographic Lithuania. Still, everything is new. Of course, the sky is still there, the Wilia River (which is called the Neris), even the sandbanks at the spot where the Wilenka, or Vilnele, flows into the Wilia; some of the trees are the same, many trees, but what else? Of course: the architecture is the same. That is important.

I believe that architecture is what lends a city its aura; everything else—the style of life there, even the landscape and climate, is in a sense secondary. Vilnius is a Baroque city. However, the Baroque generally requires space, distance, perspective; cities were already laid out along modern lines in that epoch. The Vilnius Baroque is a Baroque against a medieval background. The network of little streets is medieval: everything is crooked, crowded, entangled; above this labyrinth rise the mighty cupolas and towers of a totally different century. Nothing appears here in its totality: parts of churches, slanting walls, silhouettes sliced in half loom up around a corner; amid damp and dirty corridors the magnificent white bell tower of St. John's suddenly shoots into the sky, or a small classical square opens up. The history and human relations of the city are equally tangled. But I don't need to tell you this. During my school years half of that Vilnius was in ruins; all the churches, however, had survived by some miracle. Artillery fire destroyed one of the two beautiful spires of St. Catherine's, which was restored after a while. Of course, the Soviet authorities closed most of the churches; they made them into warehouses for paper and vodka, and later on, with varying degrees of success, adapted some of the churches as exhibition halls. In any event, their external appearance remained the same. The city and its backdrop have fused: on a clear day you can see that the lines of its pediments mirror the lines of the surrounding wooded hills—or perhaps the hills mirror them. You once wrote that even the clouds above this city are Baroque; indeed, they are.

I don't want to linger over this Baroque. Vilnius has all the European styles (except the Romanesque), and all of good quality. The mixture is really strange, but the styles coexist in a lively fashion. During my school years I was quite serious about this. I not only knew all of Vilnius's historic monuments but also virtually every window and column in them. I acquired an understanding of architecture, or at least a better understanding of it than of the other arts; I developed my visual and spatial imagination as best I could. (Unfortunately, I lack a musical imagination.) I had a few friends with the same architectural passion: we could spend hours entertaining ourselves by guessing at styles, eras, even decades, or listing from memory various Vilnius curiosities. Mikalojus Vorobjovas's book, which was published in 1940, was a great help to us. Professor Vorobjovas emigrated to the States after the war and committed suicide there. (His lovely daughter lives in New York; I met her quite unexpectedly the day after my arrival in that city.) Vorobjovas's book, which appeared only in Lithuanian, is something of a Vilnius Ruskin or Muratov. Later, I saw many cities, and my "Vilnius disease" became somewhat less severe. However, I admit that on the worst days of my life, already as a grown man, I would walk straight to the Skarga courtyard, to the little square in front of St. Ann's or St. Theresa's, and stand there and look; and it always helped.

Now I find something similar in Italy; topographically, Vilnius is very much like Rome. It even has a stratum of pagan monuments, just like Rome. Let me relate a little anecdote here. A Lithuanian student tour group traveled to Europe before the war and one of the participants described the excursion eloquently. This is a sentence from his report: "We have arrived in Florence; the city is pretty, like Vilnius, only worse." The funny thing is that I almost agree with him. At any rate, the cultural sphere of Florence and Vilnius is identical. Vilnius and Florence belong to the same world. Russia is entirely different, with the exception of Petersburg, perhaps, but Petersburg is a complicated question. As for Tartu or Tallinn—in my opinion, they have very little in common with Vilnius (other than their unhappy fate); they are Europe, but part of the Scandinavian realm.

So, quite early in life I began to perceive Vilnius's architecture as a sign. It was speaking to me about something and making certain demands. It was the lofty past amid the strange and uncertain present, tradition in a world suddenly bereft of tradition, culture in an acultural world. A culture—why conceal it?—that was in great measure Polish. But also Italian, German, French; above all, Christian (as I realized later). You say that, for you, Wilno is the possibility of normalcy. For me, it was never normalcy. In my childhood I had a very strong, although nebulous, sense that the world is out of joint, crippled, turned inside out. Later, I began to think—and to this day I still think—that by now we are living after the end of the world, which, however, does not absolve us of responsibility. In my Vilnius there were only enclaves that gave some idea of that lost normal world. Naturally, normalcy is, on the whole, a relative thing, and I suspect that human life never works out in an ordinary way; everyone dreams at times of ordinariness, although it was always an ideal average with no relation to facts. But in our epoch the most unbelievable fates are perhaps the most frequent, which is to say, the most ordinary.

Not long ago I read Thomas Mann's essay "Lübeck as a Form of the Spiritual Life." He speaks of a peaceful, dignified world, always seeking the middle way; in this world such categories as reason, duty, home are important. That has certainly changed. Those categories are no longer given to us "from the start" by tradition; they can only be a task. In other words, we have to grow into a feeling of duty, a rational and worthy life, some personal, non-mechanized spot if not in space, then in time, and grow into it with great effort, always taking into account the possibility of failure. This is the result, above all, of the totalitarianisms of the twentieth century. One of those totalitarianisms appeared in Thomas Mann's moderate fatherland, but that is a separate issue.

I don't come from Vilnius; I was born in Klaipeda, which my parents had to leave in 1939, when Hitler occupied the city and its environs. I was two years old then. I spent my childhood, or the German occupation, in Kaunas. After that I became a resident of Vilnius, one of the thousands of Lithuanians who, during and after the war, came to their historic capital. It was a thoroughly unfamiliar city to them. Before the war there was hardly any movement between Wilno and independent Lithuania, as is well known. There was a myth of Vilnius, however, very significant for the Lithuanian imagination (see below); but that is a different dimension. There were also, and there still are, Lithuanians who were native Vilniusites; they are an interesting group of people, but not very numerous and already dying out. So life in Vilnius at the beginning was an arduous sinking of roots into a new soil. In general, it was chaos.

As I said, half the city was in ruins. On the former "Georgie," every other house had been burned down. However, the wooden Helios movie theater was still standing there threateningly. (Today, more or less on the same site, stands the rather pretentious new Vilnius opera house.) The history of that street's name deserves a separate description. The Lithuanian authorities changed it to Gediminas Street but left the name of Mickiewicz on its extension. In 1950 or thereabouts, it was announced that, in deference to the pleas of the working masses, the name of the street would be changed: it would become Comrade Stalin Boulevard. It bore that proud name until the Twentieth Party Congress. One of my acquaintances, a young graphic artist, wrote a petition to the authorities at that time proposing a return to the old name. He was immediately expelled from college; in accordance with an old custom, he was drafted into the army, the Red Army, from which he returned a broken man. True, he found work in his profession later on, but he was sickly, and he died, as people whispered, from an overdose of radioactivity, which he'd received somewhere on a northern base. In the end, of course, the street became Lenin Boulevard. My generation always called it Gediminke, however, and still does. I should say that Gediminas also survived officially, because Cathedral Square was renamed after him. In that way, religion was erased from the map, and Lithuanian nationalism, although it wasn't completely liquidated, was relegated to its appropriate position—second place.

The entire ghetto (including German Street, which was immediately renamed Museum Street) was an incredible dead space, probably quite similar in appearance to Warsaw immediately after the war. The walls of the old synagogue were still standing, but they were demolished forthwith. Various other things that weren't entirely compatible with the new order were also destroyed. One morning we noticed that the Three Crosses had disappeared; they had been blown up overnight. First the cathedral was renovated and then the figures of the three saints were removed from its pediment; the press explained that they were not part of Stuoka Gucevičius's original drawings (which is true, but the cross had appeared in those drawings, and it, too, was removed). There were rumors about a large highway that was supposed to link the train station with Antakalnis; two churches (the Dominicans' and St. Catherine's) and Aušros Vartai stood right in the path of this future highway. There was also talk of building a truly Soviet skyscraper in place of St. Jacob's (a similar skyscraper was built in Riga). After Stalin's death, somehow those lovely projects were forgotten. But the whole city was surrounded by gray standardized buildings, in comparison with which the tsarist garrison architecture began to look quite respectable; such buildings effectively ruined Antakalnis and had begun to creep in here and there even in the historic center—for example, as far as Museum Street.

My high school, the former Jesuit *gymnasium*, was at the end of this street, forming, as it were, an island amid the ruins. It was large, very gloomy, and my memories of it are not of the best. Various crises of youth coincided with that sense of abnormality that I have mentioned, of a certain contortion of the world. On the very first day, I got lost in the ruins after school and that exhausting, helpless wandering about in search of my house, which lasted for a good four hours (there was no one to ask directions of because I encountered very few people and those I did meet spoke no Lithuanian), became a private symbol for me. In that early period the population of Vilnius was very small; furthermore, it was an unbelievable hodgepodge. Almost all the Jews had perished; the Poles had left en masse for Poland (or Siberia); what remained was the proletariat, the lumpen proletariat. The Lithuanians belonged either to the new Soviet elite or to the remnants of the intelligentsia, who were usually either broken or terrified. A good many Russians and other immigrants turned up: bureaucrats, officers of the occupying forces and their beautiful daughters, simple people who led a beggar's existence or worse. A strange new jargon developed from a blend of that "hereabouts" language, Russian, and bits and pieces of Lithuanian. It was a city of outlaws, and it was dangerous. Brawls and small battles erupted quite frequently, usually against a background of settling national accounts. And above all, one felt the heavy hand of the authorities.

Certainly, I experienced this differently from the majority of people, because my family was part of the Soviet elite; nonetheless, I was aware of it. Using my father's rather extensive library, I developed an interest in many things. But soon I came to recognize that they were non-issues, because certain names were forbidden, or else they were nonexistent, because certain problems were forbidden. This irritated and humiliated me. In several books, including Greek literature, the translator's name was scratched out. I asked my father what that meant and he answered that he had bought those copies in a secondhand bookstore in Moscow and had no other information about the translator. Much later I learned that he was Adrian Piotrowski (the son of Tadeusz Zieliński), who perished during the Stalin purges. There was another translator of classical Greek literature, this time into Lithuanian, whom one was also not supposed to mention by name because he was the President of independent Lithuania—Smetona. But why single out Smetona when more than half of Lithuanian literature did not exist officially (because it was hostile and bad)? Later I realized that was true of Russian literature as well. The problems of nationality and religion did not exist, which naturally aroused in me eventually a rather lively interest in both the one and the other. The majority of the ·countries in the world also did not exist. France and England were exclusively literary concepts for me, on the order of Jules Verne's islands; Poland, too. They were simply imaginary or, in the best case, belonged to the past; in the present, they were simply an indistinguishable and absolutely inaccessible (because hostile) expanse. After I graduated from the university I came across a book called *Everything about Wilno in 1913*. On one of its first pages there was a long list of foreign cities to which one could purchase a direct rail ticket from Wilno. I was curious about how many of those cities remained. I found two: Königsberg and Lwów.

Everything possible was done to uproot the past and graft on a new mentality. It is easy to understand that it was not just a matter of destroying crosses or suddenly renaming the Casino and Adria movie theaters Moscow and October (their names to this day). The new ideology was forcibly instilled in every way possible in order to degrade people, to demonstrate that man is worth nothing. The older high-school teachers and university professors, choking with helpless rage, said things that they didn't believe and that a man should probably not say at all. The poet Putinas, no longer young and universally respected, kept silent for a while, then began publishing what he was supposed to. In a novel about 1863 he smuggled in a sentence which made an impression on a great many people: that a nation must mature not only to freedom but also to slavery. I consider that sentence a form of capitulation. One should not train oneself for the role of slave. But it turns out that Putinas was also writing poems for the drawer, which are now appearing in émigré journals. He translated Mickiewicz, was admitted to the Academy of Sciences, and was catastrophically unhappy; he died after many years of such a life. He was given an official funeral.

Another poet, Sruoga, returned to Vilnius from a German concentration camp. He managed to write a book about his experiences —quite interesting, cynical, somewhat similar in tone to Borowski's. At a writers' meeting one of the Party activists literally said that the Germans probably were right to detain such worthless people in their camps. Sruoga died soon after the meeting.

There were a few brave souls, but they were the sort that in any event had nothing to lose, like the old Russian émigré Karsavin, who was a philosopher of religion; such people died, of course. But others died, too. Ultimately, people grew accustomed to everything: to obligatory parades, mandated friendships, a special language that was diametrically opposed to what they really meant to say. Later, there was conformity and relative peace. People, the educated stratum in particular, feel that daily lying is the tribute one must render unto Caesar in order to have a more or less bearable life, and they do not see a moral problem in this. Perhaps that is precisely what the authorities want.

This is a phenomenon of modern, post-Stalinist times. But one must remember that in Lithuania Stalinism really never came to an end: it grew milder, even much milder, in the sixties, but it remained itself. I think that the situation in Poland is different. Even in Russia the situation is somewhat different. Among the intelligentsia in Lithuania a feeling of powerlessness and complete demoralization predominates. I cannot imagine a member of the Lithuanian Academy of Sciences supporting Sakharov, although there are certainly some who admire him in their heart of hearts. They have a convenient explanation for this: Sakharov is a Russian problem; Lithuania is an occupied country with its own problems, and everything must be dedicated to the goal of saving the Lithuanian language and culture. Which means: keep a low profile. Only, no one knows if a culture preserved in this manner will be worth anything.

The center of opposition in Lithuania is located elsewhere. Here I return to postwar Lithuania and my personal recollections. I often heard something about a partisan war in the Lithuanian forests. It was also supposed to be one of those forbidden topics; however, it acquired such powerful dimensions that there was no way to maintain complete silence about it. The authorities naturally attempted not only to squash the partisan movement but also to slander it in every possible way. They are still doing so today: the surest path to success in official Lithuanian literature or films is to portray the partisan movement as an abomination; this is often done quite perfidiously, with a certain carefully measured dose of truth. The war was tragic and incredibly savage. I also heard about mass deportations; that was a strictly forbidden topic, but I knew that they were taking people, mainly rural inhabitants, to Siberia, where life was very hard. It was impossible not to know that. Several students from my class disappeared; I went to their house and learned that they and their family had been taken away because the father had been an officer in the old Lithuanian Army. My father's brother was sent to Siberia; efforts were made to get him out of there, but they were fruitless. He died shortly afterward; his wife and daughter returned only many years later. Acquaintances who were members of the old intelligentsia disappeared. Some of them came back; most now write very orthodox things.

You speak about the crime of 1940. We both know that this crime reached its worst proportions after the war. One out of six Lithuanians was deported, they say. This was connected with collectivization, but not only: above all, an effort was being made to break the nation of the habit of attempting to decide or even think about its own fate. It was never completely successful, and by now one can say that it didn't succeed at all. But not because the authorities didn't try.

The partisan movement was a doomed undertaking. The West, as is well known, was not interested in the situation of the Baltic countries. Every Lithuanian should be grateful to you for writing about that situation in *The Captive Mind*; unfortunately, what you wrote wasn't listened to as it deserved to be. Even now I read colossally stupid disquisitions on the subject of the Baltic states in the Western press. Somehow, people have grown accustomed to the idea that Russia always was and ought to be a presence in that territory for the sake of peace, so that everything else is an insignificant incident. True, there are wiser voices, too, probably raised more often now than in those days; this is the saving influence of Solzhenitsyn and others like him. Lithuania was more bloodied after the war than the other Baltic states; however, possibly because of this, it remained the most obstinate among them. The forest war continued up till Stalin's death and even longer; the last partisans have literally held on to this day.

There is not a great deal of historical documentation of this war, and if it does exist, it can be found mainly in the bowels of certain well-known archives. The fear of such information is enormous. Several months ago a former partisan named Balys Gajauskas went on trial in Vilnius; he received a fifteen-year sentence solely for collecting archival materials on the forest war. (I should add that he had already served one twenty-five-year term.) In the postwar period we used to hear that the partisans controlled the area to the southwest of Vilnius, near Druskininkai. There was no Lithuanian partisan movement around Vilnius itself, or else it was much smaller, because the population was not sympathetic to Lithuanianness; on the other hand, for a while there were detachments of the Home Army in this area, whose relations with the Lithuanians, it seems, were not always amicable. In the city itself, however, there was a functioning Lithuanian underground. Obviously, I knew nothing about it and I am beginning to learn about it only now; but I had a feeling that something like that was going on. A close friend of my father, the poet Kazys Boruta, wound up in jail because he knew something and wouldn't turn informer. That name is not unknown to you; I think that you translated Boruta into Polish a long time ago. After the Stalinist prison, Boruta remained a man of integrity; when Pasternak was denounced at a meeting of Lithuanian writers, he was the only one who stood up and walked out. Boruta's lady friend, Ona Lukauskaite, went on trial with him and was given ten years. She was freed after Stalin's death. Recently, in her seventies, she joined the Lithuanian Helsinki group.

The underground was infiltrated, of course. A certain Markulis, who turned out to be a KGB agent, held a lot of threads in his hands; today, he specializes in forensic medicine or, more accurately, the preparation of cadavers. I know this sounds excessively literary, but it is the truth. Ultimately, everything was crushed. In my university days it already belonged to the past; people were either in the Gulag or in the ground; among those who remained, accommodations and stabilization were setting in, especially since the regime, to use Akhmatova's words, had gone over to a more vegetarian diet. However, in 1959, I think, we were informed at a meeting of students that an organization engaged in enemy activity had been discovered in the department of philology. The members of that organization used to discuss Lithuanian problems and, it seems, wrote a few proclamations. I had no contact with those people, I didn't even know any of them by sight, but by then I had already undergone a political transformation, so I was sympathetic to them. The embers of resistance smoldered for many years—not armed resistance anymore but spiritual. I consider that to be the only morally acceptable resistance, and also the only effective one. A nation cannot acquiesce to being broken, having its face spat upon, and being ordered to joyously offer up thanks for this treatment. It is impossible to eradicate normal human reflexes, especially when it is a question of the proverbial Lithuanian obstinacy and endurance, which has been a tradition for a good seven hundred years. Lately, there has been an unbelievable flowering of Lithuanian *samizdat*, which means that the resistance has taken on a new and important dimension. It is difficult, somehow, not to pay attention to the fate of this country. I know that the Lithuanian intelligentsia can take no credit for this—at least not that segment of the intelligentsia that is visible. There exists, and in large numbers, a bourgeoisified *homo sovieticus* who modestly (and also immodestly) is acquiring wealth, is entertaining (with his heart on his sleeve) relatives from abroad, and even, at times, is beginning to travel abroad himself. He nurtures a silent, fateful hatred of the Russians, but he hates them as Russians; he finds the system comfortable, he wouldn't know what to do without the system, at least for a while. But there are also others, ordinary people for the most part.

I knew one of them; his name is Viktoras Petkus. He is one of the most unusual individuals I have ever known in my life. This large, phlegmatic Samogitian spent fifteen years in gulags. The first time, he was sent there as a minor for links with the underground, although he had never held a gun; he was released after Stalin's death, but was soon rearrested, this time for having subversive literature in his home. Among the literature cited was Selma Lagerlöf and a book by the Lithuanian-Russian poet Baltrušaitis which was published in 1911. He sat for eight years. (Baltrušaitis and Lagerlöf had been rehabilitated in the meantime.) After he got out, of course, he didn't have a normal job, but he collected one of the best libraries of books about Lithuania in Vilnius. He joined the Lithuanian Helsinki group as if it were the most natural thing in the world to do so, although he certainly understood, as everyone else did, that he would be the first to be thrown in jail. He was arrested. His trial took place at the same time as the trials of Ginzburg and Sharansky, who were his

friends; he was also a friend of Sakharov's, and was not at all a
Russophobe. I was already in the West by then, in France; I could
do almost nothing for him, other than reading all the newspapers I
could get my hands on every morning and sensing how Petkus's
stature was growing from day to day. He did not answer a single
one of the court's questions. He let it be understood that in his
opinion it was an illegal court of an occupying power. One ought
neither to cooperate with nor have any dealings with such a court.
Then he either sat silently or slept. He was given another fifteen
years.

In Vilnius I often had the tormenting feeling that its present-day
inhabitants somehow didn't belong to this city. They didn't measure
up to Vilnius. I perceived the world as deformed in part because of
that. But it turns out I was wrong. We must remember that today
Vilnius is the center of Lithuanian resistance, which, without a moment's hesitation, I can call great. My personal contacts with the
resistance were insignificant (although I had my private war with the
regime and my game of *va banque*). But it was in the air.

The authorities' attitude toward Lithuanian nationalism was always
double-edged. Naturally, they attempted to wring its neck; however,
with their other hand, they fed it a little. They would make amazing
temporary compromises with it, even in the Stalin era. I have already
mentioned Gediminas Square. In 1940 nationalism was absolutely
forbidden; however, during the war they started permitting not only
Russian patriotic bombast but, to a lesser degree, Lithuanian nationalism as well. All of a sudden it was all right to praise the great
Lithuanian grand dukes (because they fought valiantly against the
Germans). This was all very transparent (although, I must say, ambivalent); after the war, it began to get murky. Some concessions
were a tactical move in the grand game of defeating the nation. At
other times, it was a matter of the Lithuanian Soviet elite's maneuvers; in their own interest, they would quietly sabotage Russification
(as I have said, deep down that elite is wildly anti-Russian, although
all one has to do is apply a little pressure and it will do everything
it has to, and even more). Furthermore, it is, of course, easier to
rule by setting Lithuanians against Poles, Poles against Lithuanians,
everyone against the Jews, and so on. (They also made some concessions to the Poles in the Vilnius region, although these may have
been insignificant.) Well, the Russians are good bogeymen: Don't
do this or that, or the Russians will strangle us. "Song and dance"
will obviously prosper, even in the form of highly refined spectacles
for the few, and "festivals of song" are as characteristic of the regime

as are May Day parades. One should not remember the grand dukes
too clearly. However, the castle in Trakai was rebuilt; this infuriated
Khrushchev, but his picturesque anger remained a memory. There
is also a fad of historical drama with various vague allusions, gen-
erously approved by the censor and the Party critic, to be sure. In
short, in Lithuania, too, they use nationalism as an additional instrument of control (and a safety valve); less so than in Poland, but
still they use it. The attitude toward Catholicism is much more
monolithic: Catholicism is not exploited; they simply try to destroy
it. But I think that not only nationalism but Catholicism, too, is a
real power in those areas.

I can remember the tragicomic, highly humiliating, and quite frequent vacillations of the so-called national politics. Especially when
it was a question of symbols. (That regime is incredibly sensitive to
symbols.) The red flag on Gediminas tower was replaced by a tricolor
flag—not the prewar Lithuanian flag, but a new one, with a pre-
dominant splash of red. After a while, city seals were reinstated, but
that policy ended when it came to Vilnius's coat of arms, which
represented St. Christopher. After the war, the national anthem,
which was strictly forbidden during the first occupation, was again
played during parades in Vilnius, even in the worst period; but then
it was replaced with a new one, the words for which were written
by my father.

Here I must say a few words about my father. I cannot pass judgment on him and I am not about to do so. I know that he had a very
hard life. In his youth he was a leftist intellectual more or less like
Kazys Boruta or Ona Lukauskaite. Pranas Ancevičius was a friend
of his, a good friend, before his escape to Poland. That world of the
Kaunas-Vilnius intelligentsia is really very small; everything in it is
interconnected. So I had heard about Ancewicz since childhood,
although his character existed for me in a very specific perspective.
Unlike his friends, my father became orthodox. It is hard for me to
say what he went through in 1940, when he was in the puppet par-
liament with Jędrychowski. It seems that the war had a decisive
impact on him; afterward, he no longer changed, he recognized the
existing situation as the only possible situation. He was not a cynic.
He continued to be friends with Boruta, and Lithuania was not an
empty word for him. Finally, his personal situation (mine, too) was
marked by a certain precariousness, because after Stalin's death he
found out that a trial of former leftists, himself included, had been
under way but was not prepared in time. These were weighty affairs.
I admit that I am more inclined to forgive people of that generation

than I am today's *arrivistes*; at least they faced problems that people today do not face.

Vilnius University. As I said, I became a student there in an era of relative stability. Of course, there was a greater difference between my university and yours than between your university and Mickiewicz's. After 1939 the professors from Kaunas University, which was a pretty good institution, transferred to Vilnius; but when I was there they were no longer giving lectures. They were in emigration, in Siberia, or no longer among the living. A couple of them, like Putinas, whom I mentioned before, had retired. Right after the war, the level of the university (in the scholarly and every other sense) dropped catastrophically. True, the language of the lectures was still Lithuanian; but the lectures were often no more than ideological banalities or military drill. Change came very gradually. I have fond memories of a few professors. For example, Balčikonis, professor of Lithuanian, an old-fashioned lexicographer, a great eccentric, and, at the same time, a courageous man: I believe he gave almost his entire salary to repressed families. He was one of the faculty members from Kaunas. There was a Professor Lebedys, a very good specialist in the history of the sixteenth and seventeenth centuries in Lithuania. Professor Sesemann examined me in logic; he was a former Russian émigré who had returned from a Stalinist camp (where, people said, he managed to practice yoga and translate Aristotle into Lithuanian). I am deliberately writing only about the deceased. A school of Baltic studies was organized only after I graduated from the university. It drew a lot of people because it was a patriotic undertaking and yet, at the same time, neutral in a way; but not all that neutral, apparently, because the head of the school, Professor Kazlauskas, soon drowned in the Wilia under rather mysterious circumstances.

Only the walls, the beautiful library reading rooms, and the even more beautiful courtyards preserved the aura of the old university. There are nine or perhaps thirteen courtyards. We used to say that there were places in that labyrinth where no human had ever set foot. The student dormitory on Bouffałowa Hill (the *Tauro kalnas*), where I spent a lot of time, also remained from the past. All right, perhaps it wasn't only the architecture that remained, because the library did, too. It was predominantly Polish (this changed somewhat later on). Many of the books were placed in the "special collection," which meant that as a practical matter they were inaccessible; nonetheless, I did find interesting things. I learned Polish quite quickly, although the majority of my colleagues were not interested in that language. (It was easy for me, because my maternal grandmother was Polish; she was a passionate admirer of Sienkiewicz. My father, too, read Polish and could speak it a little.) I even wrote a longish paper on "Mickiewicz at Wilno University." When I was working on the paper, I read at least half of what there was to read on that topic; so I learned about the old Wilno Masonic movement (interwar Masonry was terra incognita for me, of course), the Society of Rogues, and Kontrym. After this paper my friends and I even formed a circle modeled on the Rogues, which was a risky business, considering the all-seeing eye of the KGB, but somehow it dissolved into student pranks and alcohol. In any event, I knew about the traditions of that Wilno. But at the same time I felt that my tradition was linked with Poška (Paszkiewicz), the eccentric whom the Rogues made fun of, and Daukantas (Dowkont), who had ties with the Philomaths but took a different path, becoming the first Lithuanian historian. The fate of this somewhat comic and saintly figure is quite moving. Donelaitis, the eighteenth-century poet, in my opinion the equal of the greatest poets in Europe, was and remains important to me. Here I should say something about language. Vilnius, which is now a half-Lithuanian city, speaks in a peculiar koine [common dialect], because representatives of all the dialects of Lithuania came together here; Slavic (and Soviet) jargon also exerted an influence. So the new Lithuanian poetry is in part a rebellion against this koine (in which it is helped by those old writers), in part, its ingenious transformation. *Nota bene*, the Russian iamb does not arouse any antipathy in me, because there is also a Lithuanian iamb that has a long tradition and is obviously in harmony with the spirit of the language (it's probably a question of the system of stress, but I won't develop this theme, because that would be linguistics). One way or another, Lithuanian literature—in no small degree connected with Vilnius— is my field; however, I came away from the university with a love of Polish literature, too. Also of Russian—and it is a great love.

Of course, no one taught me this. Now I would like to recall my first political experiences. In high school, I became a member of the Komsomol, and I even thought that that was the way to reform the world. Almost everyone was drawn to the Komsomol; at the university, the Komsomol members were of all sorts—they were not always dull-witted Stalinists, although those types naturally were in the majority and always had the last word. I belonged to the so-called believers, who, I think, were not very numerous. For me and a couple of my friends, the Twentieth Congress was a shock (despite what we already knew); but I can give you an absolutely exact date for my true transformation—it was November 4, 1956, the day the

Hungarian Uprising was crushed. Then came the Pasternak affair. Four of us wrote an ecstatic letter to him. I read all his poetry and memorized at least half. We tried to put together a student literary almanac, but it was stopped by the censors and was publicly labeled an "enemy" work. I was suspended from the university for one year. I consider it a blessed year. I read from morning to night. It was then that I understood what Russian poetry is; in fact, in general what literature is.

Nadezhda Mandelstam likes a game that she herself invented: she suggests that everyone name ten truly educated (and young) people in the Soviet Union. It turns out that there are only two: one linguist and one specialist in Byzantine culture. Then Mrs. Mandelstam explains why: they both were sickly throughout their childhood and did not attend a Soviet school. I was not so fortunate. But if I did manage to become educated to a certain degree, it was during that year. The university gave me only a fundamental knowledge of Lithuanian studies (and large areas of it were still inaccessible to me); there I became familiar with Marx, which I do not regret, and studied a certain amount of classical philology. A friend and I even went in search of a rabbi who could give us some idea of what Hebrew is like, but where could we find such a rabbi in postwar Vilnius? In any event, it turned out that it was possible to learn something. You can swim against a Niagara of falsehood and unnecessary information and even emerge from it, but it is impossible to pull anyone along with you; everyone has to do it himself. I confess that Moscow as well as Vilnius shaped me—Moscow, a very interesting city, because, as Zinoviev says, it has everything that the soul can desire: Catholics and Buddhists, avant-gardists and dissidents, mathematicians and girls who are better even than in Paris. True, today the majority of those girls are, in fact, in Paris. Or in London. But joking aside, Moscow is quite an experience.

I have one typical Soviet disability: I cannot speak any foreign language (other than Russian and Polish); even now, in the States, I find English very hard. True, I can read several languages, but it seems I am doomed to passivity in this area, and that pains me. Because what use are languages to someone from the Soviet Union? Western books are accessible in absurdly small numbers; periodicals are completely inaccessible; there's no point in talking about travel. So Polish was all the more important for me, and not for me alone. I knew a dozen or so people for whom it was a window on the world. We used to meet for years in the Polish bookstore on "Gediminke"; we also would get our hands on books that weren't in that bookstore—your books, for example. We would argue and joke in Polish, partly to confuse uninvited individuals, partly out of snobbery, partly from love of Polish, because we owed a great deal to that language.

This brings me to the problem of Lithuanian-Polish relations. For me, personally, the antagonism between our peoples seems a colossal idiocy; I wish I could consider it overcome. I think that a significant percentage, possibly the majority, of the younger generation in Lithuania no longer feels any hostility toward Poles. I suspect the same is true of Poles vis-à-vis Lithuanians; it may be that a sense of Polish superiority, of lordly hauteur, still lingers here and there, but then again, it may be gone. We have been run over by such an epoch that our former quarrels seem insignificant. However, the problem may be more complicated than that.

Lithuania gained its national consciousness quite late, with great difficulty and in opposition to Poland. The influence of Polish culture, especially after the Union of Lublin (1569), was enormous; I think it was positive, on the whole, although practically no Lithuanians would agree with me on this. Without Poland we would not know many things, including the concept of political rights. Our national rebirth also had typical Polish overtones, both Sarmatian and messianic, so that those models, in a paradoxical fashion, were turned against Polish cultural domination. Everything was "inside out": Jogaila [Jagiełło] was a traitor, Janusz Radziwiłł a hero, and so forth. The nation had to stand on its own feet. Sometimes it did this clumsily, succumbing to childish complexes, which can easily be forgiven, because this happens to every nation in the early stages. But complexes have an incredibly long life and turn into ballast. You speak about Poles' memories; the memory of Lithuanians, I think, is even greater: it reaches back hundreds of years. We are even proud of that, although no one knows if it's worthwhile. We remember that Polish cultural (and social) domination in Lithuania in the eighteenth century had begun to threaten Lithuanians with the loss of their language and their own historical path. Add to this a painful feeling of national inferiority stored up over several centuries and the resulting megalomania and paranoia. It's easy to laugh at this, although healthy ambitions are born here, too. I personally have absolutely no sense of national inferiority. The younger generation of Lithuanians is liberating itself from this, because in every respect Lithuania today appears to be no worse than the other countries of Eastern Europe. But certain archetypes remain and can be reborn, especially since the experience of totalitarianism generally does not favor wise and tolerant positions. A certain habit of demonizing Poles does exist. According to this mentality (which has influence, even though it is vestigial), for centuries Poles have thought about one thing only: how to attach Lithuania to Poland, denationalize, and, in general, oppress it. Poles are much more dangerous than Russians (after all, they are Catholics and Europeans). There is a very seductive stereotype of the Machiavellian Pole, who always insists on having his own way, if not by force, then by perfidy. Here, in emigration, I frequently come across this mentality and I always feel a terrible sense of shame, because, after all, this kind of immaturity is straight out of Gombrowicz. It is simply impossible to denationalize a mature nation, such as Lithuania undoubtedly is by now, even were someone to want very much to do so. This whole stereotype is inertia and a yearning to go backward. It can be useful only to the regime. It cannot, therefore, be ignored; we—the Poles, too—must steer clear of activities that can only incite or revive those feelings.

Naturally, it all hinges on Vilnius. There is a specific Lithuanian mythology of Vilnius; I believe it has played a greater role in the history of this city than, for example, economic relations. For the Poles, Wilno was a cultural center in the Kresy, the eastern borderlands; it was important, but it was still the provinces. For Lithuanians, it is a symbol of continuity and of historical identity, like Jerusalem. In the nineteenth and twentieth centuries, the myth of royal, holy Vilnius, torn away by force, shaped the Lithuanian imagination to a significant degree. This myth does not appeal to me in its entirety, especially the royalty and Grand Duchy part, but we have to admit that there is something to it. For example, Vilnius is very different from Riga or Tallinn, because it was not a Hanseatic center but was a capital city, a sacral city, and the seat of a great university as well. Nor was it a colonizing center, but developed naturally out of its terrain. Thus, the argument about Vilnius, as you have noticed, is an argument about the historical status of this city: need it be a regional center or can it be placed among the ranks of traditional East European capitals? It is also a question of the status and endurance of Lithuania. Because Lithuania without Vilnius is an ephemeral state, but with Vilnius it regains all its past and all its historic obligations.

There were no great battles between Lithuania and Poland; still, the problem of Vilnius was serious. The city gradually became a Polish (also a Jewish) enclave on Lithuanian territory. In the book I referred to earlier, *Everything about Wilno in 1913*, there are only two Lithuanian surnames: Smetona and Basanavičius (not just anybody, to be sure; the latter was the first signatory to the Act of Independence). The language of the surrounding areas was predominantly Lithuanian as late as the nineteenth century (I found out about this when I was working on Mickiewicz). In order to untie this historic, ethnic, and social knot, one would need the mind of a Solomon, and history has not been generous with us in this regard; anyway, there wasn't enough time. So people acted unwisely. Lithuanians were unable, and to this day are still unable, to forgive either the Żeligowski episode or the Polonizing fervor of Wojewoda Bociański and others; they also could not understand Piłsudski's federative ideas, and they were right, because a confederation is not created like that, even were it possible, which I doubt. But on the other hand, they did not want to understand that the Poles also had a right to Vilnius, since the Polish population and culture were dominant there. Forced Lithuanianization, just like forced Polonization, would have been an unforgivable sin. In any event, the stereotype of the "perfidious Pole" was, unfortunately, widespread in those days. Kaunas Lithuania was considered to be something like the Piedmont, whose aim was the taking of Rome, alias Vilnius. This was not a governmental issue alone; rather, it belonged to the sphere of mass emotions. And so the Lithuanians insisted on having things their way, although the triumph of Lithuanian obstinacy came about, with historic irony, in the most tragic of circumstances.

At present, however, it seems we both consider that this quarrel has been resolved. Having experienced the twentieth century, Vilnius is a new city. True, it is still the provinces, and the worst sort, because the whole Soviet Union is one horrible province. It is still an enclave, only now it is a Lithuanian-Russian enclave in predominantly Polish environs. I hope, however, that it will become the capital of a democratic Lithuania. Lithuanians, in a very difficult situation, have created the conditions for that.

It is still too early to speak about this democratic Lithuania. I think, however, that we have to keep it in mind as a possibility and a duty. We must also think about new Polish-Lithuanian relations from this perspective. We must think not about the future but about the present, because the immediate future will be the same old struggle with the totalitarian system, except that it will be carried out in more far-reaching ways, such as we have already had a taste of in Poland. Vilnius, that eternal enclave, is getting a new chance here. As a city of ethnic strata that overlap each other, it is a model for all of Eastern Europe. Coexistence and mutual enrichment must replace the old quarrels, and the antitotalitarian movement is actually the greatest help in this regard. Take, for example, the Jewish question. You are right: Vilnius cannot be the city it once was without the Jewish quarter, which was destroyed partly by the Germans, partly by the Soviets. However, the few Jews remaining in Vilnius are a significant group. Their relations with Lithuanians are not easy, because it is true that some Lithuanians—just like some Poles, Russians, and others—were provoked to commit crimes during the war. There are various reasons for this, which I shall not go into; one must also say that hundreds of Lithuanians, at risk of losing their own lives, were engaged in saving Jews. But a crime is a crime; there's no denying that. Recently, the television film *Holocaust*, which showed a Lithuanian SS legion participating in the liquidation of the Warsaw ghetto, was aired on TV; it has created a stir among the Lithuanian émigrés. Formally speaking, there was no such legion; rather, there were individuals. But people wanted to "redeem the national honor," as though it were possible to redeem something by silence, evasion, and placing the blame on the Germans, or even on the Jews themselves. The only thing this proves is the existence of complexes and a not entirely clear conscience. For me, a man from the other side, this is incomprehensible. It seems we have already overcome that complex. We know a number of axioms. First of all, that one may not keep silent about any crime. Second, that there were and are collaborators, sometimes in greater, sometimes in lesser numbers, depending on historical causes, but there is no such thing as a collaborator-nation. Third, that anti-Semitism and Sovietization are virtually one and the same thing. It is an enormous loss for Lithuanian culture that all traces of Jewish Vilnius have been eliminated, even those that could have been saved. And it is an utter shame that the exterminated Jews are not spoken of officially; only "innocent Soviet citizens" are mentioned. An understanding of these very simple things helps a great deal in untangling Lithuanian-Jewish problems and in daily collaborative work. Anti-Semitism in Lithuania—aside from the official anti-Semitism—is very weak today, perhaps even dying out. Obviously, a Jew would see this more clearly, but I have heard the same thing from Jews, too.

That same model can serve for the improvement of Lithuanian-Polish relations, and Lithuanian-Russian, although there are significant differences in each case. The matter of Lithuanianness or Polishness historically has been a terribly knotty question, because the very concept of "a Lithuanian," like the concept of "a Pole," has changed with the passage of centuries. According to one definition, Mickiewicz and Syrokomla are Lithuanians; another would

include Witkiewicz, Gombrowicz, and Milosz, too; according to a
third, Poška and Daukantas; a fourth, Lithuanian writers of the present
day; and Oscar Milosz requires a separate definition. One thing is
clear: our nations are bound together and will not be able to manage
without each other. In becoming a nation and a modern state, Lithuania had to emphasize that it is different from Poland. Today,
however, this does not have to be emphasized, because it is self-
evident. We also must not attack each other verbally, because, as I
have said, this only plays into the regime's hand. You say it is only
natural that the new Lithuanian nationalism was hypersensitive and
parochial. It may be that this was not always the case, because there
were some attempts at a dialogue with Poles which were answered
with a resounding "Never!" There were various unexpected rap-
prochements, both personal and familial, but I agree that there was
also a good deal of fanaticism and ordinary unadorned stupidity in
this, as can be said of every nationalism—French, Flemish, who
knows, maybe even Romansh. Apparently it's easier to forgive small
nations for this, but whether or not this is so, we must not forgive
ourselves. But those were relatively distant times. "Central Lithuania" itself, shall we say, is *plusquamperfectum*. The confederative
dreams of the Localists should also be considered a thing of the past;
after all, there are no Localists in Lithuania now. The very fact that
they had once existed was news to me, which perhaps reflects badly
on me; but I agree that there were some valuable ideas in that
program, which are worth remembering. A Finnish-Swedish solution
would have been a good idea, but that is probably a lost opportunity.
The same can be said of a Lithuanian literature in Polish (although
in a certain sense such a literature does exist: I would be inclined to
include *The Issa Valley* in it, for example). But above all, we have
to focus on reality. And reality is two hundred thousand Poles in the
Vilnius area and some twenty thousand Lithuanians in the vicinity
of Suwalki. There is no aristocracy among them by now and virtually
no intelligentsia; these are farmers and laborers, people who have
been oppressed by the regime and have a right to a human life. I
am furious when I see how Lithuanians are treated near Sejny, especially because it is the Polish Church, which has done so much
good, that is responsible for this. And should a forced Lithuanianization ever begin in the Vilnius area (today, there is no such thing,
because Russification is under way instead), I will be the first to say
"No!" And I hope I will not be alone.

You are right to say that it is easy to detect nationalism behind
the façade of official lies throughout Eastern Europe. It is an ambiv-

alent force, but a very dangerous one. The whole value of world culture resides in its variety of traditions and languages; but when language and ancestry turn into an amulet for saving one's life in time of slaughter, I would rather be the one being slaughtered. The humanization of national sentiments is of the utmost importance; we have to invest all our energies in it. There are some very positive phenomena in Lithuanian *samizdat*; I have mentioned them already. But sometimes one hears traditional voices, similar to those of the Endecja, only *à rebours*. However, this happens much less frequently than in the emigration, and there is some consolation in that. The Lithuanian *samizdat* has not, for the most part, been a product of the intelligentsia, yet it reaches intelligent conclusions. As for me personally, for some ten years in Lithuania and now in the emigration, of course, I have been accused of some sort of national treason. I am a cosmopolitan, a Judaeophile, a Polonophile, even a Russophile, and Lithuanians often irritate me, precisely because they are my people. For example, the Lithuanian Helsinki group was found guilty of being not Lithuanian dissidents but "all-Soviet" dissidents. But how could it be otherwise? The situation is hopeless if it is not a communal effort; besides which, we feel emotionally tied to everything that happens over there. "Over there" means not only in the Soviet Union but throughout Eastern Europe. We are East European dissidents. Or simply East Europeans, which amounts to the same thing. Vilnius is becoming one of the centers where the new East European formation is being born; perhaps this is its historic destiny. And you, too, belong to this formation; you have written about it often, and better than anyone else.

Tomas Venclova

1979

"ELEGY FOR N.N."

ELEGY FOR N.N.*

Tell me if it is too far for you.
You could have run over the small waves of the Baltic
and past the fields of Denmark, past a beech wood
could have turned toward the ocean, and there, very soon
Labrador, white at this season.
And if you, who dreamed about a lonely island,
were frightened of cities and of lights flashing along the highway
you had a path straight through the wilderness
over blue-black, melting waters, with tracks of deer and caribou
as far as the Sierras and abandoned gold mines.
The Sacramento River could have led you
between hills overgrown with prickly oaks.
Then just a eucalyptus grove, and you had found me.

True, when the manzanita is in bloom
and the bay is clear on spring mornings
I think reluctantly of the house between the lakes
and of nets drawn in beneath the Lithuanian sky.
The bath cabin where you used to leave your dress
has changed forever into an abstract crystal.
Honey-like darkness is there, near the veranda,
and comic young owls, and the scent of leather.

How could one live at that time, I really can't say.
Styles and dresses flicker, indistinct,
not self-sufficient, tending toward a finale.
Does it matter that we long for things as they are in themselves?

* Translated by Czeslaw Milosz and Laurence Davis.

The knowledge of fiery years has scorched the horses standing
   at the forge,
the little columns in the marketplace,
the wooden stairs and the wig of Mama Fliegeltaub.

We learned so much, this you know well:
how, gradually, what could not be taken away
is taken. People, countrysides.
And the heart does not die when one thinks it should,
we smile, there is tea and bread on the table.
And only remorse that we did not love
the poor ashes in Sachsenhausen
with absolute love, beyond human power.

You got used to new, wet winters,
to a villa where the blood of the German owner
was washed from the wall, and he never returned.
I too accepted but what was possible, cities and countries.
One cannot step twice into the same lake
on rotting alder leaves,
breaking a narrow sunstreak.

Guilt, yours and mine? Not a great guilt.
Secrets, yours and mine? Not great secrets.
Not when they bind the jaw with a kerchief, put a little cross
   between the fingers,
and somewhere a dog barks, and the first star flares up.

No, it was not because it was too far
you failed to visit me that day or night.
From year to year it grows in us until it takes hold,
I understood it as you did: indifference.

                                        Berkeley, 1962

"Elegy for N.N." was written in 1962, but for a long time it remained
in manuscript, as I hesitated whether to publish it at all. The poem
seemed to me shamelessly autobiographical, and in fact, it tells quite
faithfully a personal story. This is good, for poetry should capture
as much reality as possible, but a degree of a necessary artistic transformation is a delicate point. Fortunately, the person of whom I
speak has not been named; nevertheless, the situation is as melodramatic as only life is: I live in Berkeley, I learn through a letter

from Poland that a woman with whom I had once a loving relationship died recently. There are several details significant for those who read the poem in the original. The house by a lake is "beneath the Lithuanian sky," which is enough to invoke the exodus of populations at the end of World War II, when Lithuania found itself within the borders of the Soviet Union. "The horses standing at the forge," "the little columns in the marketplace," "the wig of Mama Fliegeltaub" mean that in the neighborhood there was a little town and that many Jews lived there before 1939. They were doomed once Hitler's army entered that area.

A reference to somebody dear to the heroine of the poem (a husband? a brother? a son?) who became "the poor ashes in Sachsenhausen" presupposes a knowledge of some historical facts: Oranienburg-Sachsenhausen was a large German concentration camp located near Berlin. As the Nazis placed the Poles on their list of "inferior races" close to the Jews, many were deported there, with a poor chance of surviving. By saying, "You got used to new, wet winters," I clearly state that my heroine moved after the war from her province to the territories situated to the West, formerly German, which were offered by Stalin to Poland as a compensation for the territories he had taken from Poland in the East.

Thus, the poem moves on the margin of big events in the history of the twentieth century. For an American reader that is no more than the history of East Central Europe. For me, it is simply the history of our planet—and not because I am a Polish poet, but because quite early, already at the time of World War II, consequences of what occurred in that part of the world could be foreseen. But, of course, when writing the poem I did not try to speak of history or to convey any message. I was following a true biography, though now I notice that the poem calls for copious historical footnotes.

There are two houses in the poem. One, by a lake; another, probably on the shore of the Baltic Sea ("wet winters"), a villa whose German owner has been killed, obviously in 1945, when the Soviet army overran that area in its march on Berlin. I ask myself whether I should now provide more information on those houses. The poem does not tell anything about how I became acquainted with them, whether I visited or lived there, etc. Images connected with those places are so vivid in my mind, I have so much to say on the subject, that my memory at once starts to spin a narrative amounting to a novel. Yet even though I have written two novels in my life, I have never been able to rid myself of uneasiness about that literary genre.

After all, a novelist exploits most intimate details from his or her life in order to prepare a concoction in which truth and invention are indistinguishable. A great master of such brazen operations was Dostoevsky. For instance, in *Crime and Punishment* he took his recently dead wife, Masha, for a model to depict crazy Mrs. Marmeladova, and even worse, in *The Idiot* he made comic General Ivolgin tell a tall tale on the burial of his own leg and on an inscription he placed on its tomb: the inscription, as we know today, was identical with that on the tomb of Dostoevsky's mother. To be able to sacrifice everything, even what one considers the most sacred, for the sake of an artistic composition seems to be a mark of the born novelist. But a poem does not aspire to a gossipy reconstruction of individual lives. Every poem is to a large extent circumstantial, and some familiarity on the part of the reader with circumstances behind the scene may help, provided that certain limits are preserved, so that enough of a *chiaroscuro*, of a mysteriousness, remains.

Information on the house by a lake, contained in the poem itself, must, I feel, suffice. It does not satisfy my craving for reality, yet I am aware of obstacles on the road toward capturing it. Social, political, psychological elements tempt us and tend to dilute that sort of conciseness which distinguishes poétry from prose. My commentary on the new home of my heroine would be even more prosaic. In 1945 I myself visited the "Western Territories" of Poland and to my surprise became an owner of a house previously belonging to a German: to explain why it was easy then to acquire a property—especially if you were a writer, a member of the Writers' Union—would need a whole treatise; as well as why property was practically worthless.

The poem does not explain what sort of relationship existed between N.N. and me. Love affairs between men and women are of an infinite variety, but stylistic means of expression at our disposal prove their inadequacy especially in that domain. The language tends to reduce individual cases to a common denominator proper to a given epoch. Lyrics of the sixteenth century sing of love that is not like ours, madrigals of the eighteenth century are imbued with a sensibility at which we look from a remote perspective. Similarly, love motives in the poetry of our time will be alien to the sensibility of the future. We may even suspect that a complex interplay of the mind and the flesh, making for a human sexuality so different from that of animals, constantly undergoes transformations that go together with transformations of the *Zeitgeist*. Of course, every poet is guided by Eros, who according to Plato is an intermediary between gods and men. Yet, considering the intricacies of our century, it is difficult today to write love lyrics. I have written a number of strongly erotic poems but very few addressed to a given woman. And "Elegy for N.N." is, for better or worse, an example of a rather reticent approach. It happens, though, that now, returning to the poem after many years, I discover its value as a memorial. I have brought her to life in a way and now again I feel her presence.

I discover also that this is a sad poem. Think how many dead are in it: N.N. herself; Mama Fliegeltaub, who was the owner of the only inn in the town and who stands for its whole Jewish population—as far as I know the Germans did not even care to deport them but executed them on the spot; a person close to N.N., who died in Sachsenhausen; a German owner of the villa. And all that just because I gave account of facts. But the saddest is the ending and I am not sure whether I approve of it. Probably not, which would mean that I have changed since the time the poem was written. Indifference and a feeling of distance from the world of the living have been ascribed to the shadows of the underworld, inhabitants of Hades. Upon my arrival in Berkeley in 1960 directly from Europe, I was for a long time visited by a thought that the distance separating me from the places of my childhood and youth had something eerie in it, that perhaps I found myself, if not in Hades, at least upon some unearthly fields among lotus-eaters; in other words, that I started to lead a sort of after-life. This found its reflection in the poem's last stanza. Which is invalidated by the rest of the poem. For N.N. visited me, after all. And by writing about her, I proved that I was not indifferent.

[Written in English by C.M.]

INTRODUCTION TO STANISŁAW VINCENZ, *ON THE SIDE OF MEMORY**

Were I only to praise Stanislaw Vincenz in this foreword to his essays, thereby setting up his readers for disappointment, I would be doing him no favor. There is no reason to hide the fact that the majority of those who pick up this book will put it aside after skimming several, perhaps a dozen, pages, "because who has the patience for all this." It could not be otherwise, for every age has its own manner of reading, and the manner to which we are accustomed is completely off the mark in this instance. The manner, or perhaps I should have said, the rhythm. Among contemporary authors there are those who are easily accessible, and those who are difficult, but Vincenz's "difficulty" is of a particular, almost unknown variety, because it does not stem from either the intricacy of his argumentation or an excess of intellectual shortcuts. It is easy to master this difficulty, but in order to do so we must rid ourselves of all impatience, we must somehow slow down our pulse and allow ourselves to be led by this prose that spills out in innumerable digressions and does not aim at any dramatic conclusions. A similar preparatory transformation, or breathing exercise, is required for the reading of many classical authors, if we really wish to profit from them; the same preparation is necessary for reading sixteenth- and seventeenth-century writers. Vincenz is old-fashioned, but with an old-fashionedness that does not date from just a few decades ago. This is writing in defiance of this century, repudiating all of the century's spices, that is, the assorted whips that flog the reader and thereby maintain the intensity of his attention.

Obviously: a chatty style. As everyone knows, Polish literature never had much success with the novel, but it presents itself very nicely in memoirs, chatty narratives (*gawędy*), and epistolary prose. This tradition, should it continue to bear fruit, apparently contains

* Stanisław Vincenz, *Po stronie pamięci. Wybór esejów* (Paris: Instytut Literacki, 1965).

a number of as yet unexploited possibilities. Certainly, it would be impossible to divide a history of twentieth-century Polish literature into such chapters as Poetry, The Novel, The Theater, Criticism, overlooking genres that are more difficult to define and that may well be the most interesting. It so happens that two people whose youth coincided with the years before the First World War have behaved like gardeners who cross-fertilize previously distinct species of plants: they crossed the old gentry *gawęda* with humanistic erudition, producing what we are accustomed to call the essay, although this foreign and too inclusive term does not capture the distinctive, native features of the new creation. I am thinking of Paweł Hostowiec and of Vincenz, whose "essayistic writing," which was already evident in many chapters of *In the Upper Highlands*, develops chronologically in the present volume, starting from meditations on the Hungarian landscape during the last war. It is not a good idea to manufacture categories and to cram dissimilar authors into them. However, both Vincenz and Hostowiec incline one to similar reflections on the complex of conditions, so infrequently met with in Europe, that was the necessary prerequisite for the development of this new genre. Both came from a region where civilizations, religions, and languages had interacted for many centuries, where the wind that blew from the sea was the wind of the Argonauts' Colchis and of the Ionian cities of Asia Minor. This region produced the "Ukrainian school" of poetry, suffused Słowacki's writing with its special color, shaped the young Joseph Conrad. One would be hard put to deny that such native realms were influential in producing the benevolent response to the shifting affairs of men, viewed against a background of bitter experience, that writers from this region, endowed as they are with historic memory, have achieved. But Vincenz and Hostowiec are also linked by a phase of European education, the last one, it seems, when people were taught in high school to read the Greeks and Romans in the original. Vincenz would not have spent years in the company of Homer and Plato had there been no Gymnasium in Kołomyja. Although, to be sure, once he had discovered Greece he must have become more and more certain that he had made the acquaintance of something familiar: the pastoral civilization in his native Carpathians, like all the mountainous regions of the Balkans, still preserved many features of a society that was no longer known in any other part of the world. Even today, don't researchers who want to discover how the ancient Greek bards recited Homer travel with their tape recorders to the villages of Montenegro and Macedonia? However, these elements would have combined to produce a different alloy had they not been tempered by the old gentry sensibility. It is impossible to define, but we recognize its tangible presence in Kochanowski's poetry, in Christmas carols, in songs and Italianate love poems, in baroque idylls. The transformation of the noble class into a synonym for all sorts of evil does an injustice to the other side of the coin, to the gentleness, the rectitude, the graciousness that for much of the history of the Commonwealth was the ally of religious and linguistic tolerance. Such is the tone, elusive, but ever present, of Vincenz's and Hostowiec's erudite *gawęda*, a tone that is almost courtly, with a friendly and somewhat unexpected sense of humor.

How, then, should one approach Vincenz's book? One should, I think, pretend that one is sitting in a dimly lit room, watching the flames in the fireplace consume the thick logs and listening to stories about distant lands, their rivers, mountains, and gods, about encounters with ancient poets and philosophers. The storyteller seems to derive pleasure from the telling itself, and to forget why it is that every so often he spins a new yarn from some trifling detail. He doesn't want to prove anything, and just when we think he is making a point it soon looks as if he has lost the thread and is not at all certain what it was that he was aiming at. And only imperceptibly, gradually, as we give up the desire to extract a thesis and a conclusion from the husk that encloses them, does an impishly concealed, Socratically masked intention begin to emerge·from the juxtaposition of tales.

Despite appearances, Vincenz is engaged in a very contemporary polemic, although he does not make use of argumentation in his objections. He takes the listener-reader by the hand, leads him in the opposite direction, and says to him, "Don't look there; look over here." That is how he attempts to heal him. From what ailment? From what each of us is inclined to consider as the fate of man today, from anxiety, despair, the sense of the absurd, whose true names are no doubt "godlessness" and "nihilism." The godless man can travel for many hundreds or thousands of kilometers in a single day without noticing anything that might move him, and just as space loses the value of the particular for him, so, too, does time lose value; for him, the past is obscured by a cloud of gray dust, it is reduced to vectors of motion, "lines of development"; no inn, in which it would be pleasant to stop and rest, attracts him. His nihilism is a feeling that he has lost his fatherland, both heavenly and earthly.

A fatherland is that which we love. Can one love a Heaven that has been stripped of all fantasies about it? Can one love an Earth whose expanse is changing into an abstraction?

Vincenz's endeavor depends on his carefully persuading us that much of this is our own fault. He is a pious pilgrim to the fatherland. The events in his life were not necessarily a major influence here, although they, too, attest to a certain constant striving. Vincenz arrived in Hungary in 1940, after an arduous journey from his Carpathian backwater near Kołomyja across snow-covered mountain passes. After the war, he did not distance himself from that mountain range, the geographical backbone of Europe, whose eastern spur is the Carpathian Mountains and western, the French slopes of the Alps. He settled first in Grenoble, then in a village near Grenoble, not far from the spot from which his Provençal ancestors had emigrated to the east several centuries earlier, turning into Polish gentry over there. It is probably not too wide of the mark to say that Vincenz's habits as a denizen of the mountains explain his gift for noticing the detailed texture of the landscape: more things *happen* on the same amount of space in the mountains than in the valleys. Indeed, the antidote for godlessness and nihilism that Vincenz prescribes (circuitously and secretly) is the enrichment of space and time: so that something might *happen* in them, so that our imagination might be open to it.

These days, denunciations of the world usually assume the form of denunciations of civilization and its vain repetitiveness, or of the impasse into which civilization's exceedingly presumptuous variations are driving us. Deracinated, and thus deprived of collective memory, the individual has as the sole proof of his identity only his own body, placed in opposition to a world from which the entire history of the human species has been erased as if with a sponge. The spreading cult of primitivism is tantamount to idolization of the moment when experience is severed from any communal before or communal after: this is how hope is supposed to issue forth from meaninglessness. It is no accident that the literature of the Beat Generation, for whom the "moment" is a key word, arose in America, where the always fragile bonds between human beings have succumbed to even further weakening. Entering into the artificial paradises of psychedelic experiments, they try in vain to convince themselves that they are Adam, who has not yet torn the apple from the tree of knowledge. This innocence, with an awareness of demiurges and monsters lurking right beneath it, is much too constrained.

Reading Vincenz in an age like this is a thoroughly contrary, antiprimitivistic endeavor. Humanists generally distrust a *tabula rasa*, and they are right to do so. For at every moment, whether we admit it or not, we are in the power of those who lived before us. Where there is no memory, both time and space are a wasteland; the trees and rocks speak to us, but we do not understand them. Only through memory can we learn to understand their speech. It is not for nothing that Vincenz writes in praise of Pausanias, who, while traveling through despoiled, plundered, depopulated Greece in the second century A.D., was able to divine what would later, much later, preoccupy entire generations. It is possible that I could not have written my introduction to this book by the Pausanias-like Vincenz were it not for certain of my experiences as a Polish poet caught between two fires: between history reduced to vulgar schemata and a contagious revulsion against history; for dissembling and crippled as it is, history does not fulfill any of its promises. However, if one wishes to preserve one's respect for being and not to perceive everything that surrounds us as meaningless magma, one can discover a number of positive indicators by reflecting on one's own genealogy. It seems to me that Polish literature, despite its numerous weaknesses, offers better antidotes against today's despair than the much more brilliant or substantial literatures of Western Europe. Its hopeless entanglement in historic events, which it continually grumbles about, enables it to form a sense of historical particularity that "more fortunate" peoples do without. In other words, whoever descends from this literature receives *signifying time* as a gift, and even if his efforts to decipher its meanings are in vain, he is full of curiosity about them, he does not sink into apathy, which is the mother of boredom and grayness. If, like Norwid or Brzozowski, he is conscious of this blessing, his writing will be an invitation to the energetic deciphering of meaning. It is unlikely that a sensibility like Vincenz's could have appeared within some other literary tradition. He represents, I dare say, the opposite pole that has often counterbalanced an overly functional immersion in actuality.

Man dies and we are unable to reconcile ourselves to this. When, during the war, Vincenz kept a record of his thoughts about the Hungarian landscape, he was engaged in an endeavor that many of us would not consider totally alien: there is a death-defying permanence in earth that is molded by a human hand. The end of the world will come, but for lovers who are still holding hands twenty years later, it is not the end of the world. Gods may perish, but in fact they only vanish from our sight, becoming incarnate anew and assuming different forms, so that we do not immediately recognize their heavenly origin. It is not at all surprising that Vincenz's book is, above all, a journey through Greece and Italy, countries where many such incarnations have taken place. One may suspect that its aim is to incline us to optimistic doubts about our knowledge: what if the truth of immortality is richer than expected, if nothing is ever destroyed, if the Eleusinian mysteries of Greece are still taking place?

The two names that appear most often on the pages of Vincenz are Homer and Dante. They personify the two periods of European civilization when man had a fatherland. We don't really know what Homer's fate was, and Dante spent most of his life in exile, but they are poets for whom the heavens are full of the shapes and colors of Earth, and the Earth is not empty, because the currents and whispers of heavenly forces run across it. Attempting to prophesy the future of Slavic theater, Mickiewicz viewed the Slavs as the heirs of both ancient Greece and the Middle Ages, because they wove a sense of the supernatural, of the miraculous, into all human affairs. When Vincenz was a young man, this was still most definitely true of the Hutzul peasants, which is yet another reason why Vincenz is able to approach Homer and Dante differently from scholars or even poets from industrialized regions. The "miraculous" is the liberation of the imagination, which is always spatial. The gods have human faces; an animal approaches us on a forest path, but he is both himself and someone else—there is no distance between the thing and the symbol. We understand what this means by contrast, measuring the progress of abstraction from the moment when Zwingli asked if Christ is actually present in the Eucharist or *only* symbolically present. That is why when we read Vincenz we are always haunted by the question: Is this movement that has carried us away toward absence, toward dispossession, toward the not-quite-corporeality of the imagination something that is irrevocable?

Vincenz, as is his wont, does not provide an answer. At the most, he allows us to discern from the ebb and flow of motifs, from the traces of ancient religion in folklore, from the wandering of forms, a certain archetypal permanence under the surface mutability. It seems that it is not salutary to pose overly disquieting questions, that we should rather trust our attraction to seemingly naïve rites and incantations. Under his influence, various assumptions come to mind; for example, that the intense historicity that characterizes our era has filled up our minds with the simplified, abbreviated concept of "phases" or "stages," in consequence of which everyone now assigns responsibility to the "phase" in which he lives, and goes on at great length about technology, frustration, and alienation. Or another assumption: that although there is a good deal of truth in the diagnoses of our *mal du siècle* or *Weltschmerz* (by no means the first in history), at the same time something more propitious is sketched out here, not through a return to philosophical systems that are no longer possible, but through the further intensification of historicity, until it is transformed from being cold, schematic, and impoverishing into being warm, complex, and enriching. In his anthropological ruminations, Vincenz bears some resemblance to Frobenius, who pointed anthropology in a new direction by observing that "civilized" people, by subscribing to the prejudices of naïve evolutionism, have thoroughly misinterpreted "inferior," "aboriginal" civilizations. This naïve evolutionism has endured for a long time, as is demonstrated by the (absolutely authentic) example of a certain Annie, a very young and poorly educated girl, who was already conversant with the so-called achievements of science. Annie once said, "In my opinion, those Romantic poets must have been beastly." "Why?" "Because man is descended from apes and they lived such a long time ago." Rather than laugh at the girl, we should look inside ourselves and consider whether, perchance, there isn't some of the same facile wisdom in our own fascination with the revolution that has elevated us above all humanity that came before us and deposited us on the plateaus of a barren earth. It would be impolite to assert that all we need is to wish for it and our imagination will organize cosmic space hierarchically into Dante's Heaven, Purgatory, and Hell. But in the continuous complaints about the uniqueness of our situation there is a great deal of self-torment and self-pity. We are not alone, and the miraculous has not disappeared forever, for man is a miraculous being; if we need to hunt for theses, then that would probably be Vincenz's main thesis.

I have no doubt that in such a multilayered and dense book as this, each reader will find his own pathways and will admire different sights. Let these comments of mine, then, be accepted as an expression of one reader's very personal interests.

Berkeley, 1965

LOOKING FOR A CENTER:
ON THE POETRY OF CENTRAL EUROPE

My title may suggest something profound, perhaps a metaphor referring to the psychology of modern man. But I intend to speak of
more elemental, more earthly matters, namely geography. Whoever
pronounces the word *center* implies another word, *periphery*, and a
relationship between the two, either centrifugal or centripetal. Also,
a center implies two crossing lines, vertical and horizontal. These
few elementary notions about space should be present in our mind
when we deal with the geography and history of Europe taken as a
whole, and particularly of so-called Eastern Europe. Perhaps, coming from an area which for a long time has been considered the
Eastern marches of Rome-centered Christendom makes one more
sensitive to shifting points of gravity, symbolized by the very fluidity
of such terms as *the West* and *the East*. Though my subject is the
twentieth century, when such shifts have been accelerated, I feel I
must first make a brief historical survey. My examples will be taken
from the history of Polish letters, with which I am best acquainted,
but I do not doubt that students of Czech or Hungarian or Baltic
literatures will easily find analogies.

Human imagination is constantly busy with organizing geographical space. A village or town where we live is "here," while many
important events take place "over there," at a distant, more or less
definite point. For a medieval clerk the West–East axis was perhaps
less tangible than the North–South axis, as the countries situated
north of the Alps directed their longing toward Italy and the capital
of the Christian world, Rome. In Poland for a couple of centuries
medieval Latin was the only written language, as opposed to the
spoken vernacular, and as a consequence, literary models were
brought from *outside*. Even Polish syllabic verse was invented in
imitation of the medieval Latin syllabic verse. More or less at the
same time the marvels of Italy of the Quattrocento began to acquire

a legendary dimension. A Polish poet writing in Latin around 1500, Janicius, while staying on scholarship in Italy, sang the beauty of that country, though he was wary to moderate the extent of his "Italianization" for fear that his scholarship wouldn't be renewed. The most important Slavic poet to appear before the nineteenth century, Jan Kochanowski, spent ten years in Italy as a student of humanities. And a curious anecdote might be recalled concerning his time, namely the sixteenth century. Readers of French poets of La Pléiade are familiar with a poem, "On the Ruins of Rome," by Joachim du Bellay. However, an identical poem is found among the works of his Polish contemporary Mikołaj Sęp-Szarzyński. What is more, an identical poem exists in Spanish under the name of a famous Spanish poet, Francisco Quevedo. It is quite probable that the same poem exists in other European languages, always presented as an original product. To my knowledge, nobody solved that puzzle, with the exception of a Polish gentleman-scholar, the late Jerzy Stempowski, who told me about the results of his detective work in a private letter. He discovered the source of all those poems—an original written in Latin by an Italian humanist, Ianus Vitalis of Palermo, who is today forgotten. Many similar examples of Italian influence can be found in poetry, painting, architecture, and music.

The seventeenth century not only initiated a scientific revolution but also gradually moved the cultural center of Continental Europe from Rome to Paris. Baroque architecture, Italian opera, and Italian dance tunes competed for a while with French classical tragedy, but the name of René Descartes explains why Paris proved victorious. The French language was becoming a language of letters and sciences as well as of the literary salon in a more and more cosmopolitan Europe, and it preserved that position till the outbreak of World War I.

My paper could as well be entitled "What Happened in Our Time to Paris, Once a Mecca of Poets and Painters?" A student of modern poetry in whatever language must invariably go back to Charles Baudelaire, Arthur Rimbaud, and Stéphane Mallarmé. Those were also the patron saints of bohemian groups of poets around 1900 in Cracow, Warsaw, Prague, and Budapest. The claims of Berlin, Munich, and Vienna to the position of cultural capitals of Europe were short-lived in spite of ties between such groups as Young Scandinavia and Young Poland meeting and influencing each other in Germany. For poets and painters to be "in" meant to be "in" artistic Paris. Bolesław Leśmian, the most accomplished poet of the Polish "Moderna," went through several years of Parisian apprenticeship. The roster of the Society of Polish Artists active in Paris in 1910 reads like a list of the most eminent names in Polish arts and letters of that period. The mythological aspects of Paris and the birthplace of everything new and daring was enhanced of course by the fact that great Polish Romantic poetry had been written there and a nineteenth-century precursor of modern Polish verse, Norwid, had lived there. (In parenthesis, he was as much Italy-oriented as was Robert Browning. One of the most interesting Polish long poems of the nineteenth century, *Quidam* by Norwid, deals with Rome at the time of Emperor Hadrian.)

The legends surrounding a center of attraction travel with a variable speed, and it may happen that the glow of a star is strongest at the very moment its source is dying. Paris after World War I, the Paris of Gertrude Stein, Hemingway, Fitzgerald, and so many other American expatriates, was still aglow, but signs of decline had appeared. Probably one spot in Paris could be indicative of the last acme and of the fall—this was the Café La Coupole at Boulevard Montparnasse, which together with the Café Dôme reached its peak of fame in 1926 and started to fade in 1930, never to recover, or what amounts to the same, it acquired a different, less colorful public. The Paris of the 1920s and 1930s still was sending abroad its inventions: Surrealism, even new phases of Picasso, *Le Cimetière Marin* of Paul Valéry, the Neo-Thomistic philosophy of Jacques Maritain. Yet for poets in Warsaw or Prague, the City of Lights remained primarily the home of nineteenth-century genius, above all of Symbolist poetics, much as for their painter contemporaries everything received a new beginning with the paintings of Cézanne. Two main schools of poetry in Poland of the interwar period, Skamander and the Avant-Garde, even if hostile to each other, continued, each in its own way, different aspects of the poetics to be found in the poems, notes, and letters of Stéphane Mallarmé. Native roots in the past of Polish poetry should not be neglected by a student of that period, nor the affinity with Russian Acmeism bypassed, but the French contribution probably outweighs others.

Similarities among poets of the Renaissance, whether French or Polish or Croatian, were due to their common models taken from Italy. Similarities among modern poets of various languages were due to their openness to French influence. However, it would be a mistake to reduce this to the question of fashion and of imitation. Rather, French men of letters succeeded in imposing everywhere their own conviction that what was French was universal, i.e., a norm for the whole civilized world, while the particular, different in every country, constituted so many deviations. Such a view can be traced back to the French Revolution, with its ambition of delivering a message to the whole of humanity. And undoubtedly, a certain political mythology of liberty, then of Napoleon, helped in sustaining the authority of French thought and literature in my part of Europe. If the attitude of the nineteenth-century Russians toward France was one of love-hate, the countries situated between Russia and Germany represented another nuance of feeling, close to unhappy love.

Only someone who, like myself, witnessed in 1940 the reactions of the Polish population to the news of the fall of France can realize the extent of their shock and despair. Instinctively it was taken as even more significant than Hitler's victory over Poland—in fact, as the end of Europe. And it was. After the first tentative partition of Europe by the Ribbentrop–Molotov Pact, the second partition in Yalta sealed Europe's fate. An enigmatic new era emerged for some hundred millions of Europeans who were then officially relegated to "the East"—and also for their poets.

Moscow, the capital of the empire, aspired now to the title of the center of Communism and, potentially, of the planet Earth. The premise of its precedence as a model for the future had to be universally accepted. The first decade after the war saw a gradual implementation of that premise as political institutions, the economic system, philosophy, art, and literature, first elaborated in Moscow, were imposed and copied in the newly conquered countries. Then something strange happened: a clash between two forces opposed to each other, between the traditional pull of Mediterranean civilization and of France, on the one hand, and of the new center of political power in Moscow on the other. Nowhere was that clash more obvious than in literature, especially in poetry. As a result, Moscow completely failed in its attempt to establish its cultural preeminence; on the contrary, it came to be regarded as backward and barbarian. Yet since it exerted complete political control, a curious and ominous dichotomy made its appearance, consisting in rule by a party which hadn't conquered the hearts and minds of the people. The dichotomy was kept in check as long as Western imports in styles and ideas were strictly forbidden and branded as decadent and bourgeois. The relaxation of control after the turbulent year 1956 in Poland and Hungary brought about a true invasion of everything Western, in thought, art, literature, music, even women's dresses: a sufficient demonstration that there was a vacuum to be filled. Since that moment Polish and, as far as I know, Hungarian or Czech poetry has been in form as "Western," or, if you prefer, "postmodern," as one could desire.

Such facts are usually told with a kind of glee or with a self-congratulatory smile and presented as a victory of freedom. In my opinion the matter is made a little more complex by the rather illusory existence of the Western half of Europe. Amid prosperity and technical progress it has been losing its power to inspire arts and letters, and its once famous center, Paris, has been touched by a progressive eclipse of vigor.

The military impotence of Western Europe thus mysteriously parallels or follows the weakening of its spirit. Avid for Western models, people of the Eastern half of Europe have been discovering the illusory character of Western promise. One could write a whole book on Polish poetry of the last two decades as a history of the gradual realization that former centers of attraction do not offer much in terms of values, and that a poet from the East must rely upon his own resources.

There is a curious poem by Zbigniew Herbert, "Mona Lisa." Leonardo's painting in the Louvre symbolizes the Europe of supreme cultural achievements, but a Europe that was for many years forbidden to the inhabitants of countries behind the Iron Curtain. Images of war and annihilation are the background for the representation of a dream about going one day to Paris. The narrator obviously is a survivor with obsessive memories. Those very memories make a mockery out of a meeting with Mona Lisa, an inert object. Let me quote a few fragments:

> *Through seven mountain frontiers*
> *barbed wire of rivers*
> *and executed forests*
> *and hanged bridges*
> *I kept coming—*
> *through waterfalls of stairways*
> *whirlings of sea wings*
> *and baroque heaven*
> *all bubbly with angels*
> *—to you*
> *Jerusalem in a frame*
>
> *. . .*

So I'm here
You see, I am here
I hadn't a hope
but I'm here

Laboriously smiling
resin colored mute convex

As if constructed out of lenses
concave landscape for a background

between the blackness of her back
which is like a moon in clouds

and the first tree of the surroundings
is a great void froths of light

so I'm here
sometimes it was
sometimes it seemed that

don't even think about it

only her regulated smile
her head a pendulum at rest

her eyes dream into infinity
but in her glances snails are asleep

so I'm here
they were all going to come
I'm alone

when already
he could no longer move his head
he said
as soon as all this is over
I'm going to Paris
between the second and the third finger
of the right hand
a space
I put in this furrow
the empty shells of fates
so I'm here
it's me here

pressed into the floor
with living heels

[Translated by Peter Dale Scott]

A chapter in a hypothetical book on Polish postwar poetry should be dedicated to irony and even derision in the treatment of the Western European and particularly French intellectuals. Paris in the 1950s exported a desperate vision of man's condition in the writings of its Existentialists. Though Albert Camus didn't want to be called that name, he, more than any of his colleagues, caught the imagination of Polish poets who engaged in polemics with him in poetry and prose. Camus's short novel *The Fall* provoked Jarosław Iwaszkiewicz to answer in a story entitled "The Ascent." The narrator is an average Pole who has lived through the horrors of the Nazi occupation and later of the Stalinist terror. By implication Camus is accused of contriving sufferings for his hero in a century when *real* sufferings abound. In other words, a *real* hell is opposed to a *literary* hell. Yet, in my opinion, the scorn with which Iwaszkiewicz treats Camus is unjustified and the story may be called an exercise in self-pity. Nevertheless, it merits mention, as it is highly characteristic.

Some Polish critics have considered Tadeusz Różewicz the most important voice among poets who made their debut after the war. If this is true, then a tone of derision, especially when he speaks of Western thinkers and artists, deserves particular attention. Różewicz's nihilistic poetry seems to be built upon several layers of anger and disgust, perhaps disgust with the pretense of Western Europe to exist, when its time is over. In any case, such a meaning may be read into a polemic with *The Fall* of Albert Camus. I quote from Różewicz's poem entitled "Falling":

Camus
La Chute the Fall

Oh, my dear fellow, for a man who is alone, without
God and without master, the weight of days is dreadful

that fighter with the heart of the child
imagined

that the concentric canals of Amsterdam
were a circle of hell
the hell of solid citizens
of course

"here we are in the last circle"
the last moralist
in French literature
was saying to a chance acquaintance
in some joint

he inherited from his childhood
a belief in the bottom
he certainly had a deep love of Dostoevsky
he certainly suffered because
there was no hell no heaven
no Lamb
no lie
it seemed to him he had discovered the bottom
that he was lying at the bottom
that he had fallen

Meanwhile
there was no longer any bottom
instinctively this was understood by
a certain young miss from Paris
and she wrote a composition
about copulation bonjour tristesse
about death bonjour tristesse
while grateful readers
on both sides
of the formerly so-called
iron curtain
bought her . . .
for its weight in gold
the young miss that lady
that young miss that lady
understood that there is no Bottom
no circles of hell
no rise
and no Fall
that everything is played out
in the familiar
none-too-large area
between
Regio genus anterior
Regio pubice
and regio oralis

and what was once
the vestibule of hell
has been changed
by the fashionable lady of letters
into the vestibulum
vaginae

[Translated by Magnus J. Krynski and Robert Maguire]

I do not share Różewicz's philosophy. I think his mistake consists of exaggerating the predicament of contemporary man. Certainly, our century is not a serene one. But problems confronting our ancestors were not easier to cope with, even if today we witness the fulfillment of Nietzsche's prophecy, namely, the rise of "European nihilism." Not very much comes out of wailing over the human condition as Różewicz does. Intellectually crude, he may be interesting only if we regard his poetry as a code for an obsession of a political nature, what I would call a complex of betrayal by the West. That complex may express itself sometimes as a rejoicing over the universal decay of values.

It would be wrong to underestimate the subtle and hidden relations between poetry and politics. And the intellectual Paris of the 1950s and 1960s turned with expectation to the East, masochistically assigning itself the role of a periphery of Moscow. A poem written decades earlier by the Greek poet Cavafy, "Expecting the Barbarians," acquired a new poignancy and was particularly liked by the Polish poets as an indictment of their Western European brethren. The poem is famous and I am sure many people know it, but let me recall it here once more. It tells the story of how a center, by losing faith in itself, changes through resignation into a periphery.

What are we waiting for, assembled in the public square?
The barbarians are to arrive today.

Why such inaction in the Senate?
Why do the Senators sit and pass no laws?

Because the barbarians are to arrive today.
What further laws can the Senators pass?
When the barbarians come they will make the laws.

Why did our emperor wake up so early,
and sit at the principal gate of the city,
on the throne, in state, wearing his crown?

Because the barbarians are to arrive today.
And the emperor waits to receive
their chief. Indeed he had prepared
to give him a scroll. Therein he engraved
many titles and names of honor.

Why have our two consuls and the praetors come out
today in their red, embroidered togas;
and rings with brilliant glittering emeralds;
why are they carrying costly canes today,
superbly carved with silver and gold?

Because the barbarians are to arrive today,
and such things dazzle the barbarians.

Why don't the worthy orators come as usual
to make their speeches, to have their say?

Because the barbarians are to arrive today;
and they get bored with eloquence and orations.

Why this sudden unrest and confusion?
(How solemn their faces have become.)
Why are the streets and squares clearing quickly,
and all return to their homes, so deep in thought?

Because night is here but the barbarians have not come.
Some people arrived from the frontiers,
and they said that there are no longer any barbarians.

And now what shall become of us without any barbarians?
Those people were a kind of solution.

[Translated by Rae Dalven]

In recent decades, American, not French, poetry has entered the countries of Eastern Europe as an active force. And yet it had been to a large extent shaped by Europe-oriented expatriates, like Ezra Pound or T. S. Eliot. Thus, we may speak of American poetry of our century as undergoing a rather belated transformation from a dependent into an autonomous organism, if not a center. There are signs indicating that a similar process has been taking place in my area of Europe. Its poetry has been recognized as a specific component of the international literary scene. When in the 1960s I translated a number of poems from Polish and published them under the title *Postwar Polish Poetry*, I had a very lively response, especially among young American poets, many of whom told me later that poems from my anthology influenced their own writings. They sensed in those poems something different from what they had previously found in Western European poets read in translation, perhaps more vigor, clarity, and sensitivity to historical situations. Yet some poets whom I translated, whether Herbert or Różewicz or others, were still in the phase of bitter accounts with Western Europe because of its failure to continue to exist as a *subject*, not an *object*, of history.

A visible change occurred in the 1970s, as if a new generation assumed the decline and fall of the Western center as self-evident and decided to tackle their own problems in their own way, which, in poetry, meant giving a growing role to Polish poets of the past and a priority to the moral choices of the individual in the Communist system. Such, for instance, is the poetry of Barańczak, Krynicki, Kornhauser, Zagajewski—committed, not expecting anything from outside, and fostering the development of the new power: public opinion.

The present cultural setup in Europe is strange indeed, and its future enigmatic. It is not probable that Moscow will emerge as a center of attraction. On the contrary, every year seems to advance its sclerosis in philosophy, art, and literature, while only its military power is growing. The inhabitants of the empire, if they look for inspiration from *outside*, may follow fashion that favors America; and of course the English language has been doing well all over Europe, at the expense of French. However, the differences in the political and economic systems are so great that affinities must be superficial, often based upon misunderstanding, much as the Polish independent trade unions have little in common with American unions, except for the name. One may submit the thesis that we are moving toward a pluralistic, multicentered world without a clear-cut North–South or East–West axis. Then the name "East Central Europe" would receive a new legitimacy as a certain cultural unit, placed in the Eastern orbit by force of arms and by pacts between the superpowers, but maintaining its own identity. Poetry of that part of the world, always registering the moods of a given country through a tangle of hints and allusions, may provide many insights in that respect.

And yet, if we take such an outcome as probable, we are confronted with many unknowns. Standing on one's own feet, liberating oneself from the vestiges of unhappy love for the West, is a good thing, provided it doesn't lead to entrenching oneself in a morbid nationalism. An East Central Europe composed of closed national compartments hostile or indifferent to each other would be against the vital interests of its nations. The remedy for such a division is a clear understanding of the past which, in spite of national differences, is common, for East Central Europe was ruled by the North–South axis and the East–West axis. It is quite a task, the task of bringing to light what unites those countries in their present struggle for cultural identity, and it also awaits their poets, whether they are Polish, Lithuanian, Czech, or Hungarian. A sense of history is a specific contribution of our geographic area to world literature; and if a poet must sometimes turn against the nationalism of his compatriots to remain faithful to his historical imagination, he will be vindicated sooner or later.

1982   [Written in English by C.M.]

ON NATIONALISM

A famous manifesto of 1848 began with the words: "A specter is haunting Europe, the specter of Communism." Now, at the end of the twentieth century, looking back at the history of many decades, we recognize the validity of those words written by Marx and Engels. From our perspective, however, another statement would have also been true: "A specter is haunting Europe, the specter of nationalism." It is an open question as to which of those two specters has proved its greater ability to become reality. However, while many thousands of pages have been dedicated to Communism, nationalism remains elusive, not openly confronted, and even shameful. In view of the magnitude of evil perpetrated in the name of a nation confronting another nation, as well as the absurd doctrines justifying the unique vocation of one's own nation, that reticence in recognizing the importance of the phenomenon is understandable. And yet wherever we look in the world today we see the extreme vitality of various nationalisms engaging human lives and making people ready to die in the name of a given nation.

At the end of the eighteenth century the word *nation* started to attract attention because the French nation was a great motoric force in the history of that period. The French nation was bound by the ideals of the rights of man and of the French Revolution; to be a Frenchman meant to make a choice, and in fact foreigners would proclaim themselves Frenchmen because they shared the revolutionary ideal. Spawned in a way by the philosophers of the French Enlightenment, the Revolution was bringing forward a peculiar commitment to the universal ideas of brotherhood, of equality, and of liberty as a bond of all who belonged to *la nation*. All of us who like myself have been primarily engaged in the history of literature rather than the study of history itself are aware of the central role played by Romanticism in Europe, especially in East Central Europe. *Nation* in Romanticism means something very different from *la nation* in the French sense. The origins of Romanticism were in Germany and the first Romantics were students and young poets—humiliated by the defeats inflicted on Germany by Napoleon. I wonder whether someone will write a book on the rebellious groups of the so-called Young Germany with their fanaticism, burning of books, and killing of colleagues suspected of treason, in light of what we were able to observe in the leftist and terroristic movements in Western Germany in the 1960s. Romanticism introduced the notion of the ineffable national soul that supposedly determines a given man's belonging to a nation. It was not the free choice of an individual but his birth which was the decisive factor. One was a member of a given nation by virtue of being born on a given soil, from parents of the same language as their ancestors, also because one shared the destiny of a tribe, of a race, or, as some would say, of a common historical fate. Romanticism in its political aspect was nothing else than nationalism. Perhaps only now do we embrace the implications of certain slogans popular in that epoch. Romanticism was fostered by special groups of people, and their status throws light not only upon the origins of nationalism but also on its long history including our century. Those young enthusiasts were mostly students and young literati. And undoubtedly a distinction introduced by Ernst Gellner can be useful here, a distinction between the two cultures: the so-called higher or written culture and the so-called lower or oral culture. Precisely at the moment of passage from the oral culture to the written culture in Europe nationalism was born. And it is significant that pupils of high schools and universities were its promoters while the mass of the population was largely steeped in oral culture. It was regarded by those enthusiasts on the one hand as preserving the true national soul in its folklore, on the other hand as a passive flock to be lifted up through education toward the common goal of national dignity or national independence.

For centuries the written culture was limited to the clergy and the upper classes while the majority remained on the oral level. In some countries the higher culture was of a language different from the language of the population; thus, for example, German dominated the scene in Bohemia, in Latvia, in Estonia, while in Lithuania the same place was occupied by Polish. National movements in such countries were fostered by the new intelligentsia coming from the lower classes and speaking the language of their peasant ancestors.

If it is true that the humiliation felt by young educated people as a group is usually at the source of nationalism or political romanticism, we can find a common denominator in the movements among the intelligentsia of various countries, both the countries temporarily subjugated by big powers and the big powers themselves, thus in Germany, in Poland, in Hungary, in Bohemia, but also in Russia. After all, there are parallels between national bards who appeared at that time and whom we can call *linguistic heroes*, such as Mickiewicz, Petöfi, and Pushkin. Somebody once said that Poland, after it disappeared from the map of Europe at the end of the eighteenth century, was invented anew by a few poets.

Let us consider the enormous role of literature in the development of the so-called national consciousness. And this confirms the thesis that nationalism is closely related to the existence of schools in which the young are submitted to a special indoctrination based upon the texts of venerated great writers, harbingers of a certain highly emotional tradition. This applied to the countries aspiring to independence but also to their oppressors. For instance, Russian schools in Russian-occupied Poland of the nineteenth century used the great Russian writers—Pushkin, Gogol, Turgenev—as a mainstay in their program of Russification. In view of the role of written culture, we may observe the consequences of its triumph in the twentieth century. A hundred years ago national literatures were largely beyond the reach of the lower classes, while today every child learns about the luminaries of his or her country and this adds considerably to the intensity of national feeling. There would be nothing incongruous in imagining an atomic submarine named *Dostoevsky* or an aircraft carrier named *Pushkin*. In Poland a ship was named after a modern bard, the poet Gałczyński. It is true that this is a ship of the merchant marine.

We may wonder at the chance of success of Basque, Flemish, or Catalan nationalism in Western Europe. These are belated arrivals and they pay the price of being late in their rebellion against the written culture of French or Spanish. One at least potential national movement has no chance whatever and that is the attempt to re-create Occitania; namely, the area of the Languedoc covering the entire south of present-day France. The population there till recently spoke Oc, which was considered a dialect by Frenchmen. The fact that it was the language of a sophisticated written culture in the Middle Ages didn't save it from disappearance, and the few intellectuals writing novels in it are not enough to restore its usage.

In our part of Europe we see some phenomena analogous to those of Western Europe, but on a larger scale. While the written culture in the Baltic languages benefits from the non-Slavic character of those languages, the situation is much less clear in the areas where millions speak a Slavic language at home—Belorussian or Ukrainian—as opposed to the predominantly Russian school and written Russian culture. In France, parents of Breton children do not want to send their children to schools taught in Breton, though those schools are available. And they are motivated by obvious practical reasons. It is an open question whether the Russian policy of the stick and carrot in Belorussia and the Ukraine is more effective; namely, the suppression of schools in native tongues on the one hand and, on the other, the advantages offered those who are trained in the dominant written culture.

As you see, I speak of nationalism without giving it in advance a pejorative meaning, even if it is often responsible for hatreds between various nationalities. It should be recognized as an important factor even though progressive thinkers—the socialists and so on of the last century—ascribed it to temporary circumstances and hoped that those circumstances would disappear in the course of history.

It is possible that we now stand before new mutations of national movements endowed with a nearly religious appeal, and in this connection, an arch-nationalist writer, Dostoevsky, may be quoted. For observers of the present Soviet Union his pronouncements may sound disquieting. I quote: "The object of every national movement, in every people, and at every period of its existence, is only the seeking for its god who must be its own god, and the faith in him as the only true one." Another quotation: "If a great people doesn't believe that the truth is only to be found in itself alone (in itself alone and in it exclusively); if it doesn't believe that it alone is fit and destined to raise up and save all the rest by its truth, it would at once sink into being ethnographical material and not a great people" (Dostoevsky, *The Possessed*, translation by Constance Garnett).

These are pronouncements of pure messianism, a current of thought that ascribes to a collective body the function of savior both of itself and of other nations. This transposition of the individual Messiah of the Bible to the collective is blasphemous; nevertheless, it was dear to Dostoevsky, who considered himself a Christian. We find a similar messianism, though opposed to that of the Russians, in Poland, a country that used to be called by its poets "the Christ of nations." Today factors exist which may favor the rebirth of such dreams. The first of those factors, I would guess, is the atomization of societies under the impact both of technology and, as in the countries which passed through the Communist system, of something which we could call the withering of society and the strengthening of the all-embracing state. There was a search for some principles of cohesion, some bonds surviving the destruction of organic communities. The state ideology inculcated in schools provided at least an illusion of integration, even though in some countries such as Poland the official Marxism was entering into a conflict with another set of values maintained by the Church and the family. With the erosion of the Marxist doctrine, a void was opened and it calls for being filled with something. The Solidarity movement in Poland has had many components, but the nationalist component was undoubtedly very strong. Perhaps in some Western national movements, the Basque for instance, we could distinguish a somewhat similar search for new bonds in the modernized state with its big industrial centers.

Some elements of messianism seem to be present in contemporary national aspirations, though they are perhaps modified and less drastic than in the past. In the nineteenth century Russian messianism was fed by opposition to the "decadent," horrible Western Europe, and in this respect we may see again several rebirths. In Poland it thrived on the opposition of the Catholic, chivalrous country faithful to the principles of honor, to a barbaric Russian autocracy. Today we can distinguish certain lines of continuation especially as the powerful Church in Poland distinguishes it from its atheistic neighbor to the east. It is not certain whether the idea of Central Europe, invented by a few intellectuals, has not slightly messianic connotations as it opposes "the greatest possible diversity on the smallest territory" to the Russian monolith. On the other hand, it opposes a kind of intellectual intensity, a seriousness and vigor in the arts, to the Western European slackness and sterility. Here I can quote from my preface to my book *The Emperor of the Earth*, and by doing this I engage in an exercise of self-irony: "We are now like the Dalmatians in the collapsing Roman Empire. They cared when the others wouldn't give a damn." This is how a friend of mine from Poland spoke of the difference between the so-called Eastern and Western Europeans. He might have added that although we have been attracted to the great Western European centers of learning and art for generations, our admiration has never been without reservation. Yet it is true that something new has taken place in the last decades. Changed into outsiders by the political division of Europe, we began to see more clearly than before that which Western man, submerged by everyday life, has been reluctant to admit, and the spectacle appearing before our eyes didn't seem very promising. In defense of the feeling of a sad superiority expressed in this fragment—and because it draws its strength from misfortune and political slavery—what can be invoked? Probably no more than the fact that the idea of our part of Europe as a separate entity is not limited to that of one nation but embraces several nations united by a common fate and perhaps maturing to friendly neighbor relations, which in the past was not their strong point.

People who haven't lived through the first decade after World War II have difficulty visualizing the triumphal élan of the Marxist creed then attracting the best minds in both parts of divided Europe. That era is receding into oblivion so fast that the question is being asked as to *why* so many intellectuals fell victim to self-imposed blindness at that time, while the more sensible question would be as to why some *opposed* that lure and for what reasons. Thinking of human emotional needs, we should also recognize the enormous pull of claims laid on the individual by the nation to which he or she belongs. I realized this when reading Simon Dubnov, a historian of the Jews in Russia, who describes his conversion to Jewish nationalism at the end of the last century. Allow me to quote from him: "I myself have lost faith in personal immortality, yet history teaches me that there is collective immortality and that the Jewish people can be considered as relatively eternal, for its history coincides with the full span of world history. The study of the Jewish people's past, then, also encompasses me in something eternal. This historicism admitted me into the national collective, drawing me out of the circle of personal problems onto the broad highway of social problems, less profound but more timely. National sorrow became dearer to me than the sorrow of the world." Dubnov lost his religious faith, but paradoxically this prompted him to believe in collective immortality.

A faithfulness to one nation may be endowed with a religious aura, especially when the religious beliefs are weakened or eroded. When reflecting on contemporary literature in Poland, I have an uncanny feeling that in spite of the importance and the high caliber of the Roman Catholic Church in that country there is something like an erosion of religious faith on a deeper level, much as is visible in the West and in neighboring Hungary or Czechoslovakia. I ask myself whether, in its shift to patriotism, Polish literature doesn't show symptoms of agnosticism or atheism. The central locus of the sacred is moved from the religious sphere to the political sphere of a nation fighting for its independence. Utter skepticism and an awareness of the relativity of values are combined in that literature with an attachment to one absolute: an unconditional loyalty to one's nation. By saying this I do not intend to maintain that mass participation in Church rites and in pilgrimages in Poland is basically a political phenomenon. Yet the sacred bears a double character of attachment:

to the Christian faith and to parents, grandparents, and ancestors who lived and died in the same faith.

The problem of religion in our part of Europe is closely connected with that of nationalism, and in fact, it is sometimes difficult to separate religion from intense national feelings. The issue is of great complexity, and when we treat it from a purely religious point of view, it shows some unsolvable puzzles. Of course, Christian churches are primarily concerned with the salvation of the individual human soul and, in view of that aim, establish a certain hierarchy of commitments. An individual lives in a family, a family belongs to a certain community, which by the fact of language is a national community. It oftens happens that a national bond protects certain values which otherwise wouldn't survive under the impact of the state. In such a case the churches must appear as allies of the people who defend their nationality against the oppressors. But the ties between the clergy and national movements are also of a less principled nature. In some countries the clergymen of peasant origin were instrumental in bringing about a "national rebirth," acting in the name of the people's culture against the culture of the upper classes. This happened, for instance, in the western Ukraine, where the Greco-Catholic Church contributed to the Ukrainian national consciousness, and in Lithuania, where the first poets writing in Lithuanian issued from Roman Catholic seminaries. The practical identification of Roman Catholicism with Polishness occurred in Poland during the nineteenth century because Poland was partitioned by Orthodox Russia and Protestant Prussia. To be a Pole and a Roman Catholic then became synonymous. This particular marriage of the nation and the Church led to some dramatic situations in the interwar period, because the Church was used to seeing itself as a political force. It threw its influence on the scale by backing the rightist National Democratic Party and often acting against the socialists and numerous national minorities. Of course, the position of the local clergy changed considerably during the postwar decades; nevertheless, national aspirations find a protective area in Catholicism.

This collusion of religion and national feelings must worry some Catholics, for it is full of dangers. It is difficult to forget what happened in Catholic Croatia during the last war, when crimes of genocide were committed in the name of religion as the only distinctive mark separating the Croats from the Orthodox Serbs. But it is not necessary to keep in mind such blatant distortions of Christianity.

Even if it takes Christian and humane forms, religiously oriented nationalism threatens to abolish a clear distinction between what is due God and what is due Caesar. Yet Caesar means not necessarily the rulers of the state; Caesar can also mean the society at large and a collective pressure. It seems to me that in today's Poland the danger is clearly realized by Catholic intellectuals and by at least a part of the clergy.

Let me end with a quotation from Isaiah Berlin:

It seems to me that those who, however perceptive in other respects, ignored the explosive power generated by the combination of unhealed mental wounds, however caused, with the image of the nation as a society of the living, the dead, and those yet unborn (sinister as this could prove to be when driven to a point of pathological exasperation), displayed an insufficient grasp of social reality.

[Written in English by C.M.]

Part 2

THE
GARDEN OF
KNOWLEDGE

THE COSTS OF ZEALOUSNESS

Vanity is so firmly anchored in the heart of man that a soldier, a camp-follower, a cook or a porter brags and may have his admirers. Even philosophers wish to be admired. Those who write against vanity would like to have the glory of having written well; those who read their works would like to have the glory of having done so; I, who write these words, have perhaps the same kind of greed; and maybe those who are going to read my words . . .

—P A S C A L , *Pensées**

We are so presumptuous that we would like to be known by everyone, even by posterity when we ourselves are no more; and we are so vain that the esteem of five or six neighbours delights and contents us.

—P A S C A L , *Pensées*

It is very likely that people do not all have an equal talent for pride. The question why it appears in some people early in life, in their childhood, belongs to genetics and depth psychology, fields that I find quite alien. A child with a very strong ego wants to excel in everything, right away. Because it is difficult to excel immediately in games and sports, the fear of being not-first is so paralyzing that it forces the child into last place. Then the child, withdrawing, creates a second, closed world for himself, a substitute world. My happiness ended when I was sent to school. Up till then I had spent very little time in the company of my peers and had not been subjected to *the gaze of the other*. The complexity of what went on inside me as the traumatic pattern of my life was being established between my tenth and fifteenth years horrifies me. Despite my schoolwork and my participation in scouting and the Nature Lovers Circle (wide-ranging,

* Pascal translations by John Warrington.

extracurricular reading in biology), it must have had strong traits of
something akin to autism, linked with an unbelievable training in
dissembling and pretending to be normal. In any event, my development (if it deserves that name) was completely different from that
of all my schoolmates. This had nothing to do with my literary vocation, which came later. Multilayered rumination and ironic dis-
tancing are among the sources of my later ideological conflicts.

My substitute world was not particularly egotistic; that is, it was
not constructed primarily of dreams about playing a heroic role. It's
just that it was a world of unchanging laws, painless and secure. My
imagination did not serve up fictitious plots, nor did it seek an outlet
in words, but it filled an ordered space, expressing itself in fantastic
drawings and maps of nonexistent countries. I experienced my escapes as a necessity and a defect; I would probably have given everything I had to be like everyone else, an equal among equals. My
discovery that in retreating to my own space I was behaving exactly
like a Romantic poet was arrived at under the influence of Mickiewicz's and Słowacki's poetry, probably no earlier than my sixteenth
year. Even though I had written a small amount of poetry before
then, with great embarrassment, these poems were, so to speak, a
by-product of my spatial imagination; I was not like those who, from
childhood, plagiarize the poems or novels they have just read. When
I happened upon the model of Romantic behavior, I did not tell
myself that I was a poet, but that I would be a poet, and I began to
write verse exercises for the time being, definitely classical (in imitation of Joachim du Bellay), and not bad at all, judging from the
lines preserved in my memory.

What Pascal says is absolutely true and is especially true in relation
to someone who has accepted the Romantic model (what other model
in Poland?) of the poet-bard. The no less decisive role of wounded
pride can be traced far back, into childhood, and it is necessary to
recognize in one's future fate how much is owed to the constraints
of leading one and not another existence. Our path has been marked
out and we can choose either constant intellectual activity and daily
industriousness or ruin—even were we to be cast away on an un-
inhabited island. Which of course is only a conjecture, for my vanity
has been assuaged with the respect of "five or six neighbours."

Contradiction. Pride, outweighing all miseries. Man either hides his
wretchedness, or, if he reveals it, glories in the knowledge thereof.

—PASCAL, *Pensées*

We are not satisfied with our own life as it really is; we desire to live an imaginary life in the minds of others, and for that purpose we endeavor to shine. We labor unceasingly to adorn and preserve our imaginary existence, and neglect the real.

—P A S C A L , *Pensées*

A gift: it is impossible to make an offering of anything other than the I, and what is called a gift is only a label under which the revenge of the I is hidden.

—S I M O N E W E I L , *Selected Writings*

You are under the Power of no other Enemy, are held in no other Captivity, and want no other Deliverance, but from the Power of your own earthly Self. *This is the one Murderer of the divine Life within you. It is your own* Cain *that murders your own* Abel. *Now everything that your earthly Nature does, is under the Influence of* Self-will, Self-Love *and* Self-Seeking, *whether it carries you to laudable, or blameable Practices, all is done in the Nature and Spirit of* Cain, *and only helps you to such Goodness, as when* Cain *slew his Brother. For every Action and Motion of* Self, *has the Spirit of* Antichrist, *and murders the divine Life within you.*

—W I L L I A M L A W (1686–1761), *The Spirit of Love*

I am aware, of course, that these quotations contain enough material for a fifteen-volume philosophical study. Out of practical considerations let us limit ourselves to a couple of observations. The sense of guilt because of one's own existence may well have been explained one way or another by Dr. Freud and his disciples, but I have never taken seriously these myths of my century, and at the time when I was forced to learn from experience how to cope with my feelings of guilt, I knew nothing about them. We become aware of evil at the very root of our being; that is, we encounter the vicious circle in which whatever we do that is good is a service to our *I*.

From there a transition, at about age fourteen, to contemplating the merciless structure of existence, contemplation assisted by readings in the field of biology. I don't remember if I got my hands on some pages from Schopenhauer at that time; most likely, I did. What is important is that a Manichaean temperament definitely exists, and is inclined to torments of painful ambition and at the same time to a hostile judgment of that ambition; furthermore, it is not out of the question that one derives some relief from extending the principle of evil to existence in general. This temperament, more than Indian and Persian influences, contributed to the rise in Christianity of a certain type of heresy and to the fact that these heresies endured, which does not, of course, mean that all people who are endowed with this temperament were counted among the heretics. St. Augustine was one and the same man when he belonged to the Manichaean Church and in later years when he was an orthodox Christian. The shared characteristic of these people is their distrust of Nature —both human nature and the natural world. In singling them out, I am simply guided by experience, because I have discovered, in succession, writers who have much in common with each other. They are: St. Augustine (*The Confessions*), Pascal (it's not easy to suspect Jansenists of a friendly attention to Nature), Simone Weil (who was close in much of her thinking, and openly so, to the Catharists or Albigensians), William Blake (whom many people, not without reason, have called a Gnostic), Lev Shestov (whose entire philosophy is based on a protest against the Law of Nature—although he did not like gnosis). I am using shorthand here, which may be unjustified; I beg the reader's indulgence, because I fear slipping into erudition.

The paths we will travel are carved out early in life, and that is why I have been dwelling on my school years. A sense of guilt in itself is no indication of who a given person will become, since it may be shared by people who are pure, like Simone Weil, and not so pure; that is, by those who are down-and-out in the sphere of moral capabilities. Among the latter, it is often a subterfuge that allows them to avoid behaving as they ought to. It would seem that if the cunning vanity of our I depresses us, there should be nothing simpler than subduing that I inside oneself and sacrificing it, which should make us feel less guilty. But no, nothing of the sort happens; on the contrary, it even seems that the guilt, shapeless and, to a significant degree, imaginary for the time being, prepares the voluntary acts that will thoroughly justify it. The deeper we penetrate into the woods—the woods of life, as in Dante—the greater the number of voluntary acts marked by the nasty triumph of our I— the more confidently does guilt settle in as our sovereign master. The only thing that is possible is to try to buy it off with something. Then the substitute world, which originally was a separate island, occupies more and more new territory within us and the zealousness that it exacts (writing books swallows up more time than drawing maps of nonexistent countries) generates a further skewing of our day-to-day obligations toward people. Thus zealousness, conceived in guilt, multiplies guilt, and therefore, since it is a constant flight from itself, a flight forward, we are unable to satisfy ourselves with anything: the only thing that counts is what we still have the hope of achieving.

My comments may be useful to some people, although this process is not necessarily typical. It is, furthermore, a theme with variations. From time to time it demands recognition, some universal paying of tribute to us; it makes itself known painfully and erupts in outbursts of such rage that they are restrained by reason only with great difficulty. Then again comes rebellion against what we have learned to consider our destiny: is it possible that one will be only "someone who wrote such and such a number of books" and nothing else? Must the secretly nurtured ideal of a "real human being" remain beyond our grasp and an unknown force drive us back to our penitential work? My spurts of "real humanity" were not long-lived. Only my pedagogic career, begun late in life, around age fifty, has afforded me some lasting satisfaction. In the lecture hall, facing the young people to whom I was able to offer something, I forgot about my wretchedness and felt that I had a right to exist.

1974

THE SAND IN THE HOURGLASS

*The contemplation of time is the key to human life. It is a mystery that
cannot be reduced to anything, and to which no science has access.
Humility is inescapable when we know that we are not certain how we
shall behave in the future. We achieve stability only by disowning our
I, which is subject to time and changes.*

*Two things cannot be reduced to any rationalizing: time and beauty.
One must begin from them.*

—SIMONE WEIL, *Selected Writings*

Mystery deserves respect. If man were unaware of the ephemeral
nature of his life and of all human things, he would not be man.
Beauty, whose very essence is both impermanence and the power
of the moment confronting the passage of time, would also be beyond
his reach. The words of Ecclesiastes are a model for all lyric poetry,
for he who speaks through them both affirms that he must die like
all other men and rises above his vulnerability to destruction through
the rhythm of language. In just the same way, line and color deliver
us from our I, and regardless of the filth that may have nourished
the creative act, they are transposed into the not-I.

Continual meditation on time is impossible because it would par-
alyze our actions, whispering that each of them will be in vain. People
must aspire, love, hate, establish families, earn a living, struggle.
Their days must be subordinated to the discipline imposed by immediate goals. The artistic temperament is characterized by a sensitivity to the current of time itself with its mesmerizing effect, as
when a snake mesmerizes a rabbit. One cannot refute the reasoning
of those who have seen in art and in religious contemplation a dis-
tancing from Will, the will to life, an ascent above the circle of birth
and death. That is why people can be divided into two enduring
types: people of Will and people of Meditation, which does not mean
that these types exist in a pure, unalloyed state, or that they do not

at times come into conflict with each other within a single corporeal shell.

When I was a child, no one initiated me into the dread mystery of ephemerality; I stumbled upon it myself, receiving it, as it were, as a gift from nature. The way I read a certain book for young readers is worth mentioning. It was Fenimore Cooper. It is virtually impossible to read Cooper in English today because of his prolixity. But if I remember the book correctly, it was an abridged edition, a selection from all the volumes, perhaps a translation of a French or Russian abridgment. In the first part, the hero, Natty Bumppo, appeared as a young man, the Pathfinder, the Deerslayer; in the last, as an old man named Leatherstocking. My experience of this book was so piercing, so sweetly painful, that it has remained with me to this day, as if it were just yesterday that I was in that hero's company. At that time it was naked, beyond words; now I am able to evaluate its by no means paltry dimensions and to name it. The Pathfinder traveled—in space, because in his flight from civilization he kept moving farther and farther West, to the wilderness where only Indians lived; in time, because he changed from a vigorous, carefree youth into a mature man, and finally into an old man. That was when he had his encounter with a civilization that was ruled by a different time. The region where he had spent his youth was by now densely populated; his Indian friends had perished in battles or died; for the new generations of colonists his authentic forest fatherland was only a legend and he himself was an eccentric relic with his old-fashioned, long harquebus. Completely alone, no longer sharing a common language with anyone, once again he walked away, into territory that meant exile, because it was no longer forest but wilderness— the empty, boundless prairie.

I read Cooper, then, as a symbolic parable about human fate. A young boy, I empathized with the old trapper for whom everything was already in his past. And who knows, perhaps it was Cooper speaking in a poem that I wrote later on as a twenty-three-year-old:

> *The gale combs the gray hair*
> *With its fingers and at last repeats*
> *Authentic words for those who stare*
> *into memory's abyss, open.*

By the way, just as a single grain helps to crystallize a solution, so one image in Cooper could provide the germ for my reveries about ordering space. Let us imagine a lake, surrounded on all sides by virgin forest, and in the center of the watery surface a sort of ark at anchor, a floating house. When the Pathfinder was a young man, the colonists had not yet made their way to Lake Otsego in the northern part of New York State. In the ark, unfriendly to other people and fenced off by the water from the rampaging Indians of the primeval forest, lived a retired pirate and his two daughters. Was that not the model of a completely secure state for a child's imagination?

Thus, Cooper, the Romantic American, spoke to me earlier than the Polish Romantics. When I made their acquaintance later on, I was not particularly sensitive to Gustaw's madness in love, but I was very sensitive to his grief over what had vanished—when he visited his childhood home and saw "ruins, emptiness, devastation." I was thoroughly captivated by Słowacki's "The Hour of Thought," with its heartrending tone heightened by a still classical restraint, a tone of remembrances accompanied by tears that, as I learned much later, Edgar Allan Poe considered closest to the very essence of poetry. "The Hour of Thought," unlike any other work, mythologized the streets on which I walked—St. John's, Dominican Street, and also the park grounds of the Jaszuny estate, twenty kilometers away, where Słowacki and Ludwika Śniadecka used to go out riding together.

"The sorrow of ephemerality" can also be found in the ancient Chinese poets, and in a poem that had a particular influence on the Romanticism of the Slavic countries—Thomas Gray's "Elegy Written in a Country Churchyard." As one who has been addicted since childhood to grief over transitoriness, I could not help contemplating (exactly when this began, it would be hard for me to say) the moral flaw inherent in the aesthetic temperament. If we treat what is actually happening to us or around us as already in the past, as material given to us only so we can transfer it at this very moment into the past and observe it as if it were already a memory, then such an immense distance arises in our response to the "now" that even in the most hellish circumstances (such as there has been no lack of in our era) the spectator in us preserves his coldness and impassivity; and this is indisputably inhuman. Perhaps not only coldness and impassivity, for the spectator does not lack an inclination toward sadism. After all, the aesthetic attitude is not the exclusive privilege (some privilege!) of artists. Every highly aroused and acute consciousness flees toward similar solutions and, by splitting into subject (I observing) and object (I being observed), somehow relents toward the object and even derives satisfaction from its improper behavior, as in the case of dandyism, buffoonery, and mental cruelty.

Meditation on ephemerality has always been man's companion and will never leave him; however, its tonality changes and the *Danse Macabre* of the late Middle Ages, for example, is fundamentally different from the Renaissance prescriptions about profiting from the moment because youth lasts for such a short time and life is brief. The *carpe diem* in Kochanowski's Horatian poems (translations and imitations) always struck me as rather insipid rhetoric, although I understand that, just as in the dance of death, the point here was to emphasize a truism: you are neither the first nor the last to whom this has happened.

The attitude toward passing time, even if we disposed of no other data about specific historical periods, would suffice to suggest a diagnosis. When I was reading Cooper, Friedrich Nietzsche's predictions had already been fulfilled literally, and since that time I have either had to submit to or oppose the workings of "European nihilism." Nihilistic time, to judge by contemporary art and literature, is completely devoid of values; neither its specific moments nor their duration makes any sense. It manifests itself as only a destructive, absurd force; Horace can no longer be of help, because even the pagan respect for the Great Rhythm has been lost. This also accounts for the "fainting" attitude (it was, it passed, it's gone) or the vindictive attitude (the accursed absurdity of being) toward the passing of time. Nietzsche was not the only one to notice the harbingers of this devaluing of time (and also of human life); the Russian writers who raged against Western Europe sensed it, too.

The perfect nihilist—*The nihilist's eye idealizes in the direction of ugliness and is unfaithful to his memories: it allows them to drop, lose their leaves; it does not guard them against the corpselike pallor that weakness pours out over what is distant and gone. And what he does not do for himself, he also does not do for the whole past of mankind: he lets it drop.*

—NIETZSCHE, NOTE 21 FROM *The Will to Power*, 1887
[Translated by Walter Kaufmann and R. J. Hollingdale]

Mnemosyne was the mother of the Muses. Her role demands a new rethinking under the conditions of "European nihilism." In the past, the poet would address a beautiful girl and prophesy that one day, as an old woman doing her spinning of an evening, she will rejoice: "Ronsard praised me when I was beautiful." That is, her beauty was something objective and found its reflection, as in a mirror, in the poems of Ronsard, with the difference that the image in the mirror cannot be retained, while poetry defies the action of time. That was the foundation of all representational art, whether it represented a human figure or a landscape. Memory may be unfaithful, but it finds support in the lines and the color that belong to the things of this world and that supply us with clues as to when memory is being faithful and when it is mistaken. If we wish to know what has happened, let us consider for a moment the decline of representational painting, but let us also analyze our impressions when we watch a film from fifty years ago. Film stars who were once famous for their beauty look pitiful, all decked out in their comical rags and their comical gestures; they are imprisoned in a style, in their era's mannerisms, so that it is hard to understand how they were enchanting at one time, although it is not hard to understand that they did enchant people who, like them, were also imprisoned. Film, then, hands us a nasty, distorting mirror and confirms what sociology and psychology have taught us. It is possible, in fact, that film, because it is a segment of unfolding time, is hostile to beauty, which must be motionless (movement in poetry, in music, is of a different order and, so to speak, suffers from its inability to freeze).

Because of what we have been taught, memory is assumed to be deceitful and has acquired the consistency of dreams. Since everything that one is is subject to ceaseless transformations (and because the dark domain within us demands a past that has been censored in one way or another, and because, seized by the Spirit of Time, we project its measurements into the past), it is difficult to believe in the truthfulness of memory. And yet Nietzsche distinguished between the eye that is faithful to memories and the unfaithful eye, calling the latter the eye of the perfect nihilist, and since he uncovered nihilism in himself, no doubt he knew what he was talking about. If his formulation contains a condemnation of modern psychologizing, which, by the way, did not begin with Freud, then of course I am on Nietzsche's side.

Those who pay tribute to Mnemosyne as the mother of the Muses find themselves in a peculiar trap. They tell stories about how, for example, many years ago they encountered a lion, but then they must hasten to place this event in parentheses, making us understand that to a certain extent it was a lion but to a certain extent it wasn't, because it exists only in their treacherous minds. That is why reality "faints" every so often beneath their pens, and though color is more

or less preserved, the lines dissolve like the outline of a cloud re-
flected in waves (not for nothing did Impressionism announce the
end of representational painting). In these conditions, Proust's undertaking, his desire to rescue time past, was heroic and hopeless.
His work recalls those marvelous, colorful Oriental carpets: the
paintings of Bonnard and Vuillard, woven out of fragments of "psychological time." And like those paintings, it was already passé the
moment it was conceived. For it had already been proclaimed that
memory deceives us if it does not "idealize in the direction of ugliness." In some museum of the future, Proust's volumes will be placed
side by side with Beckett's *Krapp's Last Tape*, in which the narrator,
an old man, listens to tapes of himself recorded in the distant past.
He replies to the ludicrous nothingness of his own life with mocking
snorts and grunts.

It is not for me to write the history of European culture; others
will take this task upon themselves. For me, the problem is highly
personal, because in my poems and prose my support has been the
remembered detail. Not an "impression" and not an "experience";
these are so multilayered and so difficult to translate into language
that various methods have been discovered in the attempt to grasp
them: speech that imitates the "stream of consciousness" even to
the point of eliminating punctuation marks, of becoming verbal
magma, mere babbling. The remembered detail, for example, the
grain of the wood of a door handle polished by the touch of many
hands deserved, in my opinion, to be separated from the chaos of
impressions and experiences, to be cleansed in some way, so that all
that remained would be the eye disinterestedly contemplating the
given object. I know how easy it is to find fault with my insistence
on making distinctions; all one would have to do is introduce a couple
of concepts from a handbook of psychology, but I have no interest
in them, since making distinctions at least brings us closer to the
essential line of division and practice confirms it.

I had an amusing and instructive adventure after the appearance
of my book *Native Realm* in English translation. Its introductory
chapter includes a not very flattering opinion about all autobiographical writings, because they attempt to break through the so-called
layers of consciousness; since this is a vain undertaking, time past is
falsified in them—that is also why I prefer a selection that has been
organized ahead of time, rather than a spontaneous selection. I was
told about someone who exclaimed after reading this, "Why should
I read any further if the author himself admits that he is not going
to tell the truth!" This innocent intellectual believed in the "truth"

of various devices which are reputed to open up the contents of memory, although if he were consistent he would have had to come to the conclusion that in that case only grunting, disjointed syllables, groans, as in *Krapp's Last Tape*, do not seem "artificial" and can be taken for sincerity.

What did Nietzsche have in mind when he foresaw that a "corpse-like pallor" would veil the things of the past? Another of his aphorisms from the same year (1887) clarifies this: "An extreme form of nihilism would be the view that *any sort* of conviction, any sort of accepting-something-as-true, is of necessity false, because there simply is no *true world*." Approximately ten years earlier Dostoevsky wrote his "Dream of a Ridiculous Man"; the hero-narrator in that story decides to shoot himself, under the impression that since the world exists only in his head, it will cease to exist with his death.

This question cannot easily be sidestepped: What kind of existence can be ascribed to a sunrise, for example, somewhere beside the Mediterranean Sea on a particular morning in May in the year 1215, shall we say, and also to the flowers opening at that moment, the seagull flying past, the arm of a woman drawing water from a well? Could it be, because no one sees this any longer, that it has no existence? But all the fantastic richness of the works of the human mind and human hand that European civilization has bequeathed to us, so immense that it seems to be beyond our ability to comprehend it, was made possible only because exactly the opposite answer was given. The world, the absolutely authentic world, has endured in each of its moments, independently of the consciousness of a particular subject on his journey from birth to death. Yet something that is seen by no one does not exist. This supposition has been tacitly accepted, albeit with a fundamental emendation: one supreme subject, God—who is the most subjective of subjects because although unseen Himself, He sees—has been embracing with his vision all the moments of time which lie spread out before him like a deck of cards, for they are simultaneous, beyond any "was, is, will be." The physics that would be born eventually (Einstein's) offered as yet no help; however, religion had successfully maintained its intuitive conviction about the relativity of time and space, which did not exist before the Act of Creation. The scientific conceptualization of time and space as absolute, along with its nihilistic consequences in the humanities, is a late acquisition, a part of the scientific-technical revolution or, rather, one phase of that revolution, for it shared the fate of Newtonian physics. Evidently, the particular fields of human thought are subject to a law of unequal development because we still have to wait for an understanding of what is a new phase.

Thanks to religion, over the course of many centuries the authentic world, grounded in the sight of God, offered models for the artist who hoped to approach them not so much by imitation as by analogy. Memory played an important, but a rather secondary, role in this, for it was understood that "idealization," that is, the extraction of that which is quintessential for a particular given thing, is inevitable. In the civilization that we call Christian, visionaries responded quite unfavorably to Mnemosyne, calling her "the mother of the fallen natural Muses." And they were right, it seems, because when she found herself alone, confronting a world deprived of values, she turned out to be an unreliable guide.

One recognizes the taste of a cake while eating it. At this moment, after all, as I am putting these words on paper, I am making a choice, resisting memory's various temptations. For example, memory is offering me my university studies—the "argument about the existence of the world" that was threshed out in the lecture halls, and at the same time the argument about the grounding of values—and is even expressing annoyance with me for conflating two orders of reasoning. No doubt it is better to know that this labyrinth of concepts has been erected, but it is a barren labyrinth, for there is no place in it for our own sense of anguish. If in our moments of happiness, mastery, ecstasy, we say Yes to heaven and to earth, and all we need is misfortune, sickness, the decline of physical powers to start screaming No, this means that all our judgments can be refuted tomorrow and that it is easy to mistake our life for the world. It is not obvious, however, why weakness—whether of a particular person or of an entire historical era—should be privileged and why the old nihilist from Beckett's *Krapp's Last Tape* should be closer to the truth than he himself was when he was twenty years old.

The contemplation of time is the key to human life—but one can only circle around that key, one cannot touch it. One thing is certain: not every contemplation of time is equally good; however, since it cannot be expressed in words, we can recognize its quality by the use a given individual has made of it.

"I am suffering." It is better to say this than to say, "This landscape is ugly."

—S I M O N E   W E I L , *Selected Writings*

1974

REALITY

You shall forget these things, toiling in the household,
You shall remember them, droning by the fire,
When age and forgetfulness sweeten memory
Only like a dream that has often been told
And often been changed in the telling. They will seem unreal.
Human kind cannot bear very much reality.

T . S . E L I O T , *Murder in the Cathedral*

There goes a fascist. Kill the fascist. Crash! Crash!
Also a communist. Kill the communist. Bash! Bash!
O reality! Holy mother!
For you killing spiders is as little a bother.

K . I . G A Ł C Z Y Ń S K I . Quoted from memory. It probably comes
from *Solomon's Ball* (a prewar edition)

The sound of this word is hideous; it is a literal translation of the
French *réalité*, interchangeable at times with the nature of things (*la
réalité des choses*). French distinguishes between *la réalité* and *le réel*;
Polish lacks this distinction but needs it. Reality. *Wirklichkeit*. Russian has both *deistvitel'nost'*, derived from the word for taking action,
not from the word for thing (as in Polish: *rzecz* [thing], *rzeczywistość*
[reality]) and *realnost'*.

What does this word mean? Why does everyone pay homage to
things? In common parlance this word refers to all things that act
according to their own laws and in such a way that, if we should find
ourselves on the track along which they are moving, we would be
killed. For we are fragile beings and an avalanche tumbling down
from the mountains, a hurricane, bacteria, viruses, chemical changes
in the cells of our bodies can destroy us. However, we have learned
to resist the forces of nature, and although for a significant portion
of mankind drought, floods, and soil erosion are still a danger, what
is left to us from among the elemental disasters are mainly aging and

such diseases as have not yet been conquered by science. The thing which is most threatening to us is another man, either because he is armed and we are unarmed or poorly armed, or because (and it's all the same in the end) he has the power to deny us money, that is, nourishment. The foundation of human society is still the death penalty, whether it be death from a bullet, or in prison, or from hunger, and humanitarian choruses will have no effect on this.

For us, then, reality is social above all; that is, it is such that people-things follow orders dictated to them by other people, who appear to be masters of their own and others' fates, but who in fact have been transformed into things by the so-called necessities of life. We have not made much progress in understanding how all of this dovetails, and the scientist who studies viruses or sends rockets to other planets may react to self-appointed specialists in the social sciences with a sense of well-founded superiority.

I started paying attention to this nature of things early on, convinced that a poet who refuses to recognize its weight is living in a fool's paradise. While trying to cope with it, I also managed to collect many experiences as early as the years 1930–39; that is, in a period that is virtually unknown today. Unfortunately, if a reader should wish to find out what that period was like in Poland and Europe, I would be unable to point to any sources, because neither literature nor history has achieved even a passably accurate picture. Social reality is distinguished by the fact that it is opaque, treacherous, that with its myriad guises it deludes everyone who is entangled in it. In those days there were additional reasons for befuddlement, as happens when a man has received a powerful blow to the head. Let us consider that this was going on only a few years after World War I and that although people talked a lot of nonsense, they seemed to be doing so in order to avoid thinking about what reality signified. When I was a student, I got to know a modest clerk from Poznań who was utterly absorbed in the by no means so distant past. For he had fought at Verdun as a soldier in the German infantry and had written a book about this for which he was vainly seeking a publisher. I read the typed manuscript. This report of a sojourn in the fifth or sixth circle of hell was probably more detailed and thus more horrifying than Remarque's widely acclaimed novel *All Quiet on the Western Front*. The older members of my family had in their past the years of war spent in the tsarist army, and even my beautiful cousin Ela, whose portrait, painted by Janowski, is one of the loveliest examples of Polish painting from around 1914, was a *sestritsa* [a Russian military nurse] at the time. For a vast number of the inhabitants of our country reality still meant tsarist Russia or Habsburg Galicia, and above all the world war and the 1920 campaign—perhaps even more than independent Poland itself. How well was it understood that the year 1914 was the manifestation of all of Europe's defects and of her end, that the longed-for war of nations had brought Poland to life as a posthumous creation? Pride in "one's own rubbish heap regained" counseled putting on a face that suggested nothing was wrong, but various subterranean currents were at work undermining the supports of official thinking. And just when virtually every grown man was struggling with some Verdun of his own, there came a new blow to the head: the 1929 crash on the New York Stock Exchange, mass unemployment, and Hitlerism, orchestrated by the German combatants of World War I. Soon afterward, a poet who had been one of Piłsudski's Legionnaires of 1914 wrote, "Mother, hand me my boots, / The ones from twenty years ago." The boots may not have had time to grow old but the "acceleration of history" made a few changes in the world around Poland.

When someone assures us after many years that he had a clear awareness of standing "face to face with the end," we should not believe him, because almost no one had such a clear awareness. Among writers, perhaps only Zdziechowski and Stanisław Ignacy Witkiewicz did. As one of the creators of "Catastrophism" I could, in fact, present written evidence on my own behalf, but it would be evidence of only an intuitive, poetic recognition.

Let me briefly explain where catastrophism came from. First, a rather general background, not just the Polish one. The social reality of the nineteenth century weighed upon people in literature and art, so they considered protesting against it the chief aim of their activity, although they reached out for various solutions. However, even the most abstract aesthetic theories had as their foundation a rebellion against the swirling vortex of the oppressors and the oppressed; the artist, as the only free man, had to be set against this vortex. By taking refuge in bohemian circles from the morality of the hated bourgeoisie and concluding numerous alliances with social dreamers, the writer or the artist bore witness to his heritage: the centuries-long yearning for the Second Coming. Secularization was proceeding apace, however, and if Jesus was still the central figure in utopian socialism, this Jesus figured only as an ethical ideal and a reformer. Soon it would be openly announced that Man-God and not God-Man would restore fallen nature.

In my mind, contrary to what I know about frivolous Paris in *La Belle Epoque*, the beginning of my century has a gloomy color and a shape that is, if I may say so, Russo-Anglo-Saxon. The year 1905. The Russian "stormy petrels." The American writers of the class struggle: Upton Sinclair's *The Jungle* (1906), Jack London's *The Iron Heel* (1907). And considering what I know about New York, I do not think that the picture Gorky painted in *The City of the Yellow Devil* (1906) was an exaggeration. Furthermore, a gloomy reality does not appear only in revolutionary writers. It is also present in Joseph Conrad's *The Heart of Darkness* (1902), the novel that Thomas Mann called the beginning of twentieth-century literature, and in *The Secret Agent* (1907). What symbolic titles! Let us recite them: the jungle, the iron heel, the city of the yellow devil, the heart of darkness, the secret agent. Since such grim forces as were described therein had led to the slaughter of the First World War, one can hardly be surprised that writers from various Western countries, raised on legends that remained in the wake of the American Revolution and the French Revolution, enthusiastically welcomed the Russian Revolution as (the final?) destruction of the Bastille.

Regardless of its specific circumstances as a country that had gained and defended its independence, Poland belonged to a system of linked vessels; for example, the left-wing wave in America and Germany was swelling in Poland precisely during the years from 1930 to 1933. I shall leave aside the question of so-called convictions, because they are not the issue here, although among the literati only a very few had any "convictions." A more important issue is their grasp of reality. I was filled with distaste during the rather short time that I produced social poetry. Because it is obvious that in these various collective movements, whose participants beat the drum for each other, the poet betrays himself, out of pride, out of a need for recognition. They will walk right past a good poem and not notice it, but give them a "theme" and they'll respond immediately with shouts and bravos. Already at that time a riddle had appeared that became more and more painful the further along we moved into the twentieth century. If man is dehumanized and diminished by social reality, is not his diminution confirmed by taking him only and solely as a small part of that social reality? Whence the dullness of all those works about "wrongs" that are, after all, so noble in their intent? Many clamorous poems and not a few pages of comparable prose were written in Poland and elsewhere at that time, but none of this appears to have lasted. "Catastrophism" was an attempt at restoring measure. A literary argument, the catastrophist poets' opposition to

such literary schools as Skamander or the Avant-Garde, explains less
in this context than their renunciation of "social poetry"; their accusations, which were never formulated as a theory, would have
sounded like this: You are preoccupied with reality but it is completely unreal, for you keep on about your provincial world while
everything is happening on a planetary scale, the Apocalypse is imminent, and while you strive to reduce man to *homo oeconomicus*,
there is a hidden content in the historical Apocalypse that we cannot
comprehend. Perhaps a poem such as Jerzy Zagórski's "Ode on the
Fall of the Pound" still belonged to social poetry, but there was more
to it than just a prediction of the collapse of the British Empire. The
same poet's "The Coming of the Enemy" is a surrealistic fairy tale
about the advent of the Antichrist; the action takes place on the
plains of Eurasia, near the Arctic Ocean, and in the Caucasus.

After 1939, the young poets of underground Warsaw could not
remain indifferent to such accurate forebodings by their predecessors. Nevertheless, prewar catastrophism was a threat to these young
people, because it was international in its intellectual references and
they wanted to enclose themselves in the national dimension whatever the cost. Similarly, when they encountered another catastrophism, Witkiewicz's, what they borrowed from him was chiefly his
grotesque, from his plays, whereas we, judging by my own response
at least, were influenced primarily by the historiosophical premises
of his novels. We were not, however, as pessimistic as the desperately
clowning and suicidally earnest Witkiewicz. Who knows if a totally
pessimistic poetry is even possible or, if poetry is to be at all valuable,
whether it does not always have to be hopeful? In the poetry of the
catastrophists, every so often a note of irony toward the fate that
befell them can be heard, but there is also a yearning for harmony,
for beauty, which ought to be the lot of a saved man.

And what about today, when those dire prophecies and their fulfillment (or, rather, partial fulfillment) are in the past? Our planetary
reality has split in two into the so-called West and the so-called East,
and I have drunk from both the one and the other poisoned well. I
have also become convinced that the puzzle of the thirties still cries
out for a solution.

Did the nineteenth century lie when it dreamed its dream of itself?
That can't be ruled out. But at least its great metropolis, in which
Macbeth's witches stirred their brew, speaks to us from the pages of
Balzac, Dickens, Dostoevsky; it is the stage for a human comedy
like the *cité infernale* of Baudelaire's poems; it looks at us with the
faces of the corrupt judges and venal journalists of Daumier's prints,

and with the face of the prostitute from Manet's *Olympia*. There
was something then that could be called the will of realism. That
will was still in evidence at the beginning of our century, but not for
long. Its disappearance from literature and art is more or less con-
temporaneous with the widespread dissemination of the newsreel
and the documentary, which is why people have sought to lay the
blame for this on emulation of these new, vicarious means of expression. But the true causes probably lie much deeper. Man is either a
supported being or he dissolves into mist, into a mirage. For the
nineteenth century the impetus given by Christianity still sufficed to
support man; that is, to understand individual fate as meaningful.
The advocates of Man as the Masses, industriously patching together
their social literature during the thirties, fooled themselves into be-
lieving that Nietzsche's laughter had nothing to do with them. For
no matter what our anger may be like and no matter how strong our
sympathy for the fate of the oppressed, we will have a difficult time
achieving that minimum of attention without which literature is only
paper if we remain convinced that man, whom we are concerned
about, is interchangeable, is but a bubble on the current of "processes." It is not for nothing that dread of the future rules the work
of Dostoevsky, the second prophet of "nihilism." Dostoevsky was
not a psychologist; he was, as he has rightly been called, a pneu-
matologist, and there is a great difference between the two. *Pneuma*,
the spirit, is not the same as that instrument for inscribing impressions
that once was called the soul, and the struggle for the salvation of
homo pneumatikos, despite the temptations of *homo psychikos*, is
worth the highest stakes. Dostoevsky considered himself an authentic
realist, and he was one, he could still be one, and that is the reason
why.

Having lived for a long time in France and in America, I have
been astounded by my observation that the tough and predatory
reality that surrounds me *does not exist* in the literature of these
countries. Not that it would be worthwhile to offer some formulas,
because they would turn out to be impossible. Many a formula has
been applied by writers who swear that they will faithfully describe
only what has truly taken place, will stick to the "facts," and every
time the result was, at best, naturalism. But naturalism is total
unreality—in disguise. Bundles of reflexes torment bundles of reflexes, bundles of reflexes copulate with bundles of reflexes, bundles
of reflexes murder bundles of reflexes. A world not of people but of
flies. And if man is only a fly, then why be so upset about his un-
happiness? Only a hero, in whose existence both the author and the

reader believe, can be a measure of reality. Such nineteenth-century heroes as Rastignac, Raskolnikov, Ivan Karamazov, Fabrizio del Dongo from *The Charterhouse of Parma* still *exist* to this day. The heroes that Western authors have managed to create in the last few decades are striking. The preeminent hero is, without a doubt, the youthful comic-book detective Tintin; far behind him comes another detective, a grown man, Simenon's Maigret. That's the situation in the Francophone countries. On the other hand, in the English-speaking countries, only one character seems to have truly captivated readers. It is Frodo Baggins, the hero of Tolkien's *The Lord of the Rings*, a rich allegorical novel about the struggle between the forces of light and the forces of darkness, similar, in fact, in its narrative strategy, to Sienkiewicz's *Trilogy*. Only, the young Frodo is not even a human child; he is a fantastic creation, a *hobbit*, an elf, the Englishman's daydream of himself, who lives in snug dens, drinks tea in the afternoon, and is capable of heroic deeds—but only if they are absolutely necessary.

Reality, if it is to be captured, demands a hero, but it also demands an organizing idea. This idea does not have to reside within the writer's head, because it permeates his epoch. The nineteenth century still lived with the great hope of the rebirth of man. It was no accident that I referred to utopian socialism, whose significance was enormous. Today's ideas of social justice promise everything that anyone might want, but not that the oppressed will be liberated from the power of people-things; they are therefore insufficiently exciting and their semi-paralysis turns descriptions sour while they are still in embryonic form, since they are inseparable from a sense of direction, of striving. An unseen law of phenomena turns out to be more powerful here than the wishes of numerous Western adherents of revolution, whose sense of reality appears to be on the wane, since they are unable to gain even as much recognition as their predecessors in the thirties.

There is in all these works a certain atmosphere of universal doom; especially in Ulysses, *with its mocking* odi-et-amo *hodgepodge of the European tradition, with its blatant and painful cynicism, and its uninterpretable symbolism—for even the most painstaking analysis can hardly emerge with anything more than an appreciation of the multiple enmeshment of the motifs but with nothing of the purpose and meaning of the work itself. And most of the other novels which employ multiple reflection of consciousness also leave the reader with an impression of hopelessness. There is often something confusing, something hazy about them, something hostile to the reality which they represent. We not infrequently find a turning away from the practical will to live, or delight in portraying it under its most brutal forms. There is hatred of culture and civilization, brought out by means of subtle stylistic devices which culture and civilization have developed, and often a radical and fanatical urge to destroy. Common to almost all of these novels is haziness, vague indefinability of meaning: precisely the kind of uninterpretable symbolism which is also to be encountered in other forms of art of the same period.*

—ERICH AUERBACH, *Mimesis*
[Translated by Willard R. Trask]

Auerbach's book about *mimesis* or the reflection of reality in European literature, beginning with the Greeks, was written in 1942–45 in Istanbul, where the author, an émigré from Germany, happened to be living. His above-quoted observations refer to the years before World War II. Since they are just as apt a characterization of postwar literature up till the present (except that the features he noticed have become even more obvious), we should not take his judgments lightly, nor those of writers like him when they place the twentieth century under the sign of a destructive movement that demonstrates its own continuity.

We are born only once on this earth, and only one and no other historical time is given to us. If we recognize that it is our lot to live in a decadent era, we are faced with the problem of choosing our tactics. Since man is not an animal and is in touch with the entire past of his species, and since the past, to the extent that forgotten civilizations are being rediscovered, is becoming ever more accessible, we cannot but be depressed by the thought that instead of trying to equal the greatest human achievements, we yield to inferior philosophies only because they are contemporary. It is very difficult to find appropriate tactics for resistance, and our development, if it is to be worthy of that name, must be founded, I believe, on advancing from unconscious tactics to conscious tactics. Unfortunately, the individual, because he absorbs the same things as everyone around him, is weak and is continually considering whether it is not he who is mistaken.

It would be an exaggeration to insist that man can change radically. The germ of energy which is his alone—let's call it predestination —will remain the same in evil and in good, in truth and in error; he also has certain set limits, his own ability to interpret things properly. The fundamental constructs in his life are repetitive, but they can assume a new shape. I did not stop being a "catastrophist" after the

Second World War, in the sense that losing one's sense of reality still seems to me to be deserving of punishment. But I have chosen my guides more and more consciously, and not from among the representatives of contemporary *belles lettres*, which are infected with the loss of a sense of reality. I also consciously kept apart from that plaintive whimpering that is practically synonymous with the written word these days. Having crossed a certain boundary, inside which, unfortunately, the nature of things is our mistress, one begins to treat such whimpering—and also the entire theater of the absurd, along with the attempts at traditional "realism" that are doomed to failure—as belonging to the past. A pessimistic appraisal of the powerlessness of contemporary forces, and of the literature and art that unconsciously submit to these forces, is not synonymous with a lack of faith in individual achievements or with doubts about an eventual victory of the human race over "reality." After all, consciousness, in the clutches of the epoch, is always incomplete, and as it grows older we shall at best be able to describe clearly what it is that we do not want. And that is how it ought to be, for our zealousness has its source in our nay-saying to what the age obligingly places before us.

"What is truth?" asked Pilate. "What is reality?" people ask. Such a question one should refuse to answer.

1974

SALIGIA

> Superbia
> Avaritia
> Luxuria
> Invidia
> Gula
> Ira
> Acedia

In the Middle Ages the first letters of the seven cardinal sins formed the word *saligia*, which was thought to be doubly useful since it made it easy to memorize the names of the seven sins, or, rather, failings (*vitia capitalia*), and it emphasized their unity. That much I knew, but not long ago I was tempted to look into a few encyclopedias to check out what they had to say about *saligia*. In none of them did I find even a mention of this word. What is more, Catholic encyclopedias and dictionaries of theological terms are silent about it. Priests no longer evince much interest in sins, as if they would like to ask the world's pardon for considering this one of their primary tasks for so many centuries. They mumble even when speaking of the concept of sin, and so they are not inclined to mention the old classifications in the compendia and catechisms that they edit.

In search of a certain book that is devoted to the history of the cardinal sins, I made my way to Theology Hill. For Berkeley, in addition to its university, which is splendid in every respect, also has several graduate divinity schools, for various denominations, which are located in close proximity to each other, with a lovely view of San Francisco Bay. They collaborate in an ecumenical spirit and share their rich library collections. The best known of these schools is the interdenominational Pacific School of Religion. The late Earl Morse Wilbur was a member of its faculty; he learned Polish in order to write his two-volume *History of Unitarianism*, not without a reason, for at least half his work is filled with the travels and disputes of the Polish Arians.

I found the book about the cardinal sins, but it was in storage, where rarely requested books are kept, which leads me to the conclusion that this topic is not particularly popular with either future pastors or their teachers. In fact, the list of cardinal sins compiled by the eremites of Egypt in the fourth century was always a bit of a historical relic, since the names of the sins would stay the same but their meanings kept changing. I learned from this work that the word *saligia* was popularized by Henry of Ostia in the thirteenth century, but that for a long time it was rivaled by another version: *siiaagl* (*superbia, invidia, ira, acedia, avaritia, gula, luxuria*), signifying a different ordering of the same failings. However, *saligia* triumphed, if only for mnemotic reasons, and was adopted by the Jesuits during the Counter-Reformation.

As a child, I did not receive much moral benefit from my catechism lessons. Perhaps children in general are not prepared to understand such convoluted knowledge, and besides, too many strange associations based on the Polish names for the cardinal sins would enter my mind during those lessons.

1. *Pycha* (pride) instead of *superbia*. *Pych* (punt), *puch* (fluff), *pyza* (a moon face or a round plate)? *Pyszałkowaty-pyzaty* (conceited and chubby)? Self-inflation beyond one's means? That's someone else, some gentleman, a *pyza-pycha w kryzie* (moon-faced, preening person wearing a ruff), definitely not I—in other words, this cannot apply to me. *Pycha* is classified instantly, just by its sound, whereas *superbia*, as Lucifer's attribute, has nuances of gravity, too, like English *pride*, French *orgueil*, German *Stolz*, Church Slavic *gordost'*.

2. *Łakomstwo* (covetousness) for *avaritia*. I saw in this a transgression that consisted of licking out jam jars or indulging my unrestrained craving for dessert, which may not be much of a problem today, but during my childhood desserts rarely appeared on our table. And who would have explained to me then that just such a yen for sweets was the mainspring of our civilization's grim history, that it provided the impetus for usury and the establishment of factories, for the conquest of America, the oppression of the peasant in Poland, the brilliant idea perfected by the pious citizens of Amsterdam that they could use their ships to traffic in slaves? Certainly, the mighty of this world have always wanted dessert. However, if they were at least gluttons, that is, individuals in pursuit of sensual pleasures, that wouldn't have been so bad. *Avaritia*, however, is rather an ascetic passion, as the French *avarice* and the German *Geiz* indicate. Should

Molière's *L'Avare* be translated as *The Glutton*? English *covetousness* is closer to greediness than miserliness, but it is also a stern appetite directed exclusively at money. Both meanings, miserliness and greediness, are expressed by Church Slavic *srebrolub'e*, a literal translation of the Greek *filarguria*.

3. *Nieczystość* (impurity) instead of *luxuria*. This probably had something to do with not washing oneself? With the added implication of "shameful parts"? But the Latin word meant exuberance, fertility, abundance, primarily of vegetation, then immoderate exuberance, for example in how one expressed oneself; also excess, overweening pride, and dissolution. French *luxure* preserved some of these connotations, although it means the same as Polish *rozwiązłość* (dissoluteness); *rozwiązłość*, not *nieczystość*, would have been a better Polish equivalent. By abandoning Latin here and making use of the Old German *Lust*, English has strayed too far from the original meaning, although the adjective *lusty* leans in the direction of exuberant, strong, and at one time was used in the sense of playful, merry. English *lust* suggests the kinds of changes that related concepts have been subjected to as a result of language and customs, especially if we compare it to the Church Slavic name for this sin: *blud* (which simply means "fornication"), taken directly from Greek *porneia*, bypassing the Latin. *Nieczystość*, by contrast, appears to be simply a translation of the German *Unkeuschheit*.

4. *Zazdrość* (envy) instead of *invidia*. The meaning of this word was completely unclear to me. Now, I know that its source is the Latin *in-videre*; *za-źreć*, in other words, exactly the same thing as *za-widzieć* (*zavist'* in Church Slavic). Other languages place more or less emphasis on will, yearning, although I find it difficult to say if French *envie*, English *envy*, German *Neid* adequately convey the sense of the Latin term that includes both hatred and slander.

5. *Obżarstwo* (gluttony) and *pijaństwo* (drunkenness) instead of *gula*. Originally, it meant throat in Latin; later, voraciousness and greediness, too. Gluttony and drunkenness suggested an image of laden tables, of potbellied men grunting and bellowing; obviously a grownups' sin. Only now do I wonder why Polish used two words to translate *gula*. In none of the languages I know does drunkenness figure among the cardinal sins. Church Slavic *chrevougod'e*, or belly-pleasing, was constructed on the model of the Greek *gastrimargia*; the closest thing in Polish would have been *popuszczanie sobie pasa* (loosening one's belt) in relation to both food and drink. Something unexpected happened to this failing in the course of history, perhaps because there was a time in the past when more people could indulge

themselves with *gula* than in the course of the following centuries. All sorts of undernourished people could lick their chops at the thought of stuffing their bellies just for once, and an entire poetry arose about smoked goose, kielbasa, smoked ham, kegs of beer. It was supposed to be a sin, but what else was the reward for self-restraint during Lent if not gluttony and drunkenness? And is there really a negative connotation to the French word *gourmandise*? On the contrary, if someone is a *gourmand* that's very good, it means he has a ruddy complexion, ties his napkin under his chin, and is knowledgeable about cuisine and wines; he's not a pauper. He's not quite a *gourmet*, or a connoisseur of food, but he's close to it. German *unmässig* doesn't benefit from such privileges, and the English *glutton* is also different, an insatiable gullet prone to *gluttony* or omnivorousness.

6. *Gniew* (rage) instead of *ira*. "An explosion of rage"—it wasn't hard to picture what that is. It is a short-lived physical state that is expressed in violent deeds (King Bolesław the Brave breaking into the church and in a fit of rage murdering the bishop). *Ira* doesn't present any great difficulty in translation either. *Anger, colère, Zorn*, Church Slavic *gnev*.

7. *Lenistwo* (laziness) instead of *acedia*. Polish is not responsible for the comical misunderstanding. The word is not Latin but was borrowed via the Latin directly from the Greek *akedia*, and should have been translated as *obojętność* (indifference). But for the fourth-century eremites *akedia* was the main danger, a temptation by the devil that was most severe at noon, when all nature rests in silence, motionless under the high sun. That is when a monk would be visited by sadness and boredom. He would try to resist it with prayer, but he would be tormented by a feeling that all his exertions and his mortifications were meaningless. If he allowed himself to be defeated, he would abandon his cave and just run over to the neighboring cave in order not to be by himself. If he often succumbed to such attacks, he had to return to the city, to be among people. *Akedia* was therefore a dangerous impediment for people dedicated to an intense spiritual life. Monastic instructions also devoted a good deal of attention to it later on, in the Middle Ages. It was frequently linked with *tristitia* or *lupe*, that is, sadness; it is easiest to express it with the words *nothing matters*. The transformation of *akedia* into the (physical?) failing of somnolence and indolence took place only gradually. Neither the French *paresse*, the English *sloth*, nor the German *Trägheit* conveys the original meaning. Only Church Slavic

unyn'e conveys it perfectly. Obviously, I didn't have the foggiest notion of what "laziness" was except for one of its variants, that is, my understandable repugnance for "iron necessity," that is, doing my homework.

The disinclination of clergymen today to classify sins is understandable, since the whole great edifice of distinctions, concepts, and syllogisms was erected quite late, achieving its ultimate form in Jesuit casuistry. Of course, the prestige of scientific research that sets itself the task of dissecting stuffed bears in order to see how they are constructed undoubtedly also had an influence. This stuffed bear, or man, is not studied by psychologists as a tangle of good and evil, or of values, but as the territory of certain "phenomena." At the same time, man's poor sins, in comparison with the luxuriant flora and fauna discovered inside him, have become abstractions similar to émigré governments and exiled monarchs.

Nonetheless. *Sed contra*, as Thomas Aquinas used to say. In each of us various interesting chains of causes and effects can be tracked down, but let someone else concern himself with this. When we are alone with ourselves, it is our goodness and our evil that perturb us and not those intriguing questions: Where do we come from and why are we here? And what if I should try to ascertain what the cardinal sins, so vague and foggy in my childhood, mean to me today? This would be no ordinary assignment, because it would imply that a new content is being interpreted in terms of the old *saligia*; that is, by discovering its imposing forms within oneself, one restores it to its sorrowful dignity.

Let us be candid. The seven cardinal sins were considered at most a spur to the actions that condemn one to eternal damnation, but not a single one of these seven nor *saligia* as a whole had of necessity to lead to utter damnation. For the *vitia capitalia* were the more or less universal manifestations of spoiled human nature, and this nature is not so spoiled as to leave no room for hope. Thus, in *The Divine Comedy*, when Dante and his guide, Virgil, emerge at the other end of the earth after their sojourn in Hell at the center of earth and begin their ascent to Mount Purgatory, they come upon seven terraces, each of which is inhabited by souls who are doing penance for one of the seven cardinal sins. The order of these terraces follows the model of *siiaagl*, not *saligia*, and I find Dante's reasoning convincing. Several tercets from Canto 17 are of particular importance here and are well worth citing in translation. When they reach the fourth terrace Virgil says:

"My son, there's no Creator and no creature
who ever was without love—natural
or mental; and you know that," he began.
          "The natural is always without error,
but mental love may choose an evil object [per malo obietto]
or err through too much or too little vigor.
          As long as it's directed toward the First Good
and tends toward secondary goods with measure,
it cannot be the cause of evil pleasure;
          but when it twists toward evil, or attends
to good with more or less care than it should,
those whom He made have worked against their Maker.
          From this you see that—of necessity—
love is the seed in you of every virtue
and of all acts deserving punishment."

[Translated by Allen Mandelbaum]

"Love that moves the sun and the stars" is, then, the core of all things and of each living being. In the order of nature (*amore naturale*) it does not submit to moral judgments. A stone released from the hand falls because that is what the law of gravity wants; an animal hunts another animal because that is what he is ordered to do by what has come to be called instinct. But love in the spiritual order, which is what distinguishes man and also angels (*amore d'animo*), can be mistaken. Its calling is to aspire to the first good, that is, to the source of great good, that is, to God (*primo ben diretto*). It is mistaken if it recognizes as its good something that conflicts with this chief end, and also if it itself is too strong or too weak. The seven terraces of Purgatory are an illustration of such errors. The three lowest signify depraved love; that is, love that aspired to a mistaken goal. The souls whom Dante and Virgil meet there are suffering because during their lifetimes the magnetic needle of their love (or Will) had turned toward themselves: *superbia, invidia, ira.* The fourth is the terrace of *acedia*, or insufficient, somnolent love, that love that was incapable of putting to proper use the time given to mortal man. The three highest terraces, the ones closest to the Earthly Paradise, which is located on the highest plateau of Mount Purgatory, are designated as the place of penance for souls whose love was excessive, because *avaritia, gula,* and *luxuria* derive from excess. This is rather enigmatic, because the greedy, the gluttonous, and the dissolute come out much better with their failings than do others. Their powerful will to life appears to be centrifugal, not centripetal; that is, it is directed toward the external world, toward its annexation. It is oblivious, somehow, of the annexer himself: for the greedy man or the miser, money symbolically summarizes all the delights of earth; roast meats rivet the attention of the glutton because he does not, after all, think about his own taste—taste resides in the roast; a beautiful girl charms the ladykiller with a promise of something mysterious, unrecognized. If this is so, if the centrifugal will to life is the pursuit of existence as enchantment, by transgressing a certain measure it can find satiety only in *primo ben diretto*, that is, in God; but in that case, since there is so much of it, it would lead to saintliness. But saintliness is not easy, which is why these three higher terraces exist. Which is to say, since love directed outward, so to speak, toward things apprehended by the senses, is not an error, at worst its excessive greediness would incline one to offer this advice: Either be saintly or you will have to have less of this love of yours. Dostoevsky follows Dante faithfully in *The Brothers Karamazov*; the *avaritia, gula*, and *luxuria* of both the elder Karamazov and Dmitri pale in comparison with a truly severe defect: Ivan's *superbia*, with which Smerdyakov's *acedia* is in league.*

SUPERBIA

If you are one of the thousand, shall we say, active poets of your time, you think about what will become of your works in a hundred or two hundred years. Either all your names will be listed only in footnotes to the intellectual history of the period, or one of you will rise above the fashions and collective customs, while the rest, although they had appeared to be individuals, will form a chorus obedient to its conductor, who will silence any voices that are too independent—independent, that is, of the epoch's style. That one poet is you, for you alone are right. But what does poetry have in common with being right? A whole lot. The arrangement of words implies choice, choice implies deliberation, and behind your words lurks a silent judgment about the many human matters that you have dealt with. If in your judgment (conscious, semiconscious, or unconscious) you are right, you will break through the cocoon of gen-

---

* Sergei Gessen was the first to apply *saligia* to Dostoevsky. His 1928 work, "Tragediia dobra v 'Brat'iakh Karamazovykh,' " is reprinted in the collection *O Dostoevskom. Stat'i* (Providence: Brown University Press, 1966), 199–229.

erally accepted opinions in your epoch; the others, however, will become trapped in them. For not all reasons are equal and error enjoys the same privileges as truth for only a short time. Could it be, then, that absolute criteria exist for the creations of the imagination and language? Without a doubt. But how can that be? After all, one person likes one thing, another likes something else, *de gustibus non est disputandum*. And yet everything that can be numbered among the works of the human spirit submits to a strict hierarchy. Our opinions about contemporary works are unstable and tentative, because only time lays bare the true hierarchy under the veils and piles of gilded rubbish. Nonetheless, at the moment when you hold your pen and compose poetry, you are extraordinarily confident of your rightness—and also of the erroneous assumptions of all your rivals. But isn't there a fraternity of poets who are also very different but who respect each other? There are such fraternities. The triumph of your mastery, however, is contained in the act of writing itself, and you know very well that you trust only the voice of your own daimonion.

It cannot be ruled out that this is the way things have worked up till now because "eternal glory" has gotten into the habit of crowning only a few greats. Considering that it is the *activity* (writing, painting, sculpture, etc.) that assumes prominence today and not the results, it is possible that the many millions of creative artists who are fleetingly famous will replace the few who are chosen. I was raised according to traditional beliefs, however, and therefore I am inclined to consider the sin of *superbia* an occupational disease. If we limited its meaning to overweening pride, we would ignore the rich ambiguity of its consequences, for pride and self-assurance are indispensable for the poet who wishes to achieve something and not retreat from his path.

I have held various opinions about poetry and literature in various phases of my life, so I might be making the mistake of reading into the past the views that I hold today. In the profession of "writer" I now see a certain embarrassing buffoonery. When we read the diaries of various masters of the pen published nowadays, we are overcome with pity: they really considered themselves "great." How many of them worshipped dry rot, their own renown, which was supported by a couple of coffeehouses and a handful of press clippings? That's how it is now, but my not very friendly attitude toward my profession was formed a long time ago, I think, in my early youth. Already at that time poetry, not to speak of literature in general, was *too little*. Let us assume that you are, potentially, better than your rivals (which

I did not doubt). So what? Among the blind a one-eyed man is king, and are you really going to take pride in that title? There is no question that I wanted to be a superb poet. But that did not seem to me to be sufficient. Had I aspired to the composition of a certain number of excellent poems, that would simply have been evidence of only mild *superbia*; however, I had enough *superbia* in me for it to carry me beyond any mere authorship.

I did not ascribe to myself any extraordinary abilities or talents except for one which I would be unable to define even now. It was a particular type of intelligence capable of perceiving associations between things that others did not perceive as connected. It was also a type of imagination that was particularly sensitive to customs and institutions. One way or another, I always heard this warning inside me: *This cannot last.* And if there was a certain unreality to everything that surrounded me, could works written in the midst of this unreality be real? Especially since this did not apply to Poland alone but also, although for somewhat different reasons, to all of Europe. Somewhere, Ortega y Gasset compares the artist who is born in an unfavorable era to a woodcutter with strong muscles and a sharp ax who finds himself in the desert. I wasn't familiar with this analogy at that time, in my youth; had I known it, my auto-irony would have been expressed in the following words: "You've picked a fine time, with that strength of yours, since there isn't any wood."

It was necessary to strive for that dimension where the fates of both reality as a whole and poetry were being decided. However, it wasn't reachable by words in those days. Furthermore, no one understood my poems or, perhaps more important, I believed that no one understood them, because I felt totally isolated, the more so as we drew closer to 1939. Today, I understand this as follows: Polish society has a very strong sense of the sacral, and this explains the specific fortunes of Poles in a century of advanced desacralization. What we are talking about here, however, is such an extreme appropriation of the sacral by one goddess—Polishness—that nothing else was good enough for her. The dimension that my eyes dimly perceived in the thirties did not belong to the general Polish dimension, so my place was among the "outsiders," because they were Jews or because they were Communists or Communist sympathizers. No matter where I turned, however, there was nowhere where I felt at home. A taste for "ultimate things" gave direction to my entire life, although due to various geographical-psychological peculiarities the Polish-Catholic tonality has not been dominant in this religion of mine.

Was my imagination right, then, to warn me that this could not last? Here I should draw a distinction. Grasping the "black" sides of reality, my imagination facilitated my pessimistic diagnosis, but I should try to downplay the opinion, flattering though it is, that this was my prophetic poetic gift at work. Who knows if my rejection of life in general, punishing it for being *unreasonable*, was not even more important here? This unreason, in both individual, biological life and collective life alike, has various degrees of intensity, ranging from those that can be named (e.g., economic absurdities, unsuccessful political institutions, and so forth) to completely elusive ones, though they were always inconsistent with my need for total harmony. Thus, whether the overthrow of the existing order occurred or not, its downfall would always have seemed justified to me in advance.

My *superbia* demanded punishment, and at last it has incurred punishment. For now, in my mature years, when I open my mouth and listen to myself with the ears of those to whom I speak, what do I hear? Incomprehensible babbling, which should be counted as punishment. After repeated explosions of rage (after all, I wasn't asking for much) I had to accept this immuring of myself in loneliness as equitable and pedagogically beneficial to me. Someone who writes in Polish should not harbor illusions. If the Polish custom of respect for literature as the national shrine did not go hand in hand with utter disdain for matters of the spirit, the earth would be too beautiful a place for our sojourn here.

To be polite: I am barely lifting the curtain here, conscious of the many complications that I have overlooked, for I am obedient to the discipline of language. I am limiting myself to the twofold consequences—negative and positive—of *superbia*. Does it not frequently act as a substitute for morality? As when it forbids us certain actions because they are beneath our conception of ourselves as worthy only of the highest acts? And could someone who relies on willfulness alone really get by without *superbia*? Sooner or later loneliness drives us into crises that cannot be resolved other than by some rebirth, the shedding of the snakeskin, so that what has tormented us till now no longer concerns us. True, I prefer to believe that my *superbia* has played the role of midwife at these births but that, independent of it, more noble characters have also been at work.

INVIDIA

He has what I ought to have; I, not he, deserve it—there's a model of envy. Not that I would like to be him; quite the contrary: he is inferior to me and has been unjustly rewarded, and undoubtedly, because of his inferiority, he is unable to even appreciate it (I, as the superior one, would be able to). Envy, the daughter of pride, is so widespread a failing among literati and authors that it's funny. For instance, every piece of news about a distinction accorded to others evokes in them more or less well-concealed pangs of jealousy. It is true that it is difficult to determine the extent and intensity of envy within oneself, because it is adept at disguising itself. Coming from a provincial European backwater and emigrating three times, first to Warsaw, then to Paris, then to America (always with a marshal's baton in my knapsack?), I must have been cultivating plenty of envy within myself. Let's be fair; this was moderated, however, by an exceptional talent for idolizing, so that while sternly judging some (the many), I knelt humbly before the chosen, absolutely convinced of my own utter inferiority (though they were rarely "writers").

Let us abandon the field of art and literature, however. My century should have been called the age of *invidia* and I shall explain why immediately. Social mobility, when great masses of people suddenly, within a brief span of time, change their occupation, dress, and customs, is conducive to imitation. Strong caste divisions used to make imitation difficult (for example, a bourgeois who pretended to be a member of the landed gentry was laughed at). Imitation means close observation of another and the desire to have as much as he has (money, clothes, freedom, etc.). And here is where a personality that spreads terror appears—it exists in every person as the "I-for-others" that torments the "I-for-myself." One can imagine a state in which a person is relatively indifferent to the behavior of others, if only because their station is too high (for example, wearing folk costumes because only city people wear manufactured clothes), or because, at ease with his uniqueness, he calmly tells himself: "That's not for me." However, in the twentieth century we have been forced to be ashamed of our particularity. "I-for-myself" is, after all, always a shame and a sin, although different people will cope with it more or less successfully. When a person is constantly having it drummed into his head that others are enjoying life as they should, he does not stop to think about the illusory character of this image that depicts people from the outside, that is, in such a way that every man is "I-for-others." He looks around and starts to be envious: that person over there, he's a miserable creature, and yet look at how much he's received, how many gifts have been showered upon him—he's not below the norm, I am. This "normality" or "I-for-others" is, after all, the secret of the diffusion of the "new ethics," namely, the characteristic feature of the "permissive society." Each of us has a "calling" that comprises his diversion from the norm, an appeal directed at this and not that individual. The object of envy is not others in the guise of Charles, Peter, or Ignatius, but in the guise of "normality" as seen from the outside, which we allegedly have too little of. "Reification," imitation, and *invidia* are closely interconnected.

But does the desire to become "the same as everyone else" really indicate that one is envious? So it seems. I don't have what he has, it's owed me, because if I should have it, then I would have a lot more (being myself, my individuality, of course). "Normality" will be an addition to my individuality, while, in my opinion, the essence of this other person is being dissipated in it.

If we divide envy according to its target—a small group based, for example, on profession, or "people in general," the latter would be more dangerous. It is easy to err when we don't want to accept our own destiny, which has been given to us alone, when we are unable to make our peace with the thought that some types of life-styles are beyond our abilities and would even be painful for us. When we make the effort to conform, various miseries of the "man in the crowd" reveal themselves to us.

IRA

Bah, if only it were old-fashioned anger that visits us. It is bad to turn purple in the face from fury; even worse to knock someone flat with a blow to the head and kill him in a fit of rage. Even if someone doesn't carry a hatchet around with him, he may well know the belated regrets of a hothead when it's already too late to make amends. But in addition to this age-old anger, a new, modern anger appeared on the scene when we began to feel responsible for evil as members of society and participants in history. Your guts churn, you grit your teeth, clench your fists—but hold your tongue, you are a cipher and can change nothing. And you ask yourself: "Am I crazy or are they crazy? Maybe it's me, because they go right on living and feel neither indignation nor terror in the face of their own co-responsibility." If we are born with an inclination to anger, and in this lovely century, to boot, what should we do, how are we to cope? Obviously, each person receives an upbringing; just living among others shapes him. He notices that yelling and banging his head against the wall hardly help; if he is a poet, he becomes convinced that making a lot of noise is not very useful. So his anger goes underground and emerges only in disguise, transformed into irony, sarcasm, or icy calm, from which it is often hard to deduce that fury lies concealed behind it.

I spent my entire conscious life in just such maneuvers with my own anger, never, even to this day, understanding how it could be reconciled with my (truly) asocial nature. How, in fact, are we to understand the coexistence within us of contradictory impulses and habits? All the same, my guts kept churning before 1939 and during the war and after. How is it possible, someone will ask quite justifiably, to compare what is incomparable, historical periods and systems marked by a lesser intensity of evil with those in which evil approached its own paroxysm? Unfortunately, the truth is that every human society is multilayered and multilocational. What offends our moral sense does not occur simultaneously in all strata and in all places. Even where the majority of the population is dying of hunger there are beautiful neighborhoods inhabited by the sated, who listen to good music and are interested in—shall we say?—mathematical logic. One should not imagine that those who have been swallowed by a dragon won't experience moments of perfect contentment. For example, one of my memories of felicity is the day in the summer of 1941 when, after a visit to the peasant writer Józef Morton in Chrobrze near Pinczów (we got there by way of a quaint narrow-gauge track that wound through the grass-covered hills), Jerzy Andrzejewski and I got off the train at a tiny station on the outskirts of Cracow from which we had to walk to the city proper. We stopped at a roadside tavern where, in the garden, a wandering gypsy band was playing, and then, not quite steady on our feet, we slowly entered the outlying streets, where everything, compared to Warsaw, seemed to be part of another country and another era. The hubbub of voices and the colorfulness of the crowd in the artists' café on Łobzowska Street reminded me of Montparnasse at the height of its glory. The waitress who came over to our table was Jewish, the wife of our colleague, a Warsaw poet. So happiness had not ceased to exist—although ten days later a huge roundup demonstrated how illusory are such oases.

It's not only the multiplicity of strata and locations in human society that acts as a universal law. The intentionality of our attention is another law, so that the mind transforms and shuffles all sorts of "givens." Where one person sees an injustice that cries out to heaven for vengeance, another sees nothing; where one person evinces no desire for rebellion, another uses guns and places bombs. My thinking about anger is strongly marked by years spent in America; the two zones of time and space, the European and the American, complement each other. American terrorists are not too different from a certain female poet who was quite popular in the Warsaw cafés at the end of the 1930s. Poland at that time offered many causes for anger, but this poet (from a family of intellectuals) was so loaded with hatred that according to her the system was at fault for everything—for what really ought to have been dismantled and what could not be dismantled in Poland, as well as for everything that is immune to dismantling in every collective life. It was she who wrote the rash line: "We have exchanged the Russian occupation for a Polish occupation" (as if independent Poland after 1918 was no better than tsarist Russia), but she was to suffer too much on account of her rashness for it to be worth reproaching her for this today. Her odious poem deserves to be mentioned, however, because in it our own, familiar, twentieth-century anger turns simultaneously against institutions and against, one suspects, the very existence of anything at all. The young Americans from well-to-do white families, no less disturbed by the fate of blacks in the ghetto than the Russian nihilists were by the fate of the peasants, demonstrate a boundless capacity for pumping themselves up with revolutionary rhetoric, but it would be wrong to treat this lightly. The blatant analogies with Dostoevsky's *The Possessed* are probably based on a deeper level than societal relations—most importantly, perhaps, through the figure of Kirillov, the man who condemns himself to death because, as he says, there is no God but there *ought* to be. Is anger, the mighty demon of our epoch, a Promethean outburst in the name of love of people, or is it a declaration of a grudge against a world that is too unjust for life to be worth living? Both the one and the other, I should think, although their proportions here are unclear.

It is easy to understand the anger of the oppressed, the anger of slaves, particularly if you yourself have lived for several years inside the skin of a subhuman. In my century, however, the anger of the privileged who are ashamed of their privilege was even louder. I am fairly well acquainted with this anger. Though very poor as a young man, I still knew that the couple of zlotys in my pocket was practically a fortune for the majority of people in Poland; furthermore, toward the end of the thirties I earned a lot and was able to act the role of the elegant snob. And then in America I could have served as a (doubtful) argument for the defenders of classic capitalism when they assert that "the best man wins" in it, for my work was rather appreciated. I admit that I hobnobbed with people like myself in my Berkeley and my California, people who had succeeded. "We *should* bite the hand that feeds us," one of them said to me. Perhaps. But if so, always bearing in mind the fact that well-fed, rosy-cheeked people have often gotten entangled in duplicity when they pretended that they were suffering.

ACEDIA

No one can call this failing simply laziness any longer; whatever it may once have been, nowadays it has returned to its original meaning: terror in the face of emptiness, apathy, depression. It's not isolated hermits, however, who are experiencing its sting, but the masses in their millions. A perfect reactionary would say that for their own good they should have been kept in poverty and illiteracy, so that the whip of elemental necessity would have left them only brief moments for resting but not thinking, so that they could have been protected from the influence of half-baked intellectuals exploiting the printed word. It turned out otherwise, and although the model changes depending on the country and the system, the general outlines remain the same; that is, the average man has appeared who knows how to write, read, use a motorcycle or a car. Who is also unprepared for spiritual effort and subject to the power of the quasi-intellectuals, who stuff his head with counterfeit values.

Let us not yearn for the good old days; they were not good. Certainly, the sacral daily life of the medieval city was not a figment of the imagination, for it did leave a trace in architecture and in art; but at best it can furnish a clue to the distant future, when after the present transitional phase, an ascending movement will be possible —similar, but of, so to speak, a second degree.

For the present, we are in an era when minds are being defiled, which may be the unavoidable price we pay when many human beings are granted access—not just, as in the past, the narrow stratum of the privileged. Access to what? Not to "culture"—at best, culture is reminiscent of a tightly locked iron chest for which no one has remembered to supply the key. If we may anticipate access, it will be to the "independent battles" of the human persona. Steeped in tribal customs, the individual did not need this at one time, but today, everyone is beginning to be a hermit in the Egyptian desert and is subject to the law of selection—either ascending or descending into one kind of *skotstvo* or another, to use the Russian term which, although its literal meaning is "brutishness," we are inclined, despite the linguists, to link with Greek *skotos* or "darkness."

The chaos of values makes precise distinctions impossible at present, so tributes are rendered to illusory greatnesses that are famous because they represent fashionable tendencies in a colorful and forceful manner. This age is, in addition, an age of monsters—humanity has rarely seen their like—but also, as if for the sake of balance, it has produced not a few figures of gigantic proportions, to whom it is no shame to humbly pay tribute. The mental distance between them and the mechanized man in the crowd is probably greater than that between a medieval theologian and, for example, a member of the coopers' guild. To be precise: this is not a judgment based on the level of education, for many who are Nobel laureates in one field of science do not differ intellectually, apart from their specialty, from their least-educated fellow men. Jacques Maritain used to say that the tone of this era has been set by people with weak heads and sensitive hearts, or people with powerful heads and hard hearts, whereas few people unite a sensitive heart with a powerful head. There is no better example of this than the marketplace in America that governs both the language of words and the language of images. Stupid nobility and ignoble commercial cleverness have become so interconnected that when judging journals, films, books, and television programs in terms of their educational influence, one must simply speak of a mass crime against what is called, inaccurately but not inappropriately, "human dignity."

Unfortunately, someone who will not slack off, because he knows that *acedia* (or *unyn'e*) is lying in wait for him, will soon notice that the distance between him and his contemporaries increases with every year, if not every month. One of the characteristics of intellectual work is that the same activities begin to demand less and less time; that is, one develops a capacity for abbreviations, for shortcuts. As a consequence, one loses one's taste for the words and images supplied by the market, whence the not inconsiderable problem of the new aristocracy of refined intellects who, however, as I have already suggested elsewhere, move in a different sphere than half a century ago—then, it was "avant-garde" literature and art that promised more than it was able to fulfill.

Zealous and diligent by temperament, I have worked hard enough, it would seem, that I ought not reproach myself with *unyn'e*. However, I have not done what I could have and the cause was both a flawed education and states of depression that would render impossible a fruitful resistance to the delusions of my time. Obviously, this does not mean that it would have been better had I decided to put on armor early in life, so that nothing from the twentieth century could infect me, as did one of my acquaintances from my youth, who even at that time was preoccupied exclusively with Plato. That would have been an erroneous and sterile choice. Here, *nota bene*, it would be appropriate to cite the storminess of history, which is not exactly favorable to better judgment. But only a slothful person will presume to cast responsibility onto something that lies outside him.

There is nothing new about grappling with the nothingness that encircles us; man has been faced with these trials for a millennium. However, never before, it seems, not since the times of Caesar's Rome and Hellenistic civilization, has man been so defenseless. These are the consequences of the scientific revolution broken down into small pieces and acting upon the popular imagination in this form. It is possible that the vast majority of people will submit to such nihilizing pressures and will at best search for consolation in the miraculous elixirs sold by Hindu, Buddhist, or Satanic preachers.

AVARITIA

It would seem that from time immemorial there has been nothing more universal and more classic. But although greed for money has always driven people to conquest, to oppression, although it has wiped out many species of animals and threatened the entire planet with the chemical poisoning of the water and air, *avaritia* in the present does not assume only those forms that Dante was familiar with. In those days, this failing always characterized a given, specific individual; today, it is spilling over onto mechanisms that are independent of a specific individual, and this also applies to the other cardinal sins, which seem to elude naming because they are cut off from man. For example, is it a result of greed that an oil company pollutes the ocean with its tankers? If we answer in the affirmative, then we see greed where there is no individual, and therefore neither guilt nor contrition. The directors? But they are acting not as people but as a function of the collective body, which has no other aim than the amassing of profits. They are punished for decisions taken in the name of any goal other than profit. They can, it is true, resign their positions and take up something else; this will not, however, change the actions of the corporate body, which yields only to external force.

The situation of the directors of such a corporation is probably emblematic of what confronts the various, and considerably lower, rungs on the social ladder. This or that Jones or Du Pont quietly dreams of virtue; he would eat grass, drink spring water, wear a sack tied with a piece of string; but while his yearning for the Franciscan ideal may be completely sincere, he has been "captured," alas, and there is no turning back.

The new, impersonal varieties of greed could, if necessary, be considered one of the reasons why it has ceased to be a literary theme. *Avaritia* as the sinister passion of the heroes of novels has its own history, which more or less parallels the history of the "realistic" novel. Defoe, Dickens, Balzac, Zola have successors in the West at the beginning of our century, too, primarily among American writers. In Russia, *srebrolub'e* begins its literary career with Pushkin's *Covetous Knight* and occupies a not inconsiderable position in Dostoevsky's biography (he wanted to win a million at roulette) and in practically all his works. The revolution in novelistic technique that we have witnessed took place at a time when the greedy collective, which is very difficult to describe, was already active alongside the greedy individual. But also the very flight from the realia of life somehow caused the novel to stop speaking about money. And when the human jungle stuns us with its wild growth today, literature, occupied with passive experiences and the individual's impressions, steers away from the vulgar questions: Who makes his living at what? Who is paid for what? It is characteristic that the anger of American intellectuals, who, with rare exceptions, are independent of the publishing market because they live off the universities, overlooks the crux of the matter, that is, the market, and even, on the contrary, strikes out at all limitations on the market's freedom, even though in practice that freedom serves the tradesmen-demoralizers. No doubt a powerful taboo is at work here, one of the most mysterious social thermostats, by force of which revolutionary anger at everything that *avaritia* is responsible for becomes transformed into merchandise, that is, assists that same *avaritia*.

More than other failings, it in particular, but also its absence, refers us to the vague laws of personal predestination. Success and failure, measured in money, do not appear to have an unambiguous link with greed or miserliness, although perhaps the middle groups, those who are called neither to wealth nor to poverty, are the most free of *avaritia*. In this middle group the following principle generally holds true: you will have exactly as much money as you need, but under the condition that you are not particularly anxious about it.

GULA

It is painful to think about all one's great-great-grandfathers succumbing to gluttony and drunkenness; in general, it is painful to think about the genes that one is carrying around inside oneself. The awareness that one has Slavic genes is depressing enough to make the "taste for pickled cucumbers and boisterousness" seem as burdensome as irreversible Karma; the consequences of this tendency to feasting cannot be evaded, even if subsequently they are gracefully assigned to various geopolitical causes. A simple calculation of the time spent on feasting and thereby lost to thinking over the course of centuries can explain a lot here. Idyllic feasting may testify to an inability to tolerate the world as it is, to a yearning for a gentler world; at the same time, it is one of the chief motivations of self-contempt, for revulsion at drunks in the street seems to merge with revulsion at one's own behavior in the recent past. Low self-esteem, which, to be sure, is rooted not only in this but also in a collective incapacity (so that only individuals are energetic), leads, in turn, to paranoid reflexes; self-revulsion is extended to "them," to whomever, who are guilty of everything. That is why one should also notice more than just the loud talk, stupid bragging, and jabbering in a certain type of feasting. Drunkenness itself is less important than what is revealed by drunkenness. And what is revealed is more or less the same among all peoples, with the addition of a given society's particular characteristics. It's the latter that can be the cause of low self-esteem.

I have tried to avoid the traps set by *gula* with varying degrees of success. I admit that this may be taking my practical sense too far, but I have discovered that one can "profit from one's enemy"; that is, one can ponder those things that surface whenever we carry things too far. And what comes to the fore are reflexes, whims, resentments, and egotisms too unflattering for us to enjoy being aware of them.

LUXURIA

When talk turns to dissoluteness or licentiousness, everyone pricks up his ears; I should, therefore, discourage such expectations ahead of time. For want of other attractions, above all, the attractions of the writer's art itself, the literati compete with each other nowadays in "sincerity," and it would no doubt be possible to introduce a new distinction between high style and low style based on this principle. A self-respecting author will not sink to such methods, from which it follows that *belles lettres* are not worth reading because only a very few writers in that genre stay within the bounds of high style.

Dreams of man as happy and liberated have long stood in opposition to all prohibitions and to the hypocrisy that prefers to forget about the libido's hold over us. But eliminating hypocrisy solves very little. D. H. Lawrence says that Adam and Eve's first sexual act after the Original Sin was no different, physiologically, from what they had done many times before. The difference lay in the fact that now each of them *saw*, that is to say, was conscious of his own body and his partner's body as Other; moreover, each was conscious of the fact that the partner was another consciousness. That is why they experienced shame for the first time, were conscious of their nakedness, and hid before the sight of God. "Who told you that you are naked?" God asked Adam. D. H. Lawrence sought a restoration; he wanted man to be innocent, as he was *before* he tasted the fruit of the Tree of the Knowledge of Good and Evil. This is not the place to consider to what extent we can succeed at that. That conjunction in the Book of Genesis: a man and a woman, the apple (or consciousness), shame, teaches us that in any event our words will not succeed in inhabiting the Garden of Eden and that the field of literature, or the works of the mind, can be, at best, an area on the border and, therefore, something that exists merely *in proximity* to love and death in their innocently physiological aspect.

There are a number of puzzling aspects to the "sexual liberation" of the second half of our century. Its vehemence can perhaps be explained as a reaction to the entire nineteenth century, not to the period that directly preceded it, since the years of my youth, for example, were not particularly puritanical. Let us agree that revolutions in mores do not occur rapidly; sometimes it takes decades until the so-called masses embrace a universal standard. However, even if we concede this, "liberation" is striking in its frenzy, as if it were a "feast in the time of the plague," whether because the death that threatens the individual has grown more threatening or because the plague is going to destroy the species. This frenzy has its seat not so much in the glands as in the mind, which is filled with shifting images that constantly bombard it from outside, and that are in turn obedient to the dynamics of their own form; in other words, the dose of vividness has to be increased continually. Such a frenzy cannot stop itself and it may well be that it will destroy itself, resulting in an ominous boredom. But it is also possible that it presages a new revolution, which would be a rather paradoxical result of these yearnings for innocence and normality. Science-fiction writers have already written about such visually-olfactorily-tactilely provoked surrogate discharges.

Beatrice is a powerful symbol in *The Divine Comedy*; that is, she is both a real person and a real idea of platonic love in precisely the same degree, or she is neither the one nor the other, because she appears instead of them, so that they cannot be separated. She also leads Dante to the summit—literally, because she leads him to the mountain of Earthly Paradise and even higher—assuming the leadership where Virgil ends his role; that is, where the natural sorcery of art ends.

The present antagonism toward all asceticism and even the particular fury with which it is mocked are sufficient cause for revealing a certain secret. The Divine Arts of Imagination, as Blake called them, are obedient to Eros' summons but at the same time are ill disposed to or, should we say, envious of the procreative urge. This conflict is an entirely serious one, for the arts demand of those who are faithful to them a constant striving without fulfillment, and whether or not the faithful desire it, the arts impose upon them their own monastic rule. There exist a sufficient number of testimonies to that effect; furthermore, the lives of artists and of people who have had mystical experiences can be cited together here, since the issue is the same. The coloring and expressiveness of all "visions," whether in dreams or waking, depend on a number of conditions; one of them is a high threshold of erotic energy. "Unfulfilled" love, from the Provençal ladies of whom the troubadours sang, and their Florentine sister, Beatrice, to the Romantic biographies, bears witness that the entire dualistic, Platonic tradition, which was revived by the Albigensians, responds to some truth in our nature. Or perhaps not to ours, that is, not to man's in general? Of the two types of totalism, the "permissive" will be more enduring than the "prohibitive," because in the former the arts of the imagination will wither of their own accord.

1974

THE EARTH AS PARADISE

*All appeared New, and Strange at the first, inexpressibly rare, and
Delightfull, and Beautifull. I was a little Stranger which at my Enterance
into the World was Saluted and Surrounded with innumerable Joys.
My Knowledg was Divine . . . Evry Thing was at Rest, Free, and
Immortal. I Knew Nothing of Sickness or Death, or exaction, in the
Absence of these I was Entertained like an Angel with the Works of
GOD in their Splendor and Glory; I saw all in the Peace of Eden; Heaven
and Earth did sing my Creators Praises and could not make more
Melody to Adam, than to me. All Time was Eternity, and a Perpetual
Sabbath . . .*

*The Corn was Orient and Immortal Wheat, which never should be
reaped, nor was ever sown. I thought it had stood from everlasting to
everlasting. The Dust and Stones of the Street were as precious as GOLD.
The Gates were at first the End of the World, The Green Trees when
I saw them first through one of the Gates Transported and Ravished
me; their Sweetnes and unusual Beauty made my Heart to leap, and
almost mad with Extasie, they were such strange and Wonderfull Thing:
The Men! O what Venerable and Reverend Creatures did the Aged
seem! Immortal Cherubims! And young Men Glittering and Sparkling
Angels and Maids strange Seraphick Pieces of Life and Beauty! Boys
and Girles Tumbling in the Street, and Playing, were moving Jewels.
I knew not that they were Born or should Die. But all things abided
Eternaly as they were in their Proper Places. Eternity was Manifest in
the Light of the Day, and som thing infinit Behind evry thing appeared:
which talked with my Expectation and moved my Desire. The Citie
seemed to stand in Eden, or to be Built in Heaven. The Streets were
mine, the Temple was mine, the People were mine, their Clothes and
Gold and Silver was mine, as much as their Sparkling Eys Fair Skins
and ruddy faces. The Skies were mine, and so were the Sun and Moon
and Stars, and all the World was mine, and I was the only Spectator
and Enjoyer of it.*

—THOMAS TRAHERNE, *Century 3*

The author who thus describes his childhood died in 1674 at the age
of thirty-seven. He was completely forgotten until the beginning of

our century. He owes his position as one of the leading English "metaphysical poets" to some manuscripts from which a dozen or so poetic works were published in 1903 and, shortly afterward, in 1908, *The Centuries*. *The Centuries* is composed of paragraphs, in prose and in verse, arranged in "books" of one hundred entries each, which explains the title that was assigned to the work by its first publisher.

Traherne's book is a hymn in praise of *felicity*, of man's happiness on earth. In it, the world is God's gift to man, arranged in such a way that human life should be unceasing ecstasy. Assigning *The Centuries* to the genre of devotional and inspirational literature (Traherne was a priest) tells us little about their contents. The reasoning contained in them progresses from "yes" to "no" and again to "yes"; in other words, it is presented successively: *if* man can know perfect happiness (and he can, albeit only in a state of innocence, thus, in childhood), it means that suffering, which is universal and is considered to be unavoidable, can be avoided through a return to beginnings; that is, through the recovery of a lost naïve vision, which, however, requires the fulfillment of a number of preconditions.

An emotional response to the providential organization of the world in which everything has been thought out by the Creator so as to give man the greatest pleasure was current in the seventeenth century and Traherne does not contest that convention, he only raises it to another power; but it was precisely that conformity that led to his writings being lost among the large number of similar religious tracts that are related spiritually to Baroque music. Today we marvel at the simplicity of his style, which is capable of revealing inner experience so faithfully; alas, we are also overcome by dread at the thought of how distant are the shores to which we have been swept away. There is nothing more antithetical to the twentieth century than Traherne's fundamental joy at remembering how great is *the blessing of time*—how splendid is the design that night should follow day and day night, that the light of the sun should measure out the mornings, afternoons, and evenings, that the seasons should change. In contrast, for us, time (this is the contribution of the natural sciences) has become primarily biological, which is to say, from birth to death it is composed of a countless number of parallel but incommensurable processes: in the morning a generation of dayflies was born, in the evening they died, and their brief existence intersects the longer or even shorter existence of myriads of other living creatures, including man. Nature's prodigality, or its fertility-on-the-way-to-extinction in the name of the survival of the species, began (exactly when, the reader can say) to offend us morally as if through a foreboding that that same blind fertility would soon threaten the human species and become a scandal for theology, which would be incapable of wriggling out of this inconsistency: what Providence thrust this sexual instinct upon us if we, too, will be forced to exclude the unborn from the feast of life in order that those who have been born may live? And where is Traherne, who is not at all perturbed by death, for in *The Centuries* man has not yet been transformed into a part of nature? On the contrary: each man is Unique and appears as a joyously welcomed visitor from the Abyss; he accedes to the delight of stepping into natural time as into *rhythm*.

We are, then, according to Traherne, capable of recognizing what life was like in Paradise. Young children are innocent and therefore their five senses absorb the world as it really is, in all its beauty. The Earth is Paradise—but man, when he loses his innocence as a consequence of sin, no longer knows this. However, if he acquires consciousness of his wealth and overcomes the evil within him, he will achieve the aim of his existence, namely, a renewed innocence, and once again, as in childhood, he will find himself in paradise.

I find this puzzling. One can accept Traherne's assumption when he speaks about the obstacle, i.e., sin, that from time immemorial has been identified with the victory of our ego. However, since my mind has been powerfully affected, even if against my will, by twentieth-century science, I cannot comprehend the basis for the sinlessness of the child and I must ask if this sinlessness is not a delusion. We recognize as a general rule (go ahead and count up the names of the writers who have made this analysis) that the individual human being will not be content with anything less than becoming God—because only the deity could act as a pure and absolute *subject*, capable, should he so desire, of looking at all others as *objects* and retaining the privilege that no one else's eyes will be able to turn him into an *object*. Thus, the state of sin, in adults, at least, is nothing other than the suffering of a consciousness that flings itself greedily at the world, wishing to be everything or to have everything for itself—and immediately coils up in despair within itself, ruminating on its own defeat. Yes, but that's just it, a child is pure subject, his own god, until he discovers that his power, by no means limitless, comes up against resistance (things, people). His crying or his enraged howls are his attempts to hold on to his imagined absolute power.

Where, then, ought one to draw the boundary between innocence and sin? This objection to Traherne is by no means trivial. True enough, but I am obliged to forget it in the light of one fact: the sentences that I quoted above speak the truth and nothing but the truth; I know this because I, too, have been in Paradise. Echoes, fragrances, sounds, the light of summer mornings in the countryside when I was seven have lost nothing of their breathtaking beauty, even though this all occurred so long ago, ages ago. And trying to give as polite an answer as possible to the question whether this was not an intoxication with power, I must object. When Traherne repeats the word "mine," when he says "the Skies were mine, and so were the Sun and Moon and Stars," or calls himself "the only Spectator and Enjoyer," he points to something quintessential. Because possession, undisputed by anyone or anything, is not power—power, in order to verify its being, must have recourse to deeds. If everything belongs to me, my "I" has not yet awakened; it has not fenced itself off from the world with any walls and one can say without exaggeration that it is everything that it receives at every moment, as light, color, sound, fragrance. The thought of an "I" that is distinct from a "not-I" does not appear, and this, perhaps, is what innocence is based on. Very well, but what about resistance—of things or people? Most likely we should delineate separate strata here; what is taking place in the one is not taking place in the other. As a little child I must have been an unbearable tyrant, but perhaps we are being unjust when we conjoin acquisitiveness with disinterested delight in the abundance that surrounds the child and that offers no resistance, is unable to do so, for what resistance can there be in a ray of sunlight gliding across the wallpaper?

Traherne uses a powerful argument in this connection, if we think about it seriously: he reminds us that the earth was presented as a gift not to the human race but to one man, Adam. And every man since then has been just such an Adam, which, after all, Seneca also recognized: *Deus me dedit solum toti Mundo, et totum Mundum mihi soli*—God gave me alone to the World and He gave the entire World to me alone. In such a loving union there is no struggle for power, no rivalry, for whom would it be with? Adam, by himself and in the person of Eve, who was carved out of his rib, neither felt that he was a god nor intended to become one, for were it otherwise, how could there have been a crisis—which began only when the Tempter's whisper was heard, "Ye shall be as gods"?

It would take a lot of courage to write about the Earth as Paradise today. Unfortunately, calling it Hell is about as justified as calling it Paradise, and that, as we know, is a great nuisance. But we are inclined to exaggerate when we envy Traherne's era, which was a time of revolution and civil war in England, and also of fierce religious struggles, about which *The Centuries* says not even a single word.

Two details about my encounter with Traherne. The first, from my youth. Even in England he was little known, to say nothing of Continental Europe. In France before the war only *Les Cahiers du Sud*, a periodical published in Marseilles, paid any attention to the English "metaphysical poets" or to various other phenomena that entered the field of vision of the French only several decades later. I was an enthusiastic reader of that journal, which Oscar Milosz used to set aside for me issue by issue, shipping them to Wilno in fairly large parcels, and it was there, in 1936, I think, that I came across several of Traherne's poems, printed in English, with a literal French translation.

Mickiewicz was the cause of my second encounter. To explain this, I practically have to give a brief history of Slavic studies in America. Harvard University initiated Slavic studies in 1896, entrusting the teaching of Russian and other Slavic languages to Leon Wiener, an immigrant from Białystok. His son, Norbert Wiener, is famous as the creator of cybernetics. The second center for Slavic studies was organized in Berkeley, where George Rapall Noyes, originally Wiener's student, later a graduate of Petersburg University, began teaching Slavic languages in 1901. This founder of the Department of Slavic Languages and Literatures where I would eventually be a professor was an admirer of Mickiewicz and to this day remains his chief translator into English. He did a prose translation of *Pan Tadeusz*. I did not know Noyes but I once received a letter from him on the occasion of my first essay in English, "Mickiewicz and Modern Poetry," in the Mickiewicz Symposium volume that Manfred Kridl published in New York.* In this symposium Noyes had described what it was about *Pan Tadeusz* that captivated him: the characteristic that he describes as "a childlike point of view paired with the consciousness that this is a childlike point of view." Here Noyes cites Traherne. Mickiewicz's poem, then, was for Noyes yet one more work about felicity regained.

To have been young, and then to grow older, and finally to die, is a very mediocre form of human existence; this merit belongs to every animal. But the unification of the different stages of life in simultaneity

---

* *Adam Mickiewicz, Poet of Poland: Symposium* (New York: Columbia University Press, 1951).

is the task set for human beings. And just as it is an evidence of mediocrity when a human being cuts away all communication with childhood, so as to be a man merely fragmentarily, so it is also a miserable mode of existence for a thinker who is also an existing individual to lose imagination and feeling, which is quite as bad as losing his reason.

— SØREN KIERKEGAARD, *Concluding Unscientific Postscript*
[Translated by David F. Swenson and Walter Lowrie]

One man is good and another is shrewd, or the same man acts as a good man at one time, and shrewdly at another time; but at one and the same time to perceive in connection with the same thing what is shrewd, and to perceive this merely in order to will the good, is very difficult. One man has a predilection for laughter and another for tears, or the same man is disposed variously at different times; but at one and the same time to see the comic and the tragic in the same thing, is difficult. To be crushed under a burden of remorse, and again to be a devil of a fellow is not difficult; but at one and the same time to be crushed in spirit and yet free from care, is difficult. To think one thought and to have forgotten all others is not difficult; but to think one and simultaneously have the opposite in mind, uniting these opposites in existence, is difficult. In a life of seventy years to have had all possible moods, and to leave behind a collection of samples from which to choose at pleasure, is not so very difficult; but to have one mood rich and full, and also to have the opposite mood, so that in giving the one mood its pathos and expression, the opposite mood is slipped in as an undertone, that is a difficult thing to do. And so forth.

—IBID.

1974

AN INTERVIEW WITH CZESLAW MILOSZ

RACHEL BERGHASH: *Your recent book* Unattainable Earth *consists of a process which includes being in paradise, being expelled from it, and as you say in the book: "Some are born humanized, and others have to humanize themselves slowly." How do you account for that slow process that some people have to go through?*

CM: It seems to me that every act of creative writing is a compensation for shortcomings, and that in order to be a good artist one should not be quite human. All art is a little suspect in that respect. These thoughts tortured Thomas Mann all his life.

RB: *Have you made a decision to humanize yourself after all?*

CM: No, not necessarily. I guess I tried to do that for many decades of my life.

RB: *With any success?*

CM: It is very hard to judge oneself. You know very well that we do not know our own virtues and shortcomings. It is not our business but that of the Last Judgment.

RB: *There is a philosophy in your poetry, and I wonder what you think of the philosopher A. N. Whitehead's notion that philosophy is akin to poetry and both of them "seek to express the ultimate good which we term civilization"?*

CM: I have studied philosophy and various systems of thought which are in a way like constructions in poetry. We know that philosophy is not an answer to a search for truth; it may be very honest in its

Editor's Note: This interview was conducted at Czeslaw Milosz's home in Berkeley, California, for the program *A World Elsewhere* and was broadcast on WBAI-FM New York in three parts, June 25, June 30, and July 2, 1986.

search, but it is not a more certain way of attaining truth than poetry is.

RB: *Are they similar in their search?*

CM: In a way they are similar. Personally, I am not very much in favor of writing articles and essays and am looking for a shorter and more concise form of writing. Some of my essays have definite philosophical meaning. My book *The Land of Ulro*—with a title borrowed from Blake—is, as I consider it, a philosophical book. I am very grateful to philosophy because it exists, and I remember my classes in philosophy with gratitude. But philosophy for me is good in order to forget it.

RB: *Like Kierkegaard, who studied philosophy in order to abandon it.*

CM: In a way, yes.

RB: *Do you think that philosophy and poetry are on the path of examining the obvious?*

CM: Yes. There are a certain number of questions which have been asked by philosophers for centuries and are undoubtedly related to some everyday observations of human beings. Sometimes you take obviousness and turn it into a philosophical question. There is a short poem of mine in this new volume entitled "Myness." One morning I was sitting in a university cafeteria and I listened to voices around me. As a result I wrote the following poem: " 'My parents, my husband, my brother, my sister,' / I am listening in a cafeteria at breakfast. / The women's voices rustle, fulfill themselves / in a ritual no doubt necessary. / I glance sidelong at their moving lips / And I delight in being here on earth / For one more moment, with them, here on earth, / To celebrate our tiny, tiny my-ness." This is a philosophical poem drawn out of obviousness. What could be more obvious than a conversation in a cafeteria?

RB: *In the United States poets tend to center their writing on themselves. I don't have a sense that your poems are that way.*

CM: Somewhere in Dostoevsky you read that what a man mostly wants is to talk about himself. I guess that this tendency is due to a large extent to extreme subjectivization of literature in the twentieth century, especially in the West. This subjectivization is not so strong in Central Europe, the part of Europe that I come from—Poland, Czechoslovakia, and Hungary—because there it is counterbalanced to some extent by historical experiences; the individual appears upon the background of history of the twentieth century, and upon the background of history in general, and his tendency toward subjectivism is mitigated.

RB: *I would like to subtitle your new book "The New Book of Wisdom." You have included in it, in addition to your own poems, various "inscripts" and poems from other authors that deal with significant questions and answers. What prompted you to gather these and bring them together along with your own writing?*

CM: Your question is very interesting and pertinent. I have always looked for a more spacious form to express myself. Poetry seems to me a little narrow today, in the sense that many techniques have been banned from it under the impact of looking for purity of lyricism; epic poetry, for instance, has been largely abandoned. In my new book I wanted to say as much as possible by mixing verse and prose, and by mixing quotations from poems and poems of other poets which I consider to be connected with the tone and thinking of the book. At the same time, as I mentioned before, I feel less and less inclined to write essays. It seems to me that there are too many words in articles and essays.

RB: *What about novels?*

CM: Novels are an anathema to me.

RB: *From your own poems and the "inscripts" that you have included in your book, I gather that you think that the way to deal with sin is to have a prospective conscience rather than a retrospective conscience.*

CM: Yes. There was a time in my life when I went through a very difficult period of constant retrospective thinking about my shortcomings, my sins and misdeeds in the past. A friend of mine, a follower of Existentialist philosophy, told me that I practiced what in the Middle Ages was called *delectatio morosa*, a term used to describe the way in which monks used to think about their past misdeeds and sins, meditating on them for days instead of doing what was necessary at the present. She said that our past is not static and that it constantly changes according to our deeds at the present. The things that we do in the present throw a light backward upon our previous shortcomings and deeds; every act of ours presently performed transforms the past. If we make use of them as a motoric force, for instance, that pushes us to do good things, we redeem our past and give a new meaning and a new sense to our past actions.

RB: *Would you say, then, that the criterion of being good is striving to be better?*

CM: I don't know whether we should think in these categories. Usually we are besieged by our past. We constantly think in terms of the past and the future. We visualize how we were and how we will be. We do not think very much in terms of the present.

RB: *In your book you say: "Nature soon bores me . . ." and later you say: "After all, Nature was not the object of my contemplation. It was human society in the great cities of the modern era, 'the pleasures of the depraved animal,' as Baudelaire says." Is it human capacity to deal with sin that interests you?*

CM: No, I said that the human world interests me more than the world of nature; maybe it is a heresy to say such a thing in America.

RB: *Not in Poland?*

CM: Nature in Europe lost the romantic appeal it had in the beginning of the nineteenth century. Mother Nature is not very kind. One of the writers whom I like and with whom I feel a certain affinity is Isaac Bashevis Singer. He is in a constant rebellion against God because of suffering—suffering of animals and human beings. I see nature as a constant reminder of immutable laws of suffering and devouring—animals devouring animals. I keep a kind of a grudge toward nature because everything in it which is akin to cruelty and harshness we see in the human world. This is extremely appalling to me. There is some hope of course that human beings might be kinder to each other than animals are, but it is a vain hope. In many cases human beings are worse, much worse.

RB: *You think then of nature in terms of animals rather than trees and mountains.*

CM: It is very hard to think of nature in terms of beauty alone. Nature has an enormous beauty, and I am very sensitive to it. But there is a sort of a monotony, a repetition of patterns in nature, as opposed to the great variety of the human world which is constantly kaleidoscopically changing.

RB: *In your poem "Poet at Seventy" you say that your happiness is to be alive. What accounts for that?*

CM: That is a very Faustian poem about constant youth. Until now I have been very young in spite of my age, sort of wandering and wondering.

RB: *In that same poem you say that you feel sorrow that your life is closing. Do you grieve your death?*

CM: There is a fear of death, I guess. When you are young you may be more fearful of death than when you are in advanced age, but undoubtedly there is a certain amount of grief when you are in advanced age because you are accustomed to look forward, to plan for the future, and you realize that you have little time—many plans will probably have to be suspended, though of course we never know the day or hour of our death.

RB: *In "Poet at Seventy" you also say: "And all your wisdom came to nothing," and then you say that you are making order to oppose nothingness. It is an interesting contradiction.*

CM: I don't know if this is a contradiction, because form is a constant struggle against chaos and nothingness. Had I had wisdom I wouldn't need to constantly create form in order to combat chaos and nothingness. We are constantly threatened by chaos and nothingness because life as such is an enormous multiplicity. My personal feeling about the twentieth century is that we are submerged. The things that happened in this century in the sense of horror and heroism escape our thinking and formulations. The century is largely untold. The same applies to our human lives. We are in the power of forces which escape our words and our records. Maybe that is why today everybody wants to write a novel about their life. As far as form is concerned, everything in human life is form or giving form; we enter into a relationship with the world primarily through language composed of words, or signs, or lines, or colors, or shapes; we do not enter the world through a direct relationship. Our human nature consists of everything being mediated; we are part of civilization; we are part of the human world. Writing is a constant struggle, an attempt to translate as many elements of reality as possible into form.

RB: *What are your thoughts about the form of conduct; for example, ethical conduct or heroic conduct?*

CM: Action is probably important, but I am not a man of action and I shouldn't pronounce myself as such. In action there are also many delusions.

RB: *I think of conduct in terms of motivational behavior. Socrates' death is an example of heroic conduct. Do you think that Socrates' death expressed more than could ever be expressed in writings of the Socratic dialogues?*

CM: Socrates, with his life, wrote a kind of a metaphor. Undoubtedly we can find many other similar examples which have a sort of permanent existence in the life of mankind. The question is to what extent there is a mythical transformation of acts of that sort. Maybe mythical transformations are necessary.

RB: *What do you mean by mythical transformation?*

CM: The Book of Job is centered around the suffering of an innocent man, and the meaning of suffering. Maybe the meaning of the suffering of Job is to create a parable—material for the Book of Job which transforms mythically the story of Job.

RB: *Does the answer that emerges from the Book of Job, that we can only know fragments of reality while God knows the totality of reality, satisfy you?*

CM: Yes. This is a question which I touch upon in my book, even invoking Orwell. I speak in my book about the question of the past. If the past exists only in human memories, or disappears with human memories, or if it exists only in records which can be very easily destroyed, then in fact all human beings and all the events which happened fade into a kind of mist and have no consistence, no existence at all. In order to imagine that the past is real and that those people who died, for instance, in the horrible conditions during the twentieth century, existed, we have to assume a mind embracing everything, every detail that was, that is, and that will be, simultaneously. This means that Orwell, who was agnostic, kind of searches for a solution, and the only solution is an objective reality based on God.

RB: *What moved you to write your poem "The Garden of Earthly Delights"?*

CM: I wrote this poem as a result of seeing in Prado, in Madrid, the famous painting *The Garden of Earthly Delights* by Hieronymus Bosch. I was surprised by the very enigmatic character of that painting. What did the painter want to say? It is ambiguous. We do not know whether it is praise of the earth, or praise of eroticism, or fear of eternal damnation with a very ironic attitude toward earthly delights in the spirit of the fifteenth century. My interest in that poem says a great deal about my own ambiguity about the subject, and the present ambiguity of the twentieth century about it as well. The past, the Middle Ages, for instance, had a very ascetic vision. But today we are very ambiguous. We don't know.

RB: *In your book you say: "Do I love God? Or her? Or myself?" It is interesting to me that saints, for instance, express feelings about their love for God so vividly in their writings. But I am puzzled by what it means to love God, which I understand only through actions.*

CM: I understand this very well. It is a very old problem—how to separate our love for created things, or for the world as it is accessible to us through our senses, from the idea of God, who is separated from the world. Isaac Singer is a kind of a pantheist and sees the world and God as identified. I find this a rather difficult issue to cope with.

RB: *Your poem "Father Chomski, Many Years Later . . ." which I especially love, somehow speaks to that. You say that Father Chomski refused to bow to the world and you ask: "Did I toil then against the world / Or, without knowing, was I with it and its own?" Could you talk about the difference between you and him?*

CM: We return to your first question. Father Chomski was an ascetic and a fanatic. A man who could certainly be admired for his inflexibility and his refusal to compromise with the world. I chose a completely different path and have been very often immersed in this so-called stream of life—very sensuous in a way, the opposite of asceticism. In that poem, which is sort of a question, I ask whether by doing that I went to the side of the devil, because the present world is a world of exploration, of great curiosity and of license; a world in which everything seems to be permitted. I was sufficiently on the side of the modern world to question myself.

RB: *Are you on both sides of the barricade now?*

CM: Yes. I am a man of contradictions, and I do not deny that. I have been translating the French philosopher Simone Weil, who is a defender of contradictions, and I wouldn't like to pretend to have a unified vision.

RB: *In your book you manifest a wisdom to differentiate between what is significant and what is trivial. Often it is our character that leads us*

*to that kind of insight. Do you think that yours stems from character
or from a gift?*

CM: I think that we have to pay for every gift we receive, and so I
am not very proud of my gifts, because I know that one pays. If
what you say is true, then it seems to me quite flattering, and accepting such flattering opinions I could be a very proud man. But
my shortcomings create a necessary balance, so that in hearing your
flattering remarks I don't puff myself up.

RB: *Then you must feel that a payment for possessing gifts is all right?*

CM: Yes, probably.

RB: *In one of your poems you say that you don't tell the envious
about your payments. Do you want them to think that it comes easily?*

CM: Let them. In a way I shouldn't be considered a man of talent
in America because there is a certain idea of a writer, of a poet, in
this country which I do not fit: I have never been in a mental institution; I do not use drugs; I am not alcoholic (I drink but moder-
ately); so I am probably abnormal.

RB: *Do you think that one has to be emotionally sick to be a writer?*

CM: No. I think that many people are emotionally sick and have
tremendous emotional complications, but we don't know very much
about them. With writers this somehow transpires, and people know
about it.

RB: *I am thinking of the contrast between Robert Lowell and yourself.*

CM: There were moments when I envied Lowell. I would say: "Ah,
he is clever; he has a breakdown, and they take him to a sanatorium
where he can write peacefully; while when I go through a crisis I
have to function normally."

RB: *In the commentary to your poem "The Hooks of a Corset" you
say: "I endow with a philosophical meaning the moment when I helped
her to undo the hooks of her corset." Can you conceive of endowing
meaning to that act while performing it?*

CM: The question of a certain duality between our consciousness
and our actions is a very interesting and a very tricky one. I know
people who are so literary-minded that any action of theirs, even
writing private letters, is done with the thought about the world of
art. We can also imagine various physiological functions that are

fulfilled accompanied by thoughts about their philosophical meaning. But going back to your quotation, I guess that if we are truly in love we don't have these thoughts.

RB: *Can you conceive, for instance, of anyone contemplating a sexual relationship in order to bring another person closer to God?*

CM: I cannot see a conscious design of that sort.

RB: *An unconscious design?*

CM: Yes. There is a very interesting novel written by my cousin Oscar Milosz, who was a French poet, entitled *Amorous Initiation,* published in 1910. It is a story about love for a beautiful courtesan which takes place in the eighteenth century in Venice. There is a gradual realization by the narrator and the hero of the book that physical profane love is a road toward the love of God.

RB: *In your book you say: "And when people cease to believe that there is good and evil / Only beauty will call to them and save them / So that they still know how to say: this is true and that is false." Are we too weak to realize truth without the beauty of art?*

CM: An Orthodox theologian by the name of Sergius Bulgakov used to say that art is the theology of the future. I don't know if this is true. I am not very fond of what I would call a religion of art. In the twentieth century we have witnessed a general tendency toward a certain worship of art. Art enters as a substitute for religion, and I am very skeptical about that. But, undoubtedly, there is something which should be respected here—apart from snobbery, less lofty motives, egoistic motives, or artists who make much hullabaloo about their art—because in a world where there are no certainties or strong foundations for values, people turn instinctively to art as something divine, inspired maybe.

RB: *What time and place are you transcending in your poem "The Hooks of a Corset"?*

CM: The poem is about young ladies at the beginning of the twentieth century. In the commentary to that poem I use the expression "Do you want white peacocks?—I will give you white peacocks," from literature of that time in a so-called decadent style. A serious problem is raised here, and it is that we are always prisoners of style. I mentioned before that we create form, but form changes because the human world changes. If we look at the movies from 1919 we see that the women then were very different from the women today—even their bodies were different, because of fashion, style, and dresses. Those young ladies whom I described were subject to the style of their epoch. The same goes for the various styles in painting and poetry. Our problem is that we do not see our style; we do not realize it. A hundred years from now, our dresses, our fashions, and our ways of thinking will be looked upon and maybe considered somewhat funny. In this prose fragment that I wrote there is a nostalgia, a longing, to communicate with human beings, with those ladies who had died long ago, without the intermediary of form and style.

RB: *In that commentary you write about secrets and mysteries and a search for the Real. What is the Real in a nutshell?*

CM: Searching for the Real is the same as searching for God.

RB: *In that same piece you say: "Her flesh which has turned to dust is as desirable to me as it was to that other man . . ." Do you in fact accept that?*

CM: As I mentioned, that poem is an attempt to reconstruct the era around 1900. I was not alive then, but I imagined walking in the street in Paris identifying myself with that man and that woman who are no longer alive. Philosophically, and in a certain mood of meditation, we can identify with other men. When Proust wrote about the past, all his loves and jealousies were transformed into art, into form. Art is distance and detachment. But in real life we are not detached; we are victims of our passions; we cannot identify with other men; we are jealous of them and are rather ready to kick them.

RB: *In your poem "Esse" from your book* The Separate Notebook, *you are in the Métro in Paris looking dumbfounded at the face of a girl. You say: "To have. It is not even a desire. Like a butterfly, a fish, the stem of a plant, only more mysterious." The girl leaves the train and you are " . . . left behind with the immensity of existing things." Was there a sense of frustration that led you to write that poem and a sense of relief after you wrote it?*

CM: Undoubtedly a sense of frustration before I wrote it, but no feeling of relief after that.

RB: *What happens after you write a poem such as this one?*

CM: As far as I remember, I jotted it down expressing my frustration and my longing without paying much attention to it. After a while, that poem became very important to me because I noticed that I expressed in it something essential to me.

RB: *Let's take this experience as a paradigm. If the frustration is not relieved, how does writing affect you personally?*

CM: We discussed the question of writing as fighting chaos and nothingness. After having written such a poem I am relieved for the day. I did my share of fighting nothingness and chaos. For one day that is enough.

RB: *You have received the Nobel Prize and many other honors and awards. How does this affect you?*

CM: Those things act on me in a very peculiar way. I am unable to change the opinion I have of myself because I received the Nobel Prize. Very often, when I am with other Nobel laureates, I catch myself thinking that they should be very dignified company. Then I suddenly recollect that I am one of them. The problem concerning this is a practical problem; namely, that I would like to have my work assessed not on the basis of being a celebrity but on the basis of its value. I look for people who are on very close terms with me so that they will say frankly what they like and what they dislike.

RB: *In the last section of your book you say: "Not to enchant anybody. Not to earn a lasting name in posterity." Is this a wish or a resolution?*

CM: It is a good question. To be completely honest, I would like to enchant, but a very selected group of people who are ideal readers in my mind, not the reading public at large. (There may be a kind of haughtiness in selecting a very few happy people who would be able to appreciate my work.) But that wasn't what I wanted to say in that section. What I wanted to say is that if you are going after enchanting people, you may be a little inclined to make compromises, to be a follower of various fads of a given time. When I say "Not to enchant anybody," I mean that I follow my own need for order, for rhythm and form—here, now, before my own piece of paper— and I use them as weapons or as instruments against chaos and nothingness. "Not to enchant" is a concentration upon my own struggle, not upon my contact with the readers.

1986

Part 3

ON
LITERATURE
AND
WRITERS

A POET BETWEEN EAST AND WEST

The Kingdom of art increases and that of health and innocence declines on this earth.

—THOMAS MANN, *Tonio Kröger*
[Translated by H. T. Lowe-Porter]

A long time ago, in my youth, I read a story by Thomas Mann, *Tonio Kröger*. That story was written before World War I and was constructed upon a premise then quite generally accepted in artistic circles. According to that premise, art and literature are intimately connected with abnormality or sickness and are even its function. Mann remained faithful to that premise in all his *oeuvre*, from *Buddenbrooks* to *Doctor Faustus*. Undoubtedly that view on the sources of art also influenced my literary generation to some extent, but it seemed to offend us and we tended to reject it as too obviously marked by romantic irony—and decadent.

I am separated from the moment when I read *Tonio Kröger* not only by the passage of years. Unfortunately, I must say, and let me use a pathetic expression, my eyes have seen at least a part of that horror which belongs to the very essence of the twentieth century. And that experience did not relegate to the past the problem brought up by Mann's story; on the contrary, it gave it a greater poignancy. Now I would agree with Tonio Kröger that literature is not a vocation but a curse; I can also add new arguments as to its unhealthy character. I am even ready to make a frontal attack against the art of the written word, particularly against its transformations in our time.

"The artist must be unhuman, extra-human," says Tonio Kröger; "he must stand in a queer aloof relationship to our humanity; only so is he in a position, I ought to say only so would he be tempted, to represent it, to present it, to portray it to good effect. The very gift of style, of form and expression, is nothing else than this cool and fastidious attitude toward humanity; you might say that there has to be that impoverishment and devastation as a preliminary condition."

I believe all that is true, and I understand it better now than in the years of my youth. For then "humanity" was for me an abstraction, while now it has the shape of emaciated prisoners in their striped garb, of corpses in the streets of the Warsaw ghetto, of a hand with a pistol in a window that will be changed in a moment into a gaping hole by the fire of a tank. A "cool and fastidious attitude" in the face of such scenes is a moral monstrosity, but it is precisely that monstrosity which lies, in Mann's opinion, at the foundation of art. And to deny that there is truth in his premise would be of no use. It does not matter that a poet, an artist, may preserve that same cool attitude *toward himself*; that is, that he becomes double, a man who, while being led to his own execution, still remains, with one part of himself, a detached, ironic observer. From a moral point of view that distance is hard to accept, and poetry, which owes everything to this distance, must be morally suspect.

But I do not intend to lead my attack in the name of ethical principles. Let us assume, following Mann, that art grows out of abnormality, out of a more or less hidden demonic possession, and that a kind of moral detachment makes up part of that abnormality. As we have often heard, art, by its very being, by its very *esse*, redeems the dark neurotic operations from which it stems. I prefer, by the way, to narrow the scope of my considerations and by "art" I will mean poetic art. It consists in joining words in such a manner that a unit called "the line" not only acquires a power of affecting contemporaries but is felt by generations as something necessary and natural, like the spirals of a shell. Yet there is a prerequisite, and that is a relation, let us concede, an enigmatic one, between the words of a poem and reality, always a reality of a given place and time. An imitator of Horace would today create only rhetoric. Besides, the example of Horace may indicate that the laws of the relationship between poetry and reality are different in every period, since Horace was filling his poems with philosophical maxims that must have looked like clichés to his contemporaries. And yet, whatever those laws of relationship are, old theories proclaiming that art is mimesis always seem to preserve their validity, even if we no longer confer upon art, as was done in the Middle Ages, the highly honorable title of a grandchild of God—for art imitates the daughter of God, that is Nature. By now advancing a thesis unfavorable to the art of joining words, I take into account both my impressions as a reader and my meditations as a practitioner. My thesis is: Poetry, and in general literature, prove to be less and less potent in the presence of what reveals itself in our century as reality, which means that it changes into an autonomous activity of the language, *écriture*, and as a consequence the very reason for its existence is open to question.

What do I consider reality? Probably not the same thing as an American poet does. I will choose a case which is perhaps extreme, but significant. When I came to California, I dedicated much time to the poetry of Robinson Jeffers. In my opinion he is a poet of great stature, unjustly thrown down into near-oblivion from the pedestal he occupied in the twenties. Jeffers deliberately opposed avant-garde fashions deriving from French Symbolism and, in clear-cut, transparent syntax, described in his poems what was for him the most real, the shore of the Pacific near his home in Carmel. And yet, when reading Jeffers, I discovered that those orange-violet sunsets, those flights of pelicans, those fishing boats in the morning fog, as faithfully represented as if they were photographs—all that was for me pure fiction. I said to myself that Jeffers, who professed, as he called it, "inhumanism," took refuge in an artificial world which he invented using ideas taken from biology textbooks and from the philosophy of Nietzsche. I also realized to what extent I dislike nature. I do not want to say that I am insensitive to the beauty of mountains, forests, oceans. Simply, nature, very much present in the imagination of American poets and so often identified by them with reality—without doubt very real when we enumerate the elementary facts of our biological existence, "birth, copulation, and death," is for me, in this century of mine, a huge museum of inherited images. The struggle of poetry with the world cannot take place within a museum. Precisely in California, perhaps more acutely than in any other place, I have felt that the problem of my time should be defined as Poetry and History.

Thus, I hear a question: Do I mean poetry confronted by History as a cycle of horrors: pacts between big powers dealing in human herds, battles, massacres, concentration camps? No, not at all, though it cannot be denied that such events are for poetry a sort of test: then it finds out how much reality it is able to bear. A countless number of anti-Nazi poems written in the years 1939–45 in Poland, in terrorized cities, in ghettos, in prisons, in extermination camps, gives new substance to the contention of Thomas Mann that "the artist must be unhuman, extra-human"—for the authors of those poems were merely human, and to the extent that they were human, they lost artistically, so that their poems taken together make a huge and poignant document of several thousand pages; but a document is not art. I have seen in my own case that a serious conflict arises here. For today, from a distance, those poems of mine which moved my underground audiences in Warsaw seem to me weak, while those which then looked enigmatic as to their intentions and were cruel, full of offensive mockery, now seem strong. That conflict also manifested itself when, in Warsaw, in 1942, I was preparing for print an underground anthology, *Invincible Song*. Fanatically attached to my standards of quality, I rejected those poems which were not up to my requirements, because of their banal vocabulary or trite rhymes, but I knew at the same time that I was wrong, for it was precisely those bad poems which were most effective as an emotional charge, as a weapon.

It may now be a cause for surprise that I read into this a problem. After all, *Inter arma silent Musae*—the Muses fall silent at the time of war—and how slight is the trace left in poetry by the Napoleonic wars, by the American Civil War or World War I! To this I answer that historical analogies are misleading and that the problem definitely exists. And it can be formulated as follows: The written word encountered in our time a completely new phenomenon in the guise of a totalitarian state organization—and I do not refer here to the slaughter of populations by the will of a ruler, of the Genghis Khan type. Nor do I feel that it is correct to place the events of the first half of our century in a rubric entitled "the past," for there is a strong possibility that *L'Univers concentrationnaire,* to use a term introduced by David Rousset, was only the first of *forms* taken by an emerging Leviathan, an apocalyptic Beast. People who were confronted with it for the first time, whether in its Nazi or Soviet variety, dimly perceived that all the known concepts of man and of society disintegrated and a *new dimension* unveiled itself, not because of the magnitude of the crime, but because of its impersonal nature. For that reason the behavior of language facing such a new social form, the inability or ability of language to cope with it, must be a basic problem for a poet.

This problem has been given attention in a book which reaches probably deeper than many sophisticated treatises of structural analysis. It was first presented at the Sorbonne as a Ph.D. dissertation in sociology by a colleague of mine from Poland, Michał Borwicz, and was published in 1954 under the title *Écrits des condamnés à mort sous l'occupation allemande* [*Writings of People Sentenced to Death under the German Occupation*]. The author, using materials gathered from all over Europe, analyzes the urge felt by those people to leave a testimony and to communicate their knowledge, which they sensed to be completely new, radically different from what was until then known about reality. But as the author proves, they were doing it in a language inherited, *conventional*, proper to a social milieu which had shaped them before their key experience. If we take this as a struggle of language with reality, the data gathered by the author indicate that language was losing, retreating into ready-made *topoi* and formulas, and even behaving as if these provided a refuge. Probably similar conclusions to those of Borwicz will be reached by scholarly investigators of the rich literature (songs, poems, inscriptions) written in Soviet prisons and concentration camps.

But what has all this to do with poetry written here, in America, or in England, in France, now, in the last quarter of the twentieth century? In dealing with that poetry I should be loyal; that is, I should limit myself to a personal declaration: Rarely do I find in it what *I myself* consider to be reality. I assume that in our century something has been born which we try in vain to name, and to which I give the provisional name of a new dimension of man and of society. I assume also that poetry, unless it is conscious of this and stays in that frontier area where it should strive to grasp the new dimension, by necessity lacks that vigor of being which is necessary to redeem the abnormality and moral ambiguity attending its birth. Relations between Poetry and History do not mean, in my view, that a poet should constantly visit in his imagination places of human suffering enclosed with barbed wire. I am against an obsessive turning back, and in my poems written in California I put much effort into leaving behind things past. Yet I cannot remain indifferent when I hear widespread opinions on the events of the first half of the century, often completely departing from historical truth. According to those opinions, there is a natural course of events, for man is everywhere the same in whatever state and system he lives. That natural course of events was disturbed by incomprehensible cataclysms unleashed by monstrous dictators, but everything leveled off, or, if not yet, it will level off in the near future. As a bumper sticker I recently saw read: ONE EARTH, ONE HUMANITY, ONE SPIRIT. Such reasoning by-passes the possibility that the presumed "disturbance" was the first phase of something new and that we all, as a species, are menaced by implementations of an idea: that of the state conceived as an owner of human beings, both of their bodies and of their souls. Since such a state must also be an owner of their language; that is, giving to words such meaning as it desires, a moment may be near when the apparent similarity of people living in various political zones will be reduced to their having two eyes, two hands, and two legs. For now what above all is being undermined is the millennia-old belief in the autonomy of a human molecule endowed with an orbit of its own—and an expression has even been coined: "death of man."

My attack is not directed against poets of the West but against poetry of today in general, therefore also against myself. Suppose I am right in my criticism. Yet, as a poet whom I dislike, Mallarmé, said, Poetry is not written with ideas but with words. As are all my contemporaries, I am subject to the directives dictated by a certain style. Were I not looking upon myself as a good craftsman who has written a certain number of professionally satisfactory poems, the matter would be just academic. As it is, I feel I both have the right to attack and deserve to be an object of attack.

As Borwicz's book demonstrates, a paralyzing and incommunicable experience is conveyed by ordinary people, not artists, in a language of inherited stylistic conventions. Those conventions are periodically broken by art, thanks to, in the words of Mann, a "cool and fastidious attitude toward humanity." The history of poetry in our century has been a series of breakthroughs, one quickly succeeding another, so that the language of poetry is today very distant from that of the year 1900. Yet the speed with which new varieties of style succeed each other is matched by the speed with which they are set as conventions and changed into common property. Let us notice that transformation of discoveries into clichés speaks in favor of the theory of art as mimesis. That is why today, any time we try to find a name for a new form, of a bureaucratic Leviathan, we pronounce the words: *Surrealism*, *Kafka*.

Kafka should be invoked here, for his appearance is simultaneous with a historical mutation that escapes our definitions, though philosophers and sociologists come forward with many terms. Whatever the core of Kafka's neurosis (and his personality confirms the theory of Mann), he had a strong resolve to remain faithful to reality. At the same time, his *oeuvre* proves that so-called realistic description had come to its end, because it is possible only when there is a describing individual endowed, as I said, with an orbit of his own. Kafka, like his heroes, cannot act; he is acted upon. Moreover, he is in the power of forces characterized not only by omnipotence but also by anonymity. One can describe things if they possess tangible shapes, while completely different tactics are indicated when we confront a dragon that is either invisible or, if he becomes visible, may be this or that. Kafka applied such new tactics, replacing a description of characters and events by parable and metaphor. And that is a change important for poets who write after him.

As a literary genre, poetry during the last couple of centuries had for its companion another literary genre, the novel. Suddenly poetry is alone. Everything points toward the demise of the novel, probably unable to survive the end of old-fashioned descriptive narrative. The solitude of poetry will bring about serious consequences, but we do not understand them as yet. Poetry does not supersede the novel, to occupy the honorable place it held in the era when the novel was still a country-fair genre. Just the opposite is true, as if the blame incurred by the novel, less and less read by the cultivated public, extended to *belles lettres* as a whole. And yet the quantity of poems and publications of poetry, not read anymore by anybody, increases at a terrifying rate. Language, liberated from aims and duties, seems to speak by itself to itself. Not to act but to be acted upon—this Kafka perceived as a tragedy, but it is possible that half a century after his death we agree with a remark made by the Polish writer Witold Gombrowicz, much earlier than it was noticed by the French Structuralists: that it is not we who speak the language but it is the language that speaks us.

Yes, it is undeniable, the power exerted over us by the language is a great discovery of our century. We can express no more than the language of our time and place allows us to, and this is known not only to poets but also to rulers who change the meaning of words for their own purposes. But precisely resistance against that limitation, in the name of reality, prompts me now to attack the art of the written word. For, while realizing the autonomous tendencies of language, we may look beyond language for a tangible criterion, and this is not the same as to say with resignation that there is no such criterion. Of course, by bringing in reality, I expose myself to many misunderstandings; years in a seminar in philosophy would not exhaust the implications contained in the term *mimesis*. Also, I risk inviting the phantom of realism together with all the epithets usually accompanying it. But most of the so-called realisms have little to do with reality, often no more than an inscription on the gate of a concentration camp: *Arbeit macht frei*.

To sum up, I rebelled in my youth against the portrait of the artist I found in Thomas Mann's *Tonio Kröger*, against his connecting creative activity with neurosis, with internal "impoverishment and devastation." I believed in health, strength, and sometimes even imagined a model poet as a happy giant. Later on, I learned that the presumed health of happy giants was just an appearance masking demonic possession, and I myself stopped pretending to be a strong man. I experienced how painful it is to realize that it is not the most noble, most human impulses which are allies of the poet but rather his "cool and fastidious attitude"—even if he writes a poem against inhumanity. Out of that realization grows an exigency addressed to poetry: poetry should strive toward a sufficient degree of *being* and thus to redeem its original sin. And if I agree with Thomas Mann when in *Tonio Kröger* he says that poetry serves as "a sort of revenge on life," I would not like the revenge to be taken at the expense of our human world.

1977   [Written in English by C.M.]

SWEDENBORG AND DOSTOEVSKY

Q: *You say it should be possible to write a study titled "Swedenborg and Dostoevsky." But there is an enormous literature about Dostoevsky in many languages and, admit it, the very fact that no one has yet come up with such an idea does not inspire confidence in your thesis.*

A: An entire lengthy section would have to be devoted to an explanation of why this is so. It would be a section about the "blind spots" in people's sensibility in the first half of the twentieth century. Ultimately, the entire canon of Dostoevsky studies can be delimited roughly by the dates 1900 and 1950. I say "canon" because that is when the basic works about this author which delineated the main methods of interpreting him were written. The first phase coincides with the period of Russian Symbolism, and it would be the main subject for discussion in the article.

Q: *Why the period of Russian Symbolism in particular?*

A: Not only Russian. Symbolism, regardless of its variations in different countries, had to be sensitive to its own genealogy. We have been taught that the great patron of Symbolism was Baudelaire. One of his works is even cited as a sort of program. (When I was a student in Paris I had to memorize it.) This is the sonnet "Correspondances." But both the title and the contents of this sonnet are taken from Swedenborg. Both Balzac's generation and the generation that succeeded it—Baudelaire's—borrowed extensively from Swedenborg, though they rarely admitted this. Later on, however, the period of the "scientific worldview" developed in Europe and Swedenborg became decidedly taboo, someone who could be studied only by maniacs, his followers, members of the Swedenborgian Church of the New Jerusalem, which has been active chiefly in America. Let us not forget that Symbolism, as a literary and artistic movement, is

very much entwined with the sobriety of the "scientific worldview";
after all, these poets and painters and critics were raised on positivist
beliefs. In rebelling against them they often went quite far in their
weird directions. Nonetheless, no one knew by then what to make
of such an extreme case as Swedenborg. It is fairly symptomatic,
then, that the Russian critics who wrote about Dostoevsky prior to
1914 had no interest in knowing about the great Swedish master of
the imagination.

Q: *Does this mean that things changed at some point and that today
there is a different perception of Swedenborg?*

A: I shall give a couple of examples of bafflement dating from the
first half of the century. In 1922, Karl Jaspers published his book on
schizophrenia, in which he analyzed Strindberg, Van Gogh, Swedenborg, and Hölderlin as typical schizophrenics. In 1936, Paul Valéry wrote an introduction to Martin Lamm's book on Swedenborg,
which had been translated into French from the Swedish. Lamm's
book is painstaking, positivistically sober to the point of dullness in
its abstention from coming to any conclusions; after reading it, however, it is difficult to agree with Jaspers's thesis that Swedenborg
suffered from a mental illness. And yet the amiable Swedenborg,
who was universally well liked in Stockholm social circles, wrote
about his travels through Heaven and Hell and insisted that he could
easily transport himself into the spirit world while walking, for example, in his garden. Thus, Valéry is at a loss and, rejecting suspi-
cions of both charlatanism and madness, tries to explain
Swedenborg's particular "states" as the borderline between sleep
and waking. Despite Valéry's cleverness, this is weak and uncon-
vincing; what is more, Valéry unmasks himself, and not only himself
but all his contemporaries, by confessing to a double standard. Because this is what it comes down to more or less: only the world of
"scientific laws" is real, but above it there rises an ethereal structure
of epiphenomena, creations of the human mind that deserve to be
treated with perfect tolerance because they are arbitrary, beyond
truth and falsehood, subject only to the law of their own form.

Symbolism, impeded as it was by nineteenth-century science, had
no confidence in itself; the language of images, the language of strata
that are deeper than consciousness, became the center of attention
for psychologists and anthropologists somewhat later; if we are talking about a broader compass, it came much later. In this case only
such cultural facts as the transfer of the polemic between the followers of Freud and the followers of Jung to Anglo-Saxon soil could

favor a new reception of Swedenborg. Let us note that Swedenborg wrote almost exclusively in Latin, and although there were individuals in the Romantic generation who knew Latin quite well, he was read on the European continent in a small number of French adaptations. Later on, when knowledge of Latin declined, he became an even more inaccessible writer. But this was not the case in the Anglo-Saxon countries, where translations of his works, beginning with the earliest editions in the eighteenth century, never disappeared from the book market. In America in particular he had his admirers; one of them was the philosopher and theologian Henry James, Sr., the father of William, the philosopher and creator of pragmatism, and Henry, the novelist. Swedenborg made his first appearance in the orbit of literary studies only recently, and even then indirectly, thanks to the growing significance of Blake, who was dependent on him in many ways. But the veritable explosion of "Blakeology" is in the second half of our century.

I do not think, however, that at present the tools that would allow us to comprehend the figure of Swedenborg have been developed anywhere. What is essential here is the seventeenth- and eighteenth-century scientific revolution and the resulting secularization of thought. Swedenborg was a general scientist, as was common at that time, for he was a geologist, a member of the Royal Mining Commission, a physicist, and a physiologist, whose ideas, in the opinion of historians of science, were brilliant. Until he experienced a severe internal crisis when he suddenly realized where science was leading: to the weakening of the Christian religion and—in its further consequences—to the overthrow of all values. From this crisis a new Swedenborg emerged—a visionary and a theologian. Let us not concern ourselves here with the question of where to draw the line between "normality" and "abnormality." If true schizophrenia begins where communication with other people breaks off, then any suspicion that Swedenborg or Blake was a schizophrenic is unfounded. The difficulty we encounter lies in the fact that the role of literary convention in the formation of the Swedenborgian visions, or whatever we call them, is undoubtedly highly significant but not easily defined. The eighteenth century loved to create apparently "true" stories about travels and adventures, so it is not surprising that it also gave us, through Swedenborg's pen, descriptions of otherworldly journeys. It is just that the symbolism here achieves a truly great tension and the frustrated, subjective symbols of the poets around the year 1900 appear pallid in comparison. While Swedenborg's language (like the language of those who traveled through the extramundane world before him—Dante and Milton) makes use of symbols with fixed, immutable meanings, his entire system, described in this language, contains strong features of eighteenth-century rationalism—it is this fusion that so confounds and disturbs his readers.

Q: *In what sense would Dostoevsky fit into such a study?*

A: In a dual sense. First of all, one would have to consider the probable influence of Swedenborg on the author of *Crime and Punishment*. Second, Dostoevsky's Christology becomes somewhat less enigmatic when it is compared with Swedenborg's Christology.

Q: *Obviously, one would need to know if Dostoevsky was familiar with Swedenborg's writings.*

A: In Leonid Grossman's book *Seminarii po Dostoevskomu*—I am citing an authority here—we find a list of the books that the novelist had in his private library. A. N. Aksakov's books are listed there, among others. He was one of the less-well-known Aksakovs, the one who was interested in spiritualism. Dostoevsky wrote about the Petersburg spiritualistic séances in his *Diary of a Writer for 1876*. But we are interested in Aksakov as the translator of Swedenborg into Russian. *De Coelo et ejus mirabilis, et de inferno* was published in Leipzig in 1863 in his Russian version; an adaptation or translation (it's hard to check which since the book cannot be found) of five chapters of Swedenborg's interpretation of the Gospel according to St. John was also published in Leipzig in 1864; and again in Leipzig, but much later, in 1870, Aksakov's work on Swedenborg appeared. Dostoevsky had all three books in his library and was obviously interested in the subject, since he collected them. Grossman, in the commentary that accompanies his list, notes: "Particularly worth noting is Dostoevsky's interest in Swedenborg." "These books may have had an influence on Zosima's mystical speculations about prayer, hell, and our ties with other worlds." To the best of my knowledge, no one has followed up on Professor Grossman's suggestion.

Q: *The study of influence is a thankless field. It is usually difficult even to determine what intermediaries served to convey a particular idea or thought to a given writer.*

A: Certainly. Dostoevsky had two French editions of the works of Balzac in his library, for example. And he had read some Balzac earlier, in his youth. Although Balzac had a very poor, secondhand knowledge of Swedenborg, he admired him greatly, and we can consider Balzac's "Swedenborgian" novels, such as *Séraphita* or *Louis Lambert* as "intermediaries." Let us, however, limit the scope of our inquiry to just one of Dostoevsky's works, *Crime and Punishment*. He began writing this novel in Wiesbaden in 1865, and it is well known that during his stays abroad he was starved for Russian books. So it was probably then that he purchased or was given Swedenborg's work in Aksakov's translation, which had just been published in neighboring Leipzig. The fabric of symbols in *Crime and Punishment* is so rich that it is difficult not to think about Swedenborgian *correspondences*, or, in Aksakov's translation, *sootvetstviia*. According to Swedenborg, these are "objective" symbols that inhere in the very structure of the universe—and of language. But let us leave it to others to track them down and narrow our field even further by limiting ourselves to the figure of Svidrigailov. He is one of the most puzzling characters in Dostoevsky, beginning with his name, because how, all of a sudden, does the Lithuanian Prince Svidrigaila become transformed into a Russian *barin*? The noble Dostoevsky family, which derived its surname from the Dostoevo estate near Pinsk, which had been bestowed upon it in 1505, has left its traces in the criminal chronicles of the Grand Duchy from the sixteenth century. We know from a book written by his daughter Liubov (or Aimée, as she signed her name in emigration)—a book that is misleading and full of outright stupidities but nonetheless contains some priceless childhood memories—that Dostoevsky used to emphasize his descent from that family. The surname Svidrigailov, derived from the prince who ruled the eastern (therefore, the ethnically Slavic, not Lithuanian) part of the Grand Duchy, might suggest the author's special identification with that character (although obviously Dostoevsky is all his characters). Also, let us not be too positive that the main character is Raskolnikov, because it could just as well be his gloomy alter ego, Svidrigailov. Despite Dostoevsky's fascination with crime without any pangs of conscience, which dates from the period of his imprisonment in Omsk, Raskolnikov appears to be treated with a greater distance than his diabolical acquaintance, who is never exorcized throughout the entire novel. One might even risk the assertion that there are two crimes in this novel and two punishments, and that, furthermore, the second crime, Svidrigailov's, is the "correspondence," the equivalent of a feeling of guilt in and of itself.

For what is the source of Svidrigailov's problem? He does have human lives on his conscience, but he is only apparently a superman beyond good and evil. In fact, he hates his nature, which, in his opinion, is capable only of evil, and he believes that a man such as he deserves eternal damnation. That is, he commits the sin that theologians define as first among the sins against the Holy Spirit: "despairing of God's mercy." Svidrigailov moves through the pages of the novel like a phantom, as if he were already beyond life. He prepares his "journey to America," which, on his lips and on Dostoevsky's, signifies a journey to Hell—let us remember, for example, how Kirillov's and Shatov's stay in America is presented in *The Possessed*. Of course, Svidrigailov has in mind not a journey but the execution of a sentence against himself and he finally commits suicide. He is thoroughly reminiscent of the damned as described by Swedenborg, and even the similarity of the first syllables of their two names, *Swed* and *Svid*, suggests this, perhaps through involuntary association.

Swedenborg's Hell is constructed from "correspondences"; that is, everything that surrounds the damned is a *projection* of their spiritual states, and this is so because every visible and tangible object has its own secondary and even more real existence in the human imagination, where it serves as a sign of value, that is, of either good or evil. The jaws of Hell that Swedenborg describes frequently have the appearance of grim streets in the poorest districts of great cities, of London in particular, where he lived for a long time. They are, then, pictures of life in time, but already preserved beyond time. At the same time, God does not condemn people to Hell. The damned find images of heavenly joy repulsive and it is precisely from the book translated by Aksakov that one can learn that they flee the society of bright spirits, seeking the company of those who are like them. In *The Brothers Karamazov*, in Zosima's teaching about Hell, Dostoevsky also speaks about a completely free choice of "place," although this word is inexact, since "place" is only the projection of an inner state.

For our purposes what is important is the multiplicity of hells in Swedenborg. There are as many of them as there are individual human beings. Let me take down from the shelf the very book that Dostoevsky read and quote from it, in English translation:*

> Every evil includes infinite varieties, the same as every good. That such is the fact will not be comprehended, by those who only have a simple idea respecting every evil, as respecting contempt, respecting

---

* *Heaven and Its Wonders, The World of Spirits, and Hell: From Things Heard and Seen* (known as *Heaven and Hell*).

enmity, respecting hatred, respecting revenge, respecting deceit, and respecting others of the like nature: but be it known to them, that every one of those evils contains so many specific differences, and every one of these, again, so many other specific or particular differences, that a volume would not suffice to enumerate them all. The hells are so distinctly arranged in order, according to the differences of every evil that nothing more orderly and distinct can be conceived. It may hence be evident, that the hells are innumerable.

[Translated by Rev. Samuel Noble]

Svidrigailov, when we meet him on the pages of the novel, is already seeking places in this life that can serve as correspondences for his bored despair, his *acedia*. Despite the fact that he is wealthy, he chooses miserable furnished rooms, third-class stinking restaurants, and cheap filthy hotels. If I have said that Swedenborgian "correspondences" have an objective character, then I should introduce a correction here, for certain phenomena are ambivalent and their function as symbols changes depending on their connection with other phenomena. This is true of rain and dampness in *Crime and Punishment*: for Svidrigailov they are not life-giving but grim, and are associated with his internal stagnation and collapse. A comparison with a similar function of rain and dampness in Dostoevsky's depressing story "Bobok," about the conversations of the dead in a cemetery, comes to mind here.

Svidrigailov imagines in a singular manner just what awaits people after death, and especially what ought to await him. The following dialogue between him and Raskolnikov is one of the strangest conversations in world literature:

> "I don't believe in a future life," said Raskolnikov.
> Svidrigailov sat lost in thought.
> "And what if there are only spiders there, or something of that sort?" he said suddenly.
> "He is a madman," thought Raskolnikov.
> "We always imagine eternity as something beyond our conception, something vast, vast! But why must it be vast? Instead of all that, what if it's one little room, like a bath-house in the country, black and grimy and spiders in every corner, and that's all eternity is? I sometimes fancy it like that."
> "Can it be you can imagine nothing juster and more comforting than that?" Raskolnikov cried, with a feeling of anguish.
> "Juster? And how can we tell, perhaps that is just, and do you know it's what I would certainly have made it," answered Svidrigailov, with a vague smile.
> This horrible answer sent a cold chill through Raskolnikov.

[Translated by Constance Garnett]

Q: *I admit that for the first time, because of this insertion of Swe-denborg, this conversation is no longer an incomprehensible leap of Dostoevsky's fantasy, a macabre witticism, as it were.*

A: Even if this is my discovery, and I think it is, I attach greater weight to my observations about Dostoevsky's Christology than to the question of "influences." I'll come to that in a moment. For now, let us pursue our earlier line of reasoning. In my opinion, what testifies to a deeper, more profound, more subterranean identification of the author with Svidrigailov rather than Raskolnikov are Svidrigailov's dreams prior to his suicide. The obsessive motif of an offense against little ones, of the rape of a child, surfaces in them. Dostoevsky was not "our Marquis de Sade," as Turgenev called him. The rumors that linked this motif to Dostoevsky's biography should not concern us; it is sufficient to state that a wrong committed against a child, usually a young girl, is perceived by his heroes as a moral horror; I need only recall "Stavrogin's Confession" from *The Pos-sessed*.

Svidrigailov first sees in his dream a coffin covered with flowers, and in the coffin is a very young girl, practically a child. We are free to assume that this underage Ophelia drowned herself because of him. But the first dream is only a preparation for the second, which is much more horrifying. In a hotel where he is living (this is what he dreams), he finds a little girl, a five-year-old, abandoned, crying. What follows is Svidrigailov's dream about his own goodness, be-cause he soothes her crying, lifts her up in his arms, carries her to his room, lays her on the bed, and covers her with a blanket. And then his dream about his own goodness suffers a decisive blow. Svid-rigailov suddenly feels that she is looking at him from under her half-closed eyelids, and her gaze is the gaze of a courtesan. Mediated by this dream, two of his thoughts, which might be expressed as follows, break through to the surface: "Whatever you touch is corrupted"; "Innocence and goodness are an illusion, for even if we are inclined to ascribe them to Nature, Nature knows only those impulses that accord with her law of reproducing oneself and of death." Similarly, the hero of "The Dream of a Ridiculous Man," when he visits the earthly heaven, contaminates innocent prelapsarian humanity by his very presence. The link between the thoughts of Svidrigailov that I have introduced here is not terribly clear, but it does exist: Nature, that is to say, two times two equals four in *Notes from the Under-ground*, or the indifferent machine in *The Idiot* (the digression about

Holbein's painting *Christ in the Tomb*), only deserves our protest in the name of our human values which it does not recognize. Svidrigailov says to himself more or less: "There is nothing inside me but aggressive drives and they are in harmony with the world order, which is too evil to be God's order, and I know that no attempt at breaking out of my skin can be successful." Svidrigailov commits suicide out of revulsion—at himself, and at everything. He is one of those who "cannot behold the living God without hatred, and . . . cry out that the God of life should be annihilated, that God should destroy Himself and His own creation," as Zosima says in *The Brothers Karamazov*.* To be sure, the reader will probably perceive a certain noble-mindedness in this moral revulsion and that is why Svidrigailov, despite the fact that he is in the power of Ahriman, is not generally numbered among the irrevocably black characters.

The rape of the child in the chapter about Svidrigailov's last night achieves the significance of a "correspondence"—i.e., it symbolizes his sense of guilt, not necessarily because of these or other deeds, but simply because he is what he is. What Svidrigailov actually did, and whether the young lady in the coffin is his victim, we do not know, and that is not the point, just as in "Stavrogin's Confession" one cannot be completely certain that he did not invent his rape of Matryosha. I do not want to attribute this device—the symbolism of dreams and nightmares, for example in Ivan Karamazov's conversation with the Devil—exclusively to Dostoevsky's reading of Swedenborg, because no one could prove these or any other borrowings. Let us move on to the second thread.

Q: *Would it not be appropriate to concentrate on Zosima's teachings, in accordance with Grossman's supposition?*

A: No, not in the least. It would not be a search for similarities aside from a single fundamental similarity: the intellectual situation. Swedenborg, who was born in 1688 (he died in 1772), was reacting to the great Industrial Revolution that began in western Europe in the seventeenth century. Like Pascal before him, who wanted to write a great apologia for Christianity; the notes known as *Les Pensées* are the fruits of that endeavor. Simplifying things to a certain extent, let us say that Swedenborg at the time of his crisis was seeking the strategy that the Christian should adopt toward the pressure of images derived from science. In western Europe the revolution was not

---

* Translated by Constance Garnett.

so violent, because it took place gradually over the course of a couple of centuries, while the Russian intelligentsia of the nineteenth century faced those same ferments suddenly, receiving them in a conglomerated form. Dostoevsky truly wanted to be a defender of Christianity, although the enemy had already planted itself inside his internal fortress. There is a reason why Dostoevsky has been compared so frequently with Pascal. But a comparison with Swedenborg would turn out to be, I believe, no less, and perhaps even more, fruitful.

In its attack on Christianity, rationalism progressed from timid forays to an open battle: it started from so-called rational religion, sincerely propagated by people who considered themselves good Christians. When the clergy in England warned against the "monster of Socinianism," their anxiety was well founded; even John Locke, for example, though he denied it publicly, had many publications from Raków in his own library and read them attentively, as is demonstrated by the marginal notations in his own hand. In fact, the first link in the process of secularization in Europe was the rebirth of the Arian heresy in the sixteenth century, from which a straight line leads to all the theses that proclaim, whether openly or not, that Jesus was a noble dreamer, a reformer, an ethical ideal, but not God.

Swedenborg grasped the very essence of this process, since his theological system, in conflict with the Lutheranism in which he was raised, and also with all other denominations, is the exact opposite of the Arian tendencies toward sundering the unity of the three hypostases of the Holy Trinity. Swedenborg accused all the churches of falsehood in that they appear to profess one God in the Trinity but in fact they instill in the faithful a belief in three gods, which, because this is an assault on reason, must lead to its opposite, and thus to a completely atheistic rational religion: *Deus sive Natura.* The significance that Swedenborg attached to the Gospel of St. John and the Apocalypse indicates he adhered to the hermetic tradition that stretched all the way back to the Gnostics. "In the beginning was the Word," that is, Christ, and Swedenborg proclaims the great secret: our Father in Heaven is Man. It sounds as if we were reading the old Gnostic texts. In these old texts the human quality of God is opposed to the non-human quality of the Archonts, who rule the world, or to Jehovah; man does not belong to the god of nature precisely because he has a higher ally, above the god of nature, in God-Man. There is no such dualism in Swedenborg, but it may very well be contained in his system *implicite.* In general, when someone places the highest value on the Gospel of St. John and the Apocalypse among all the books of the New Testament, this should give us pause, and it is curious that these were also Dostoevsky's beloved books.

Q: *It would appear from this that one promising area of research would be Dostoevsky as a novelist of a Manichaean revival.*

A: That is too broad and specialized a topic. Following Bakhtin, we acknowledge that we are dealing with a new novelistic genre, that is, the polyphonic novel; we cannot place the statements of individual characters into the author's mouth, since the contents of those statements is negated by other, opposing voices. True, Vasily Rozanov, for example, made quite a convincing argument when he tried to prove that the Grand Inquisitor expresses the most personal, the most despairing conclusions arrived at by the author of *The Brothers Karamazov* after many years of meditation. But the Grand Inquisitor believes that the world is in the power of the Tempter, "the great spirit of nonexistence"; he decides to serve him because the divinity incarnated in Jesus is, when measured by the order of both nature and human society, absolutely feeble, incapable of changing anything in the laws of life. However, let us consider the views of the Grand Inquisitor as only one pole, for Dostoevsky wished to create a counterweight, an opposite pole, in *The Brothers Karamazov*; the elder Zosima and Alyosha serve this purpose. Swedenborg comes in handy here because he observed that the only way to slow the progress of an atheism that identifies God with nature is to emphasize the idea of the God-Man. Dostoevsky did the same, only in his mind, which was always inclined toward extremism, this took the form of a radical "either—or": if Jesus died and did not rise from the dead; that is, if he was only a man, then Earth is a "diabolical vaudeville" and one should become a Grand Inquisitor in the name of pity for people—in order to transform the miserable "rebellious slaves" into happy slaves.

Q: *A number of Orthodox writers have called Dostoevsky the greatest theologian that Eastern Christianity has given rise to.*

A: This opinion cannot be sustained. Anna Akhmatova used to call both Tolstoy and Dostoevsky "heresiarchs," and I suspect she was not mistaken. As is well known, in Dostoevsky every negation is expressed with extraordinary power, whereas he had no idea how to produce an image of a truly good man, even less so of a God-Man. The entire development of his thought could be framed in a single question: How did he understand Christ in his youth and how did he understand Christ when he wrote his last novel?

When Dostoevsky was a member of the Petrashevsky circle and read George Sand and Fourier, his ideas were the same as the ideas of the utopian socialists, for whom Jesus was an ethical ideal, the precursor of their imminent, easily realizable perfect society. Therefore, the metaphysical dimension was completely ignored. His experiences at hard labor caused Dostoevsky to understand how very much depends on whether one recognizes this dimension or not. His letter to Fonvizina, written in Omsk in 1854, is frequently cited in the literature about him, but very few people, apparently, notice the crucial, perilous decision expressed in it. Let us reach for the text again:

> I'll tell you of myself that I have been a child of the age, a child of disbelief and doubt up until now and will be even (I know this) to the grave. What horrible torments this thirst to believe has cost me and continues to cost me, a thirst that is all the stronger in my soul the more negative arguments there are in me. And yet God sometimes sends me moments at which I'm absolutely at peace; at those moments I love and find that I am loved by others, and at such moments I composed for myself a credo in which everything is clear and holy for me. That credo is very simple, here it is: to believe that there is nothing more beautiful, more profound, more attractive, more wise, more courageous and more perfect than Christ, and what's more, I tell myself with jealous love, there cannot be. Moreover, if someone proved to me that Christ were outside the truth, and it *really* were [Dostoevsky's italics] that the truth lay outside Christ, I would prefer to remain with Christ rather than with the truth.

> [Translated by David Lowe and Ronald Meyer]

Let us consider what this means. Faith and reason have often been contrasted, but the opposition of faith and truth is quite unusual. Meister Eckhart, who is not known, after all, as an admirer of reason, said: "If God were able to distance himself from the truth, I would hold to the truth and let God go." Just at the same time in the mid-nineteenth century when Dostoevsky was in Siberia, in Denmark Kierkegaard was conducting his great attack on reason, but for him truth was on the side of faith.* Dostoevsky's choice is tantamount to granting all the trumps to his opponent, that is, to the progressive

* "The truth is precisely the venture which chooses an objective uncertainty with the passion of the infinite"; "But the above definition of truth is an equivalent expression for faith"; "Faith is precisely the contradiction between the infinite passion of the individual's inwardness and the objective uncertainty." Søren Kierkegaard, *Concluding Unscientific Postscript*, trans. David F. Swenson and Walter Lowrie (Princeton: Princeton University Press, 1941), 182.

spirit of the nineteenth century, leaving for himself the figure of Christ as no more than a dream which it is difficult to live without. But one of the attributes of a dream is that it tends to get out of control, it easily loses its clear contours. In my opinion this letter is the confession of a potential heresiarch.

Q: *When do the consequences of such a choice appear?*

A: Not immediately. Briefly, I would describe the changes in the figure of Christ in Dostoevsky's works as follows: at first, Christ is the moral leader-ideal of utopian socialism; then he disappears for a long time, making himself known only indirectly, for example in *Crime and Punishment* when Sonia and Raskolnikov read the chapter from the Gospels about the raising of Lazarus from the dead or in the epilogue to the novel, when the peasants, his fellow prisoners at hard labor, hate Raskolnikov, who is an intellectual and therefore, in their opinion, an atheist; finally, Christ reappears as the hero of the Slavophile utopia and tsarist autocracy.

Dostoevsky's obsession with portraying children is eloquent in this regard. The society of children is a society of immature beings who are, however, capable of goodness if a mature and noble person should appear and succeed in organizing them. The first attempt at evangelical portraiture of their Christ-like leader is Prince Myshkin in *The Idiot*. During his stay in Switzerland he is surrounded by a group of children; through his meekness he eradicates their bad habits and changes their attitude toward the half-crazed Marie. But Dostoevsky did not succeed with Myshkin. Because Myshkin is utterly lacking in egotism, he is inhuman, and in the end he sows devastation all around him. Judging by his example, one would have to doubt the possibility of uniting the two natures—the divine and the human—and be inclined toward accepting the opinion of the Docetists, who proclaimed that Christ only seemed to have earthly features. So Dostoevsky renewed his efforts in *The Brothers Karamazov*.

There are two adult organizers of a society of children in that novel. One of them is the Grand Inquisitor or, if you prefer, the author of the poem "The Legend of the Grand Inquisitor"—Ivan Karamazov. Let us note how many times the Grand Inquisitor uses the word *children* in relation to the people whom he rules. The other is Alyosha and the fraternity of twelve schoolboys, quite obviously a foreshadowing of the Church as a theocratic community. The only problem is that however powerful and brilliant in every detail is the Legend of the Grand Inquisitor, the chapters about the boys (along with the chapter in which the excessively caricatured Poles appear) are artistically weak, melodramatic, and offensive to the reader because of their falseness. That *The Brothers Karamazov* remains a masterpiece despite these chapters testifies to Dostoevsky's greatness. It is actually a novel about power. The power of the corporeal father (Fyodor Karamazov) is opposed to the power of the spiritual father (the elder Zosima) and this antinomy holds. Even though the skeptical Lev Shestov used the word *lubok* (a cheap woodcut sold at fairs) to refer to both characters—Zosima and Alyosha—the biography of Zosima is convincing precisely as a genre patterned after the lives of the saints. The moral of this juxtaposition is the following: It is forbidden to rebel against secular power (the father) even when it is evil, but people (the sons) will rebel if there is no spiritual power alongside the secular. The second opposition concerns the future: a leader who is in a pact with the Devil and a leader who acts through love alone. The disproportion between the immense vision of the Legend of the Grand Inquisitor and the troop of boy scouts performing good deeds under Alyosha's leadership is jarring. Artistic failure bears witness to something: therefore, this is a focal point for those Dostoevsky scholars who suspect Dostoevsky the Orthodox publicist of hypocrisy toward himself.

Q: *Does Christ represent a specific principle of social organization in Swedenborg?*

A: Not at all. But the accusations that the Grand Inquisitor hurls at Christ are actually the accusations of a utopian socialist who had dreamed that his teacher would want to march in the vanguard and bears a grudge because he does not wish to do so. So he has a new dream: perhaps Christ will serve as a model for a society which someone will first convince about the virtues of fraternity—and so the model for the Kingdom of God on earth becomes a boy scout troop.

Q: *It ought to be said in defense of Dostoevsky that there is no other example in world literature of a novelist having such boundless ambitions. He inherited the novel as a not very refined genre, and even today his admiration for such authors as Victor Hugo and George Sand amuses us. But he transformed this genre into an instrument for expressing the clashes among the most important ideas about man's fate and made such strides in this direction that quite possibly his failures can be justified, because the novel has only a limited weight-*

bearing capacity. A theologian or a poet has the benefit of greater powers than a novelist has.

A: Dostoevsky the novelist defends himself quite adequately. He should also not be completely ignored in our deliberations as the publicist-author of *Diary of a Writer*, but that particular activity of his indicates how very much he required illusions.

Q: *If I understand you correctly, the similarity between Swedenborg and Dostoevsky would have led to an exceptionally sharp consciousness of the consequences for religion inherent in the development of the exact sciences. This is the link between them; that is, in a certain sense, Dostoevsky was struggling with atheism in its eighteenth-century form.*

A: The atheism of old man Karamazov is Voltairean. And the comic liberal, Stepan Verkhovensky from *The Possessed*, is, if one were to measure him by the Western criteria of that time, a little like a character out of Rousseau's romances. As a result of tempestuous historical events, above all of the Industrial Revolution, the sharpness of the religious problematic was dulled in Western Europe and the voices of a few individuals became a crying in the wilderness. In nineteenth-century *belles lettres* no one said as brutally as Dostoevsky what, it now seems to us, had to be said, especially about indifferent Nature as Law, about "two times two equals four." A search for other similarities with Swedenborg would probably not be justified, because Dostoevsky's political daydreaming appears to have served him as an alibi in the confrontation with metaphysical difficulties.

Berkeley, 1975

DWIGHT MACDONALD

Dwight Macdonald is a totally American phenomenon—if one can call a person a phenomenon. To America's eternal glory, it has a tradition of privately published political pamphlets, of small journals that are read by a thousand individuals, of discussions in which pacifists, conscientious objectors, and various shades of anarchists engage in splitting hairs. This tradition is becoming more and more difficult to maintain due to the conglomeration of the assets needed if the public is to be reached: the cost of publishing a journal is incomparably greater today than it was, for example, in 1850. Nevertheless, the tradition has not died out. Obviously, from a realistic point of view, it is easy to demonstrate that this subcutaneous current of American life is not particularly significant. Realistic assessments, however, often lead to false conclusions. Because there exists a specific American type—the completely free man, capable of making decisions at all times and about all things strictly according to his personal moral judgment—this country has had its Thoreau, Whitman, and Melville, to name just the greatest.

From 1944 through 1949, Macdonald published a journal, *Politics*. For the broad reading public, it was an extraordinarily forbidding organ, because of both its dense columns of small print and its peculiar, eccentric manner of posing problems. The journal was therefore read mainly in New York's intellectual circles. One of the authors it introduced was Simone Weil—before she achieved her posthumous fame. The impact of *Politics* in both America and England, and even in France, was not insignificant, I believe, even though the journal had a limited circulation. Today, there is already something like a clan of post-Marxist writers who are trying to begin from the foundation—that is, to see the contemporary world as it is and not to accept as given any terms that are in general usage. *Politics* belonged precisely to that clan.

The Root Is Man (1953) contains articles from *Politics* accompanied by the author's commentaries. The commentaries provide his current, often revised, position; Macdonald does not shrink from appending a note: "This paragraph now seems nonsensical to me." We are able to follow the meanderings of his thought, and that freedom, that breath of man in the lines of print, is invigorating. What a shame that these texts cannot reach Poland; by their contrast with the obligatory style over there they would have said a great deal about the essence of unfreedom, which is most horrifying when it enters the blood, when it appears *normal*.

The book begins with some observations made in 1944 on the responsibility of the Germans. Macdonald, who is very well informed about Majdanek (it was the first camp that journalists were allowed to visit), about the organization of the concentration camps, the gas chambers, the crematoria, the extermination of the Jews, takes a stand against theories of collective German guilt. In a totalitarian state, the individual can do nothing. The German people are neither worse nor better than other peoples. Every nation in the same circumstances would be capable of ALL crimes. An opinion such as this may arouse objections. However, let us not forget the date. Macdonald is taking a stand against the madness of patriotic-propagandistic hatred that, as he perceptively foresees, will turn into love for the good, honorable Germans—for such is the logic of events. Both that hatred and that love, according to him, belong to the sphere of mythology exploited by the greatest enemy of man—the state. Hatred of Germans "as such" serves to justify the bombardment of civilian populations, which is probably meaningless as a military tactic, and the raising of the slogan of "unconditional surrender" (Macdonald does not like Roosevelt) that will delay rather than hasten the end of the war.

In a note that takes into consideration subsequent events, Macdonald comments:

The Russian blockade of Berlin in the winter of 1948-9 produced a dramatic reversal of the wartime roles of two aggregations of people, the U.S. Air Force and the population of Berlin. The former changed from executioners into relief workers delivering coal and food instead of bombs to the latter, who in turn were transmuted, in our press, from cowardly accomplices of one kind of totalitarianism into heroic resisters against another kind. Since these reversals had very little to do with any free-will choice or action by the human beings who made up the two groups, the episode struck me as an ironic verification of my objections to the concept of collective responsibility . . .

Man lives in history but is not at all comfortable there. Even at best—by which I mean in a smallish, integrated community like the ancient Greek city state—there is always a desperate struggle between what the individual wants and what happens to him as a result of living in society. (The process of hauling the individual about like a bale, or a corpse, and cramming him into some badly fitting context of ideology or action—this is what is euphemistically called "history.")

To illustrate how Macdonald views the fate of the individual in today's world, it is worth repeating a rather instructive story that he recounts on the basis of a report by Orwell (in the London *Tribune* of October 13, 1944):

Among the German prisoners captured in France there are a certain number of Russians. Some time back two were captured who did not speak Russian or any other language that was known either to their captors or their fellow-prisoners. They could, in fact, only converse with one another. A professor of Slavic languages, brought down from Oxford, could make nothing of what they were saying. Then it happened that a sergeant who had served on the frontiers of India overheard them talking and recognized their language, which he was able to speak a little. It was Tibetan! After some questioning he managed to get their story out of them.

Some years earlier they had strayed over the frontier into the Soviet Union and been conscripted into a labour battalion, afterwards being sent to western Russia when the war with Germany broke out. They were taken prisoner by the Germans and sent to North Africa; later they were sent to France, then exchanged into a fighting unit when the Second Front opened, and taken prisoner by the British. All this time they had been able to speak to nobody but one another, and had no notion of what was happening or who was fighting whom.

It would round the story off neatly if they were now conscripted into the British Army and sent to fight the Japanese, ending up somewhere in Central Asia quite close to their native village, but still very much puzzled as to what it is all about.

Macdonald's articles are polemics and it is important to determine whom he is addressing. His opponents are those whom he defines as *liblabs*. These *liblabs* (liberal-labor) are optimistic advocates of progress "on scientific foundations," manufacturers of rose-colored glasses that are meant to prettify distasteful reality. This does not mean that his words have a tone of hopelessness, of bitterness, or that he speaks as a defender of the status quo. His ideal is a socialist society based on the freedom of individuals. However, he opposes those nineteenth-century illusions that are marked by hubris, by that pride which, according to the Greeks, always precedes the fall of a hero. In other words, he belongs to the same broadly conceived family as Simone Weil, Orwell, Camus. This is a position that is particularly hard to maintain because it supplies its own counter-arguments to the shallowest minds—those who understand absolutely nothing about the distinctions, the fundamental propositions that are involved, yet bellow, "Didn't we tell you so!"—which has its Polish equivalent in the expression "Nonsense, my good man, one must live and that's that. Shit is always the same everywhere; only the flies are different."

Macdonald was once a Trotskyist. He opens his polemic against the *liblabs* with a quote from an article that Trotsky published in November 1939 (in *The New International*). Since practically no one knows it, this quotation deserves to be reprinted:

> If this war provokes [Trotsky wrote], as we firmly believe it will, a proletarian revolution, it must inevitably lead to the overthrow of the bureaucracy in the USSR and the regeneration of Soviet democracy on a far higher economic and cultural basis than in 1918. In that case, the question as to whether the Stalinist bureaucracy was a "class" or a parasitic growth on the worker's state will be automatically solved. To every single person it will become clear that in the process of this development of the world revolution, the Soviet bureaucracy was only an episodic relapse.
>
> If, however, it is conceded that the present war will provoke not revolution but a decline of the proletariat, then there remains another alternative: the further decay of monopoly capitalism, its further fusion with the State and the replacement of democracy wherever it still persists, by a totalitarian regime. The inability of the proletariat to take into its hand the leadership of society could actually lead to the growth of a new exploiting class from the Bonapartist fascist bureaucracy. This would be, according to all indications a regime of decline, signalizing the eclipse of civilization . . .
>
> However onerous the second perspective may be, if the world proletariat should actually prove incapable of fulfilling the mission placed upon it by the course of development, nothing else would remain except openly to recognize that the socialist program based on the internal contradictions of capitalist society ended as a Utopia. It is self-evident that a new minimum program would be required—for the defense of the interests of the slaves of the totalitarian bureaucratic society.

Trotsky's hopes for a revolution of the proletariat were not realized. Another, pessimistic variant of his prophecy is being realized instead. The proletariat can be either (1) used by professional revolutionaries to introduce Communism according to the Russian model (Macdonald proposes a new name for this regime: Bureaucratic Collectivism); or (2) it can act within the framework of a benign trade unionism that has nothing in common with socialist slogans. The founder of the American Federation of Labor, Samuel Gompers, was a Marxist. "In the early seventies, New York City looked like Paris during the Commune," Gompers wrote in his autobiography. But where are the snows of yesteryear? This complete cutting off of all escape routes, or, as Trotsky put it, "the decline of the proletariat," demands the revision of many ideas which the *liblabs* hold dear.

Above all, the idea of Progress, which, after growing like an avalanche since the end of the eighteenth century, found its fullest expression in Marx's system. "We who reject Marxism are indebted to Marx for the very fact that the boldness and intellectual grandeur of his work make it possible for us to formulate more clearly our own position in the process of distinguishing it from his; this is the service which any great thinker renders to his critics," says Macdonald. Summarizing Macdonald's conclusions as concisely as possible, we can say that he sees the dual character of Marx's thought, which on the one hand, considered the liberation of the individual to be the goal of revolution and hence opposed the state (whose overthrow was to be accomplished by a revolution), and on the other, established laws that were supposed to lead to this goal out of "iron necessity." While many of his historic predictions are being validated today, the ethical contents of his work, so closely linked with nineteenth-century optimism, lie in ruins.

The old order is ending in many countries, but the bourgeoisie has been replaced not so much by the proletariat as by a new political ruling class. The process is taking place from above, not from below, and is moving in the direction of nationalism and war. Not the liberation of the masses, but their enslavement; not the Kingdom of Freedom, but the Kingdom of Necessity. The worker's chains are becoming visible. Under capitalism, they were concealed. The worker met the purchaser of his labor power in the marketplace and a financial transaction took place. "The Roman slave was held by fetters," says Marx; "the wage laborer is bound to his owner by invisible threads . . . His economical bondage is both brought about and concealed by the periodic sale of himself, by his change of masters, and by the oscillation in the market price of labor power."* Today there is no "oscillation of prices," no "change of masters." There is just one master: the state. The whole mechanism was per-

* As quoted by Macdonald.

fectly clear in Hitler's Germany, as it is today in the Soviet Union. Furthermore, Marx did not give sufficient weight to the significance of war as a phenomenon in the history of civilization. War has become a goal in itself.

> . . . the effects of the technical measures that must be taken to fight a modern war have become more important than any political effect of the war's outcome . . . The existence of powerful warmaking apparatuses, with economies and social institutions deformed to support them, and the quite justified fears of every nation of attack from every other nation—these factors are the key to the problem, rather than the expansive needs of capitalist imperialism . . . or the "contradiction" between Soviet collectivism and American private capitalism . . . The machine is out of control and is grinding away according to its own logic. Here is another example of "reification" ("thing-ification"): things created by humans developing their own dynamic and imposing their own laws on their creators.

The concept of "the left," according to Macdonald, is indefensible today. A "leftist" must decide if he is a "progressive" or a "radical." The progressive believes that we live in a single world that is controlled by laws which can be discovered by scientific methods. The greater the number of laws discovered, the greater is man's power over his surroundings: progress. The radical sees the limitations of science. He assumes that our world is not single but dual: (1) a world of laws revealed by science; (2) a world of values.

"By 'scientific method,' " says Macdonald,

> I mean the process of gathering measurable data, setting up hypotheses to explain the past behavior of whatever is being investigated, and testing these hypotheses by finding out if they enable one to predict correctly future behavior. The essence is the ability to accept or reject a scientific conclusion by means of objective—and ultimately quantitative—tests whose outcome is unambiguous: that is, there is recognized to be a universal standard *independent of the individual observer*, which forces *every one* to assent to a given conclusion if it can be shown to meet the requirements of this standard.

He continues:

> By "value judgment," I mean a statement that involves the notion of "Good" and "Bad" in either an ethical or an esthetic sense. Such a judgment is always ambiguous because it involves a qualitative discrimination about something which is by its very nature *not* reducible to uniform and hence measurable units; the "personal feeling" of the

observer not only enters into judgment but is the chief determinant of judgment. It is impossible, therefore, ever to solve a moral or esthetic problem in the definite way that a scientific problem can be solved, which is why one age can build on the scientific achievements of all past ages, whereas it is notorious that in art and ethics no such progress may be observable.

Progressives follow Marx and Dewey, "each of whom has made a Promethean effort to unify the two worlds by deducing values from scientific inquiry." Values are considered to be *illusory*: it is taken for granted that they are only a reflex, a reflection of some deeper reality that scientific knowledge is capable of discovering; this reality is historical in Marx and psychological in Freud, for example. Values are quite real as phenomena, but they are derivative.

Science, however, is incapable of answering our fundamental question: What should we desire, how should we live? The *liblabs* raise a hue and cry when this point is raised, because they are embarrassed. An ethics based on scientific principles is an impossibility.

"I have discussed this problem of values with Marxists and Deweyans a good deal of late," says Macdonald.

> They generally begin by assuming as "self-evident" that Man ought to want Life rather than Death, or Plenty rather than Poverty; once some such assumption is made, then of course they have no difficulty showing how science can help us reach this End. But if the assumption is questioned, it soon becomes clear that it is based on other assumptions: that "Man" means "most people of the time and place we are talking about," and that the "normal" or "natural" as defined in this statistical way is what one *ought* to want. It is understandable that their answer should take a quantitative form, since science deals only in measurable quantities. But if what most people want is one's criterion of value, then there is no problem involved beyond ascertaining what in fact people *do* want—a question that can indeed be answered by science, but not the one we started out with. For this answer simply raises the original question in different form: why *should* one want what most people want? The very contrary would seem to be the case: those who have taught us what we know about ethics, from Socrates and Christ to Tolstoy, Thoreau, and Gandhi, have usually wanted precisely what most people of their time did *not* want, and have often met violent death for that reason.

Please don't hold it against me that I am using too many quotations. All reviews fulfill pragmatic functions. People in Poland will most likely not read Macdonald and I am trying to give them a sense of these quarrels, seemingly taken from the era of Plato, in the hope that I can contribute in some measure to blowing on the flames and making as many sparks as possible begin to fly.

According to Macdonald, man must therefore accept the fact that he lives simultaneously in two worlds. The sources of values and actions are within the individual. Free will, even though it may operate in a rather constricted sphere (because there is much in man that is subject to determinism), does exist. The historical relativity of values has been overemphasized in our times in both ethics and art. We must not forget about the unchanging element that allows us to make contact with the peoples of past civilizations.

This, then, is the line that separates "progressives" from "radicals." Among progressives, one should add, the most consistent are probably orthodox Communists (for example, it is hard to accept as successful the backbreaking efforts of the "heretic" Mascolo to maintain a balance between the two worlds). However, as soon as we cross the demarcation line and find ourselves among those who accept the independent existence of values, we are faced with the age-old questions: Where do values come from? What guarantees them? Simone Weil, for example, or Jaspers, replies that all values vanish like mist unless you accept the Absolute. Macdonald dismisses religion. Values for him are, so to speak, pragmatically absolute—if these words are not mutually contradictory; obviously, we can discover a link with Lao-tse, but not with an inhabitant of Saturn. "The root is man." Here Macdonald comes close to Camus.

But what is to be done? Macdonald himself reminds us that the best thoughts come to nothing if they do not influence action. The goal is clear: man must be returned to himself, which is possible only in a society in which people enter into direct relations with each other and in which, therefore, economic and political organisms are sufficiently small so that the individual can fully understand their functioning and take an active role in their life, shaping them by his own free and uncoerced will. Macdonald quotes some lines from the young Marx: " 'For Hegel, the starting-point is the State. In a democracy, the starting point is man . . . Man is not made for the law, but the law is made for man.' " When you get down to basics, it is irrelevant whether the individual feels helpless in relation to the state, the party, or the trade union. What, then, should be done? Macdonald expresses a skeptical attitude toward the possibility of wider action today. He seems to think that we are living in a preparatory period and that an awareness of the mythological character of the various ideological tomtoms is seeping very slowly into consciousness. He summarizes his advice to "radicals" under five headings:

1. Negativism. An automobile is racing at full speed toward a precipice. Seeing the radicals sitting on the side of the road, the passengers cry out contemptuously, "Yaahh, negativists! Look at us! *We're* going somewhere, *we're* really doing something!" [50]

2. Unrealism. During the First World War Dewey urged his fellow countrymen to participate in it. His disciple Bourne saw in the war what Dewey's realism prevented him from seeing: a catastrophe, the end of nineteenth-century dreams.

3. Moderation. For the Greeks, the "geometry of virtue," as Simone Weil calls it, was the main topic of discourse. Western civilization has ceased to understand this. It is necessary to own up to our ignorance, to live among contradictions, not to bind up our wounds with all-embracing systems.

4. Smallness. While he was in the resistance movement, Camus published *Combat*; after the war it achieved a large circulation. Camus became one of the most influential journalists in France. And then he quit, because, as he confirmed in a conversation with Macdonald, while writing for the larger public he was unable to talk about what is real and true.

5. Self-ishness. "Phoo, you are worried only about saving your own soul." But isn't it better to save one's soul than to lose it—and, what is most important, not gain the world? It is hard to love all of mankind. It's too large. Let each individual ask himself as a first step toward political action and political morality what it is that satisfies him, what it is that he wants. Direct human contacts should replace abstractions.

Macdonald has been called a crank, a utopian, an eccentric, and so forth. It is not without a certain hidden agenda that I have attempted to summarize "Macdonaldism." I realize that many of the ideas of this American radical would not strike the countless Poles, Jews, Czechs, Lithuanians, Ukrainians, etc., who are floating like globules of fat on the great Western soup, as particularly alien. Since they have no possibility of any wider action, they are surely able to appreciate his betting on slow processes in the human mass and his belief that one man counts or, if we are lucky, three or four men, linked by friendship. Macdonald seems to pin his hopes on the fermentation concealed beneath the surface, which is not automatic, and to which everyone can contribute. Toynbee's assertion that the millions of émigrés are like the Roman proletariat who became the yeast of Christianity is probably an exaggeration. Nonetheless, there is something in this anticipation of new movements, now that the forms of action that existed up till the present seem, in all likelihood, to be leading to miserable outcomes.

Brie-Comte Robert, 1954

JEFFERS: AN ATTEMPT AT DISCLOSURE

This essay is an exploration of particular variants of the American and European imagination. Before taking the first steps, it will be appropriate to consider several motivations for selecting one direction rather than another. The work of the American poet Robinson Jeffers (an already closed body of work, because Jeffers, who was born in 1887, died in 1962) was the deciding factor. When I started translating his poetry, the thoughts that were stimulated by an attentive reading of these works—and one is never so compelled to attentiveness as when translating—kept leading me, via the play of similarities and differences, deeper and deeper into the history of modern American, Polish, Russian, and French poetry, and from there to the characteristic features of a civilization that finds its expression in poetry. These ideas formed into several trains of thought that became more and more distinct as a result of personal experience, and the theme—Robinson Jeffers—allowed me to crystallize some vague intentions I had to tackle some painful problems that are not often raised in print.

In turn, however, one must ask what is the meaning of someone having a desire to translate a given poet; what is concealed in this? There are translations that are done by chance or under contract; but if the translation is undertaken out of unconstrained desire, the question Why? is justified. The simplest response is to say that a reader who liked the poems wants to see their equivalent, even if it is imperfect, in his native language, and thus becomes a translator. This sentence, if you examine it closely, assumes that the discoverer's pleasure is incomplete if it is not shared with others; since it would be possible simply to belong to a coterie of the poet's admirers in his own country, the sentence also assumes that a community so constituted is felt to be imperfect, that we seek a fuller one, with people who are closer to us, because we are bound together by the powerful bonds of history. Finally, the aim of "enriching" one's native language—the diligence of a mouse dragging a seed it has found back to its hole—permits us to conclude that the translator sees a sort of "empty space" in his own home, in his home of sounds and intonations that he has known since childhood, and desires that it not remain empty. And one might even suppose that in the first contact with the original, the ever-present background of one's own language is the decisive factor: what is at work here is surprise, a feeling that one has stumbled across layers that remain unexploited in one's own language—which is to say, possibility colors reception. Thus, an apparently simple assertion is by no means simple, because it expresses in abbreviated form relations between the individual and the collective, as well as the impulses arising therefrom.

The translator's decision is preceded by a dual evaluation: of the selected work and of the so-called literary life into which the work will be thrown, having acquired its new linguistic shape. The more conscious the translator is of his goals, the more carefully does he calculate his moves, keeping in mind the fact that everything that exists in a given language combines to form a situation that is continually being transformed by even the most trivial human acts. The scales of the present fluctuate between the past and the future, and every little lump added to one of them has significance. This element of will leads one into so much trouble that translation becomes an intentional act.

The wave of modernity traveled across Europe at the end of the nineteenth century and engulfed Poland. The patrons of the first avant-garde movements were Western masters: Baudelaire, Rimbaud, Nietzsche. Ever since, revolutions and transformations have been acccompanied by scrutiny of foreign celebrities, selected according to the likes and dislikes of groups and schools, while at the same time the internal logic of these new movements has grown stronger. Could it be that now, in the second half of the twentieth century, this shameful derivativeness is being repeated and that the poems of Robinson Jeffers will be one of the means by which the next fashion, this time Anglo-Saxon poetry, will be established?

Poetry in our century, as many people understood or intuited, is mutilated by the contradiction embedded within it. Two equally legitimate tendencies intersect each other and frequently destroy each other. This is not the sole contradiction, and all art lives by impossibilities, but this particular contradiction lends weight to accusations of babbling and prophecies about the end of poetry. On the one hand, it is clear that the poet cannot be only an instrument for the transformation of sensual data into more or less autonomous "objects," because his imagination is infected by ideas that are everybody's concern, and if he withdraws into a space where these ideas allegedly have no access, he discourages and disenchants his readers, despite the admiration of a few connoisseurs. On the other hand, if he decides to draw upon everything that he is as a man, i.e., as intellect, impressions, emotions, passions, he is gripped by a totally understandable fear of the pressure of speculative thought, which is in its very essence hostile to art and allied with ethical yearnings. And yet poetry is above all a lantern dispelling the darkness; the poet dwells at the very limits of where human consciousness can reach, and although his instrument is completely different from a philosopher's instrument, when he renounces his brain or employs it only to build experimental houses, he is tormented by deficiency: why, before he sits down in front of a sheet of paper, does he judge, evaluate, dispute, and yet nothing of this penetrates his poetry, that temple of hieratic rituals? Why is his throat constricted, and why is he unable to speak in a full voice?

In the period of my literary schooling, even though it was a rich and fruitful period, Polish poetry was characterized by a peculiar dualism. Lyric discourse was engaged in quite widely, especially in relation to politics, reviving the fervor of the Romantics. At the same time, numerous contending programs were derived from wonder at the "magic of the word" (whether as melody or as a system of metaphors), apparently self-sufficient and offering protection against demands put forward by shallow natures, with their unending concern for conceptual meaning. However, the discourse too frequently resembled rhymed journalism, and (for those who didn't submit blindly to the incantations and gestures) highly conventional attitudes could be glimpsed beneath the ritual activity. I anticipate the rebuke that I have not placed a high enough value on the multiplicity of layers in a poem and the transmission of intellectual weight through color and tone. Deficiency arises when literature resides at a level lower than the highest threshold that is accessible to the mind at a given time; this is divined instantly.

That this dualism I have mentioned is not something I have just concocted out of whole cloth can be confirmed by reading Bolesław Leśmian's "Treatise on Poetry," dating from 1937. This is a defense of the liberated word (L.L., *langue lyrique*) against the conceptual word (L.S., *langue scientifique*), against King Rat, as Leśmian calls it, or journalistic depersonalization. And Leśmian was not mistaken; he had a right to say this, especially because he was probably the only poet-philosopher at that time, the creator of a worldview that is impossible to convey other than through the liberated word, and so he blended divergent elements to his own satisfaction.'

It is possible that one could ascribe this dualism in large measure to French influences. French poetry, beginning with Baudelaire, was always rushing straight ahead in a panic, chased by the specter of classicism, which had gradually debased poetry to the level of very elegant prose, and by the specter of its terrifying uncle, Victor Hugo, the annihilator of all discursiveness through an excess of eloquence. Even the very nature of the language, the most precise of all languages, the richest in syllogisms, compelled writers to revolt, to rebel against unbearable discipline in the name of the freedom of a purely poetic idiom. French Symbolism, in turn, fertilized Polish as well as Anglo-Saxon and Russian poetry, but its reception in each literature differed, depending on the impetus supplied by the past and on local conditions. Due to causes which I will not inquire into here, in Poland this reception was too exclusively aesthetic. Poets managed to ignore or to simplify the intellectual violence, the system of appraisals of civilization that comprised the virtual core of Baudelaire's creative work, or Rimbaud's, or Laforgue's (or even more, of Verhaeren's), by evincing a sensitivity to melody, color, and mood above all. However, as soon as verse was harnessed for so-called duty, Romantic automatic responses could be heard. Despite numerous shifts and transformations, the two tracks underwent parallel developments for several decades.

The years of the Second World War were a moment of shock and nakedness. The horror of events was so enormous that few poets in history have had to face anything like it; it compelled them to either undertake a total reassessment or recognize the meaninglessness of art. Reality did not deal kindly with the theories of aesthetics. But duty, which naturally imposed itself at the time, was like a lead weight attached to one's leg, dragging one down into an abyss populated by romantic spirits, whereas every automatic response disarms one intellectually. Poetry that has been disempowered like that is ready to awaken in the power of political superstitions. In our century, this dilemma, just like the entire contradiction presented here, is not the property of one country alone, but it kept on stubbornly returning in Poland. It is uncertain whether solutions exist, but whoever recognizes that poetry can be saved only if it does not flee into the *ineffable* or serve as an ornament for journalistic slogans understands, at the very least, just how high the stakes are. The stakes are man's fate, which is forever eluding our understanding; which is to say, thinking (in poetry) has an immense future.

So, a new beginning was necessary. Polish poetry was, however, in my opinion, like a hunter deprived not only of his bow but even of the wood and string to make a bow. Before indicating what to hunt for and how to do it, it makes sense to try to put something in the hunter's hand. That is, it was necessary to repair the workshop where bows are manufactured. Immediately after the war I extended a friendly welcome to the poetry of Tadeusz Różewicz, not because I agreed with his hunting, but because Różewicz, moving as in a slow-motion film or like a man who has gone deaf, refused to accept anything that struck him, a castaway, as a luxury from the past. That was valuable. Given such an obvious need for a new beginning, the usefulness of translations also became apparent.

Here, an understanding of a phenomenon that goes hand in hand with the acceleration of history came into play. More and more, humanity is living off itself, and if it does not perish or revert to the Stone Age, it will consume itself in greater and greater doses. This means that wherever, in time or space, man has revealed his creative abilities, what he has achieved will be studied all the more closely and even appropriated emotionally as their own by all members of the species. This universalization demolishes the model of cultural centers which used to be located, as a rule, in a number of cities in Western Europe; it also demolishes the division into "better" and "worse" literatures, and in place of imitation it introduces mutual exchange and interdependence. The fruits of excavations in Asia as well as inexpensive reproductions of the Dutch masters and recordings of Renaissance compositions bear witness to this movement, as does the growing familiarity of Europeans with American literature. An increasingly comprehensive knowledge of, for example, the history and literatures of the East Central and East European countries is also inevitable; up till now this has been impeded by the appearance of exoticism. Movement inward, toward the past, and outward, toward all the continents, can be slowed down artificially in the name of doctrines, but the effectiveness of applying those brakes will be short-lived.

I cannot deny, however, that as I wandered through American, Latin American, and French poetry, and even looked in on Chinese poetry, I was guided less by a universal cultural curiosity than by the desire to ascertain whether somewhere there might not be some omens of victory over the illness that weighs so heavily upon poetry. Sometimes, too, as in my translations of Latin American poets, what interested me was their vividness and exuberance, a poison to be used against the victorious King Rat, who, in the first postwar decade, was terribly self-confident and convinced that he would succeed in covering everything with his beloved grayness. This transient interest ended, it is true, when I noticed that importing a colorful baroque into Poland was like carrying coals to Newcastle. For some reason I just couldn't warm up to poetic France. It was foundering deeper and deeper into professional perfectionism or straining at "engage-ment," which, to tell the truth, the tradition of Polish poetry has in excess. Among Polish poets I could see some hope of escaping from the crisis: if someone was spitting out his words through clenched teeth, like Różewicz, because too much had come crashing down on him, that was a good sign; among the French, even St.-John Perse was enclosed inside a chalk circle by the elevated nature (*la grandeur*) of his style. If Paris was contributing to the renewal of the arguments about man's freedom and responsibility, this was taking place entirely outside poetry, and a born poet, Albert Camus, was writing in prose.

Most likely, American poetry is so nourishing because its devel-opment has not paralleled Europe's, just as the entire development of the United States has not been parallel. This poetry entered into European affairs twice. First through Edgar Allan Poe and his role in the shaping of French Symbolism. Second through Walt Whitman, who had an impact on more than literary circles at the beginning of the twentieth century. A certain Gavrilo Princip was a young poet in Belgrade, and like all members of his group, he was intoxicated with Whitman. By shooting the Archduke Ferdinand in Sarajevo, he unleashed the First World War. Poets, in other words, should not be taken lightly, although it would be an exaggeration to assert that Whitman was at fault.

Next, American poetry experienced its modern crisis, which was triggered in large measure by European viruses. A battle was raging in the name of "free verse," which was by no means an alien concept to readers of the Bible and Whitman. At the same time, French Symbolism had to be reconciled somehow with strictly American habits of thought: with a long-standing ambivalence about acceptance or rejection of the elephant—here, the elephant was not Poland but "vulgar" industrial society; with the religious gravity of the heirs of Protestant austerity; with literary forms that marked the abandon-ment of elemental lyricism—the monologues and dialogues intro-duced by Robert Browning allowed the use of masks, which impose intellectual discipline. Thus, the French import was passed through an entirely different filter for American poets than for Polish and Russian poets at the beginning of the century. Baudelaire, for ex-ample, emerged as not so much a defender of the right to pain as a traveler through the Dantesque hell of the modern city, and this motif of the *cité infernale* was further developed by T. S. Eliot.

It is well known that the young T. S. Eliot schooled himself in the works of Jules Laforgue, taking from him irony, emotional restraint, and the free use of colloquialisms and popular songs. But even such modified borrowings from Europe bypassed a number of excellent "born" poets, and I must confess that although I was once drawn more to the American Europeans, who I felt were closer to me, I gradually came to appreciate the others more. Snobbery, the ever-present factotum of all art in our era, is often a benign force; unfortunately, its promptings imposed, as they still do, far too much conformity. In painting it urged a non-figurative image, to the point of calling the human arm or leg a monument of bad taste. In poetry it favored submersion in the substance of language, to the point of proclaiming prosaic communication an error. One should not underestimate the virtues of such a control, because it compels struggle and prevents the routine. But too often it rewards the effete, who withdraw from the wider game into their own pain. The American poets, with roots in their country, were too preoccupied with the tangible, real world to allow themselves to be terrorized by fashion. One of them, Robinson Jeffers, pushed his quarrel with fashion into utter contempt. One could call his artistic program old-fashioned (if that program were not the only one possible): the artist confronts *what is*, armed with his craft, and this craft must be good. He knows that he will never exhaust reality and that his defeat is inevitable, but his work is defined not by the closed systems of verse form or a canvas's dimensions but by the eye directed at—it doesn't matter what we call it—the object, being, *être*. Jeffers expressed this in one of his dialogue-poems.* A poet is complaining that "I hate my verses," because they are "pale and brittle pencils," "cracked mirrors," impotent in relation to "the splendor of things"—as if one could capture "the lion beauty, the wild-swan wings, the storm of the wings." To which Jeffers responds: Is this loathing, which in the final analysis is nothing other than self-loathing, loathing for one's shameful subjectivity, really all that important? The "wild swan of a world" will never be the hunter's game, but one should love the "mind that can / Hear the music, the thunder of the wings," the eye, because it is able to remember. "Love the wild swan." That is, either movement toward the object or movement away from the object toward one's own doubt (which immediately leads to the building of

---

* "Love the Wild Swan."

"ideal objects," since they, at least, can be mastered). Here Jeffers touches upon the necessity of ontological choice that is concealed in the principles of modern art. It seems that the dualism that reduces poetry to exercises in a linguistic laboratory can be overcome only if one chooses the wild swan and not oneself. The beast is so unusual that we must strain all our powers, and so we grow indifferent to rules that command us to beware of indecency, that is, of indicative sentences in the colloquial sense of the word.

Jeffers can be a model and an example in one thing only: the stubbornness with which he strove to give poetry the greatest possible intellectual objectivity, to fill it with his own worldview based on the cult of the Permanent Thing. But when the thing is understood differently, an attempt to transfer his devices mechanically will come to nothing, while the Thing observed by Jeffers is too hopeless to attract anyone, and this, no doubt, is the reason why in America, too, Jeffers, who is more straightforwardly brutal than his contemporary William Faulkner, has no imitators. Only in this one aspect, in the force of his assault, has Jeffers strengthened me, because if at different points on this earth, independently of each other, there arises a similar disinclination for dualistic poetry, there is something in this; it is persuasive evidence that one has not fallen victim to one's own delusions.

In the introduction to his *Selected Poetry*, Jeffers says:

> Long ago, before anything included here was written, it became evident to me that poetry—if it was to survive at all—must reclaim some of the power and reality that it was so hastily surrendering to prose. The modern French poetry of that time, and the most "modern" of the English poetry, seemed to me thoroughly defeatist, as if poetry were in terror of prose, and desperately trying to save its soul from the victor by giving up its body. It was becoming slight and fantastic, abstract, unreal, eccentric; and was not even saving its soul, for these are generally anti-poetic qualities. It must reclaim substance and sense, and physical and psychological reality. This feeling has been basic in my mind since then. It led me to write narrative poetry, and to draw subjects from contemporary life; to present aspects of life that modern poetry had generally avoided; and to attempt the expression of philosophic and scientific ideas in verse. It was not in my mind to open new fields for poetry, but only to reclaim old freedom.

And the no doubt inevitable correction:

> Another formative principle came to me from a phrase of Nietzsche's: "The poets? The poets lie too much." I was nineteen when the phrase

stuck in my mind; a dozen years passed before it worked effectively, and I decided not to tell lies in verse. Not to feign any emotion that I did not feel; not to pretend to believe in optimism or pessimism, or unreversible progress; not to say anything because it was popular, or generally accepted, or fashionable in intellectual circles, unless I myself believed it; and not to believe easily. These negatives limit the field; I am not recommending them but for my own occasions.

He did not recommend them, but elsewhere he observes that at times lying is epidemic among poets and "then it is called a poetic tradition or a new movement."

While enlarging the sphere of poetry's authority, Jeffers avoided writing prose. He did not scribble any short stories or novels, did not practice journalism or, with rare exceptions, criticism. Pressed to do so by his friends, he brought himself once to make a statement which I quote in its entirety, because it complements my own arguments very nicely:

I promised a few words for this page. When I considered what to write about many subjects offered; but each wanted to be said in verse, or had been said in verse already, or being too trivial for verse was too trivial for use. Yet others write poetry and prose, too, both brilliantly. It is an age of specialists, except in writing. Here, since the workman would not specialize, the work tended to. Edgar Poe lived ahead of his time and formulated the tendency, saying in effect that there is no poetry but lyrical poetry. The belief became orthodox. Arthur Symons announced it as beautifully as possible; no one nowadays can put his world into a poem as Dante did; he may put it in a series of novels, like Balzac, but poetry in a too complex world can deal only with essences; it has withdrawn to an ivory tower, "where it sings, ignoring the many voices of the street." Obviously a man has more to say than can be sung in a tower of ivory, and while this conception endures the poet will be seeking other vessels for his mind. The thoughts that might have fed the poem will flow into prose stories, criticism, philosophy. Perhaps they will be more at home there; but the drain might leave poetry only a lean imitation of music. There is something to be said for storing all the corn in one barn, and it seems to me that this is my unique and final appearance as a prose-writer.

Jeffers made exactly the same demands on poetry that I had once made in my conversations with my poet friends. Of course, I hadn't had the foggiest notion about this, since I did not even know his name. I have become convinced that the leap beyond the chalk circle of "pure lyrical poetry" is very difficult, that there are completely objective obstacles inherent in the anatomy of the hand and in the taste of readers, even those ideal readers for whom we can only yearn. Consequently, thoughts which cannot be expressed in verse would push me, alas, in the direction of prose, and more than once I could sadly confirm that the reader in my century has quite lost the habit of concentration that is indispensable if poetry is to be accessible. That is, he has been disaccustomed by the constant repetition of the idea that poetry is only a reflection of internal, incommunicable states. How frequently has a poem disappeared in a void, but the very thing that was concentrated and compressed in it achieved wide recognition when the author duly diluted it in an essay or an article.

"Storing all the corn in one barn" is a backbreaking undertaking, so it seems Jeffers had to fail? When he died, his work was entering the university canon and being analyzed in seminars, but I doubt professors of literature will support the judgment voiced by the young critic Dwight Macdonald in 1930 (and rather widely held at the time) that Jeffers was the greatest poet America has produced, of infinitely greater range than his contemporaries Robert Frost, who is too provincial, or T. S. Eliot, who is too unabashedly intellectual, like a student who has swallowed all wisdom. American poetry has gone down a road that Jeffers did not want for it; it has grown denser, chasing after intensity within the boundaries of its microcosm, and its helpmate in this has been the criticism that usually accompanies "incomprehensible" poetry: structural and psychoanalytic criticism. Although no one has denied Jeffers the title of great poet, his fame has slowly ebbed, and having decided now to tackle his creative work, at least I am not paying tribute to fashion, which he hated so intensely. Let us admit that Jeffers disturbs us, forcing us by his practice to reflect on how one loses, on how much one must lose, in order to win. His long narrative poems, which are essentially novels in verse with characters enmeshed in a tragic plot or (this may be closer to the truth) tragedies not for the stage, demand of the reader dedication and strong nerves. The discovery that man is *une passion inutile* was not made in France: Jeffers discovered it earlier and derived radical conclusions from it; his world of incest and murder stands out in its cruelty even against the background of all the "black" literature to which the twentieth century has inured us. Each of these long poems as a whole seems to me to be a failure, which suggests that obstacles are greater than the will of poets. Nonetheless, were it not for that craving for the all-embracing, there would be none of the fragments and shorter works that assure Jeffers a lasting position that will surely endure as long as the English language endures, and I will hazard a prediction that the eclipse of his fame is only temporary, occasioned by the fear that cultural subtlety experiences when it comes up against a work that is "all of a piece."

What is essential is that this breakneck quality, its impulses, are no different from those that the young Jeffers used to chase after when he went mountain climbing in California. Instead of succumbing resignedly to the diminution that was being forced onto poetry, he established the earth in his verse, just as it appeared to his thoughts, his eyes and imagination, and he was not satisfied with the fragments, the crumbs of impressions. If Dante could erect his cosmos on a vertical line between Hell and Heaven, shame on his heir if he does not construct a Cosmos that conforms to contemporary man's understanding, i.e., if he avoids hard and clear declarations: I believe in this, I do not believe in that. Therefore, to tell the truth, whatever is written about Jeffers ought to carry the subtitle "Worldview and Poetry." Let us skip the utterly modest little fields that have been plowed, irreproachably to be sure, by those scholars who are capable of extracting opinions even from Tolstoy in order to dissect his "art" separately. Let us return to the old, honorable method: "The poet says that . . . ," even if that method is employed in a not altogether naïve way, or, at times, perversely. This is a great relief for many people (including me) after the numerous fine points and astounding little discoveries achieved by modern criticism since poetry began to speak enigmatically, in the language of the Sybil.

Courageous and truthful, Jeffers did not want to include in the Thing studied by him, that is, human fate on a small planet of the solar system, anything that he himself had not verified. His worldview is defined by non-acceptance of the haziness of beliefs that are universally held only because they are a source of consolation. Unflinching, extreme positions are characteristic of him. They are (1) rejection of Christianity; (2) rejection of so-called secular humanism and the idea of Progress. Obviously, the question arises: What is left? Only Spinoza's *Deus sive Natura* and *Fatum*.

This is very unpleasant, repellent, and when the majority of people consider themselves Christians, progressives, humanists, Marxists, etc., Jeffers's poetry has to pay a price—which is part of the rules of the game he is playing.

But here many other questions intrude. From where, how, and why? Did Jeffers look more bravely than others at the image of the universe that is shared by all who live in this era of science and technology? Is he a link in the chain of names that testifies to the continually intensifying predicament of religious faith—from Pascal's battles with Montaigne's skepticism, to Kierkegaard's acceptance of Christ as a "scandal," to Nietzsche's cry that "God is dead," up to the contemporary debate among Protestant theologians that was initiated by Rudolf Bultmann's pronouncement and his theses on the need for the "demythologizing of Christianity"? Did Jeffers probe a sore point for atheists and agnostics who believe in progress (always, despite everything) even though they realize they have reconstructed the Judaeo-Christian conception of history for their own benefit alone, and that therefore their faith is no better protected from corrosive paradoxes than is Christian faith? Or was Jeffers a puritan from New England, yearning for the Kingdom of God and disenchanted when he reached the Pacific and the promise projected into space was not fulfilled? Or was he, perhaps, above all an heir of the transcendentalists from Emerson's and Thoreau's circle, who found comfort in a nature indifferent to the ugliness of industry and commerce? Whatever he is, nothing can be unraveled here if the individual threads are not separated and we do not follow where they lead—to the America not only of Jeffers but of his parents or grandparents, to the Europe not only of the last two centuries, to the works of those writers who are most helpful, when we want to reproduce the changing images of the great All that are continually being revised by man.

Figuring in the background, instead of philosophers, are two patrons of modern literature, American and Polish: Herman Melville and Cyprian Norwid. Both of them were strangled by the noose that was tied around their necks by the simple fact that they were born when they were, Melville in 1819, Norwid in 1821: the noose of material progress, together with its price of evil. England for Melville, a newcomer from a rural American valley, is the hovels of the port districts of *Redburn* (Glasgow); the "City of Dis" in *Israel Potter* or New York in *Pierre* is like Norwid's poems about the gloomy streets of London and Paris told in prose. Both men strove to understand how much truth and how much falsehood there are in the adjective *Christian* when applied to the domination of matter by humans. And both voluntarily destroyed their own fame, abandoning readable writing in favor of the symbol and the ironic parable—until Melville's final, thoroughly enigmatic novel, *The Confidence Man*, where the Mississippi River steamer *Fidèle* is virtually identical with the steamer *Civilization* in Norwid's story. Only, Norwid did not sail as an ordinary sailor on whaling ships and did not accumulate that knowledge about the elements, about the monsters of the land and seas, the trees and plants, that contributes to Melville's richness and lends his craziest digressions an almost textbook-like precision. Norwid was also not fortunate enough to desert a sailing ship on one of the islands of the Marquis archipelago instead of worshipping his beloved from a distance, and to spend several months there among gentle cannibals in the company of Fayaway, who was assigned to Melville according to the rules of hospitality and was immediately loved by him. Therefore, he could not totally condemn the evil energy of the white man, the Christian and power wielder, countering it with the natural, pre-Christian paradise, nor could he strip his contemporaries of their frock coats and long dresses so that they might cast off the morality of guilt and merit along with their garments, while in stark contrast stood: tattooed nakedness, innocence, brotherhood, a stoic acceptance of life and death. But Norwid heard the speech of ruins and the reality of the nineteenth century, hostile to all innate goodness, was for him a moment in the progression from–to: from the Crucifixion and the Roman catacombs to that tomorrow when "martyrdom will become unnecessary on earth."

The noose that strangled Melville and Norwid was the same, but each of them strove to loosen it in a different way; for the time being, let us not attempt to judge which way was better. Let us only emphasize that for Poles, who have been exceptionally powerfully marked by Romantic historicism (and, like it or not, also by the Marxism born of that historicism), the coupling of Christianity with historical Movement, in which Norwid was by no means an exception, whether in Poland or in Europe, seems familiar and obvious, while it is difficult for them to achieve insight into writers who are indifferent to historic hopes or, at the very least, suspicious of the Christian New Testament.

The antagonistic reflex that Jeffers's return to pre-Christian thought evokes in a Polish reader (and it is a return, above all to the Stoics) inclines one to introspection. It cannot be ruled out that this meeting is the meeting of Norwid and Melville—through their representatives. However much time has elapsed since the age of the steam engine, what is going on here is a clash between someone for whom the most important problem is "Man and History" and someone who concentrates on the problem of "Man and Nature."

If I concern myself with Jeffers's philosophical contents, this is not a contradiction of my own aim, which is the defense of poetry.

Certainly, one cannot defend it in any other way than by demonstrating that when the L.L. (*langue lyrique*) was set aside as its exclusive property, like a reservation for a vanishing Indian tribe—as Pius Servien attempted to do in interwar France with all the trappings of science—this was no favor to poetry. Poetry is necessary only where the poet participates in man's struggle with the meaning of the verb *to be* (and this will never stop as long as man lives on earth), and an essay in the field of literature or, more precisely, comparative literature can fulfill its obligation only insofar as it goes beyond literature.

I had almost completed this chapter when I came across Jan Józef Lipski's review of a new volume of Różewicz's poetry. He writes:

> Incidentally, I would like to draw attention to the astonishing consistency with which contemporary lyric poetry, constructing its vision, is taking on a role that for centuries has traditionally been reserved for philosophers—at the same time, the constructions, individual solutions, bah, frequently even entire formulations hark back, wonder of wonders, not to the philosophical tradition of the nineteenth and twentieth century that is closest to us, but to considerably more distant times, to the Greeks, and thus to the birth of European thought.

Has this role been reserved for philosophy for centuries or only relatively recently? Furthermore, a phenomenon that pleases the critic is emerging in defiance of the international code of poetics. This code, despite the appearance of renewal, has kept in force prescriptions that were already promoted as orthodoxy when Jeffers was a young man; the term *lyric*, even though it has its uses as a convenient trademark, carries in its wake all sorts of remnants of the code. Whatever has emerged in postwar Polish poetry that is truly significant has broken, more or less consciously, with these remnants, and does not easily submit to confinement within the orbit of the "lyric." However that may be, and although we could argue over where the paths are leading, these few sentences that I have just quoted demonstrate a kinship.

It ought to be clear by now that I view poetry as an addendum to religion (which is the exact opposite of poetry understood *as* religion), of religion in the broadest sense (whether or not it can be derived from *religare*, to bind); at the same time, the yearned-for fusion can be theistic or atheistic. The muscles and nerves of the mind are visible inside the word *religion*; that is why it is better than

Weltanschauung. Poetry that shies away from participating in man's fundamental effort at unification changes into an entertainment and dies. Jeffers's poetry, however, is not like that, which is why I approach it with the gravity it deserves.

Berkeley, 1962

ON THE POETRY OF ALEKSANDER WAT

I wanted to write a lot, a whole lot, about Aleksander, who was my friend. I tried arranging my thoughts, but I have come to the conclusion that I will not succeed in this. I will not succeed out of excess: his life leads into the most sensitive, the most tortuous affairs of our century. And also into the mystery of physical pain, the impotence of our proclaimed protest against the order of this world. There were periods when I saw him almost daily. It was not easy: to be powerless to do anything, only to participate as a witness. I still have too much shame and anger in me to be able to speak about this calmly. I have not forgotten the names of a couple of writers in Poland who called that Job a malingerer and a con artist while we who stood by and watched it happen were horrified by the monstrousness inscribed in existence.

By what miracle does someone create a poetic work of such quality only after the age of fifty and, furthermore, in those fleeting moments of relief, of clarity, left to him by a disease? For several decades Wat's high position in literary circles was actually the position of a talker rather than a writer. He was labeled a "fiction writer and translator." In Mayakovsky's notes from his stay in Warsaw there is a sentence: "*Wat—urozhdenny futurist* [Wat is a born Futurist]," but this, too, was the result of personal contact, the intuitive guess of a mentality that was as rooted in the twentieth century as could be.

This is how I see it. Wat had accumulated such a vast store of knowledge about our century that he was struck mute. A leftist intellectual—and then a descent into the abyss for seven years. Dostoevsky's four years of penal servitude figure in books about him as an example of a pivotal experience capable of transforming the writer, but Wat told me enough about his own penal servitude in Russia and Russian Asia that I dare to consider his knowledge deeper and more horrifying. It was unmovable, it demanded some expression, and thus arose the intention of writing a great book in prose.

It was to be a *summa* of compassion, sympathy, analysis. He was unable to write such a book. In the first place, because his cultivated, refined, fastidious, hypercritical mind demanded too much of him; most likely no one will ever write a book like the one he envisioned. Second, he would barely have gotten down to work and the illness would return. If, however, there had not been this constant wrestling with his gigantic intention, there would probably have been no poetry. Wat's hand, constrained by the excessive demands of his intellect when he tried to tell his story in prose, was free when he made marginal notations, perfunctorily. Such was his too scrupulous nature: for example, he was afraid to agree to give a lecture because he had to prepare for it as no one else prepared, although this was absolutely unnecessary; those who knew him knew that it was sufficient to provoke him, as if accidentally, and he would speak magnificently, brilliantly, for an hour, two hours, in Polish, in Russian, in French. He left behind, on tape, recorded stories and memoirs that encompass the major portion of his life's odyssey. It is a rich mine—but for me, Wat was and is primarily a poet.

One ancient metaphor sees in art a pearl that is the creation of a diseased shell. Another makes reference to the nightingale who sings beautifully because his eyes have been gouged out. Contemporary poets are ashamed of the old metaphors and ashamed of their own feelings. They have allowed themselves to be terrorized by those nitpickers who dream up ever more novel disciplines, which may be clever and convenient for those who aspire to university appointments but are lethal for someone who believes that a poet and a theoretician can coexist in the same individual. I read, reluctantly and antagonistically, the various structuralists who proclaim that it is language that controls us and not we who control language; this is exactly the way a wolf would read treatises written by honorable bespectacled ladies about how to trap animals. Wat stepped outside the bounds of literary fashions; at the most, they amused him. It could not have been otherwise, since every one of his poems was a hastily scribbled notation, with the feeling that time is short, that it was a moment of grace if he was free to register something before another attack bowled him over and the painkillers dulled his mind for long weeks or months. In defiance of what are virtually universal principles today, his poetry is unabashedly autobiographical; it is a stenographic record of his suffering. Jarosław Iwaszkiewicz called it "the thorny bush of our history." If this poetry is astonishingly modern, having nothing in common with the fluent autobiographical lyricism of the Romantics, it is because this "born Futurist" encompassed all the contradictions and all the ailments of our times. Wat appears whole in his poetry, just as he was in his relations with his friends. Wise with a too bitter wisdom, childlike, egotistical, inclined to euphorias and enthusiasms, pricking those rosy balloons of his with macabre humor, jesting, howling with dread, threatening God for His cruelty and accepting of His judgment, a believer and a non-believer, a Christian and a non-Christian, a witness to the crimes of our era and a witness to the events of five millennia, carrying in his blood the memory of what King Solomon said in bed to the Queen of Sheba. An extract of self-mockery and of tragedy constructed according to the logic of dreams; the germ of his poetry should be sought in dreams: some are simply dreams that he wrote down, although, to be sure, every dream undergoes revision, as we know, and justifies *écriture automatique* to only a limited extent. "Liberated words" were expected to bear fruit, but after the first Futurist (or, as Wat preferred to say, Dadaist) attempts they were enslaved in Polish poetry for several decades by the poetry of both Skamander and the Avant-Garde alike. Those of Wat's poems that I have managed to translate into English fascinate the young in Berkeley and San Francisco because they are zany—like Marx Brothers films. But, in fact, what attracts the students is probably something that is rarely met with in the sad buffoonery of zany contemporary literature: electrically charged contents, a percentage of felt truth.

"He dwells neither in its temple nor in rooms that he has himself chosen." Wat wanted to bequeath to posterity a great work in prose; all the faces of the wronged, the humiliated, the tortured who visited him in his dreams demanded this of him. This does not mean that he was unsure of the value of his poetry, but he appeared to treat it as stages of a monumental striving. We might say that it was forced upon him by the broken rhythm of his existence, by the incessant pendulum of hours sacrificed to and stolen by pain, so that only brief note-taking was within his grasp. On occasion, poets have created masterpieces by concentrating on a single genre, meticulously refining it, but it may well be that dazzling phenomena in literature more often emerge almost in passing.

New hierarchies are taking shape these days in twentieth-century Polish poetry; more than one honored name is being eclipsed and others are slowly emerging into the foreground. I would place Wat's poetry very high in this new hierarchy, but not because I am writing this immediately after his death. I do not believe in all those avant-garde posturings, in ever newer versions of aestheticism, because these things are not for people. The chaos of criteria is so dense that Wat's poetry, which is hypercontemporary, technically exquisite, zany, bears a surface resemblance to those performances of the faint-hearted and the vacuous who, despite using yet another formal device, have nothing to say. It will be seen eventually that a universal grievance found expression in his egotistical grievance; its severe and simple outlines, concealed in a thicket of allusions, will be unveiled, and several of his poems will appear in popular anthologies in the vicinity of "About Fridrusz Who Was Killed by the Tartars at Sokal in the Year of Our Lord 1519," which is as much as any poet can wish for.

No, the truth about our era will not be portrayed in an epic poem, in a *War and Peace*, or in a profound sociological analysis. At most, flashes of insight, halting words, brief sentences:

> *Journey to Sicily*
> *The colors that I delight in—*
> *The butterfly flutters away from them*
>   *with loathing.*
>
> *The flowers that I paint—*
> *don't put them in a vase:*
>   *the vase will break.*
>
> *The landscapes that I row through—*
> *Bosch could not have endured them:*
> *He did not suffer like this.*

Shamelessly private? Or, through this privateness, as universal as one could hope for, only different in this case from what goes on in impersonal descriptions of a world of anti-colors, anti-flowers, anti-landscapes, paid for by Wat (because it is "I" who delight, paint, row)?

I recommend to future researchers that they focus on the range of Wat's poetry: from the lamentations of a biblical prophet to the almost mathematical wit of his gnomic maxims. It is not that Wat never thought about poetic technique, that he was not continuously in search of a technique of his own, which would be malleable enough to suit his purposes. He aspired to assure poetry a greater *capacity*, which could be as thoroughly destroyed by lyrical "purity" as by garrulousness. In his conversations with me he would describe this more or less as he did in the May issue of the London periodical *Oficyna Poetów*, which is devoted chiefly to his work: " . . . my so-called formalistic interests seem to be aimed solely at locating and maintaining myself on the narrow boundary between prose prose (God forbid, not poetic prose!) and poetic poetry (definitely not prosaist's poetry)."

If I had to introduce Wat's poetry to a Polish reader who was totally unfamiliar with it, I would most likely begin with some poems whose instrumentation is simple and whose thematics link historic events with motifs borrowed from the Old Testament. For example, "Hebrew Melodies," about his sojourn in exile in Asia:

> On the Babylonian shores we were sitting, exhausted.
> "Sing!"—the guards were shouting—
> "Now sing, and sing lively
> a war song of Zion and a mournful hymn to Yahveh.
> Let the music of slaves caress our ears!"

> We would sing—
> were our song a poison!
> We would sing—
> were its words a dagger!
> We would sing—
> were our song a curse—
> and not a joy, not freedom, not a blessing!
> What do they know of Yahveh, Baal's worshippers,
> what do they know of the sweet pith of Zion's songs!
> And there were among us those who sang for the strangers.
> The Just Lord struck their lips dumb with leprosy,
> their harps are smashed, their candelabra trampled into dust
> and their houses shamed by dereliction.

> [Translated by C.M. and Leonard Nathan]

Next I would read a poem about night in a Soviet prison, from "Nocturnes":

> Was spricht die tiefe Mitternacht
>
> —Nietzsche

> What does the night say? Nothing.
> The night
> has a mouth
> sealed with plaster.

The day—why, of course. It chatters.
Without caesuras, hesitations, without a second
for deliberation. And it will chatter on like that
until it collapses and dies
of exhaustion.
And yet I heard a scream
in the night. Every night. In the famous
prison on the Lubyanka.
What a beautiful contralto. At first
I thought it was Marian Anderson
singing spirituals. But it was a scream
not even for help. In it
were beginning and end
so fused there was no knowing where
the end ended
the beginning began. That
is the night screaming.
That is the night screaming.
Although its mouth
is sealed with plaster.
That is the night screaming. Then
the day commences its tralala
until it collapses and dies
of exhaustion.
The night—it will not die.
The night does not die
though its mouth
is sealed with plaster.

Then the poem "Easter," which refers to the spring of 1943 in Warsaw:

In a two-horse carriage
an orthodox old man
with a top-hat on his head
drives away from the synagogue
swaying and talking to himself:
I am the king, I am the king, I am the king.

The men stand in a double row
The women watch from windows

The children hang garlands
The gendarmes kneel in the street.

Then Yahveh stretched out His hand
swept the top-hat from his head
planted a crown of thorns.
And the orthodox old man
in the two-horse carriage
rode straight in to heaven.

Smoke hangs over the city
Garlands of hanged children
The women lie in the street
The gendarmes stand in a double row.

Next, a poem about his own illness, which takes the shape of something inflicted *from the outside*, a prison, and thus somehow the personal is merged with the historical:

In the four walls of my pain
there are neither doors nor windows.
I only hear: a guard is walking
back and forth beyond the walls.

His muffled hollow steps
pace off blind duration.
Is it still night or dawn already?
It's dark within my four walls.

Why is he walking back and forth?
How will he reach me with his scythe,
when within the cell of my pain
there are neither doors nor windows?

Somewhere the years must be flying
from the fiery bush of life.
Here, a guard walks back and forth
—a specter with a blind face.

Now, at last, it would be time for the only religious sonnet in the history of Polish poetry that is about a Christ who, in the name of compassion for mankind, *does not want* to rise from the dead:

The man from Arimathea laid Him in the grave
and covered it over with a block of stone.
And sat down to repent, to weep for hope,
that is merely illusion?

At night two seraphs approached.
They rolled away the stone, saying, "Rise, O Lord!"
And gave Him their hands, that He might rise and go with them,
so that the resurrection of the Lord might come to pass.
"I shall not rise!" He said to them. "I shall not rise until
man, too, is set free
from death and pain."

That Joseph has long since ceased his repentance.
And turned into dust . . . But He is still awaiting
the liberation of man.

I don't believe that an introduction such as the one I have proposed would be unnecessary or unjustified. People write about poetry today in a far too convoluted fashion, as if in the final analysis it doesn't all come down to efforts at naming our common fate as the condemned men in Pascal's dungeon. I would like it to be noted that in the poems I have cited there is no devaluation of the world, such as is found in contemporary nihilism. Wat was not a nihilist; that is, he did not attack the value of existing things, taking revenge on them for the fact that the subject (I, we, they) is condemned to suffering. The radiance and splendor of nature, of architecture, of works of art, of human joy, of the ever-renewed happiness of new generations are always present—a radiance and splendor that remain untainted by the fact that individual or collective fate has forbidden me or us to rejoice in them. In this, I think, lies the maturity of Wat's poetry, distinguishing it from the art created by all those who do not admit that they are only indulging in self-pity when they don the mask of men who sit in judgment over God—which, intellectually, is an appropriate occupation only for fourteen-year-olds. It is precisely the grievance of Wat-the-sufferer—because it is so personal, so obviously attached to a specific "I" or "we"—that protects him from those generalizing impersonal forms (one walks, one lives, one consists of, one does not consist of, etc.) and from pseudo-philosophy. I would number among his greatest achievements the little notations of homage and wonderment at the dignity of reality that are like pen-and-ink sketches, for example, "In a Bar, Somewhere near Sèvres-Babylone"—but the instrumentation here is lavish, intricate, and I promised to begin with the most simple. It will suffice to cite some shorter descriptions that are in no way inferior. In "Songs" Wat used a motto that confirms what I said a moment ago about his objectivity through subjectivity (the reverse of the singers of generalized disgust and revulsion). This motto, from A. Lang's *Homer and Anthropology*, goes as follows: "It is the nature of the highest objective art to be clean. The Muses are maidens." Which is followed immediately by this landscape, observed from a vantage point that I know well, from La Messuguière, a writers' colony near Grasse:

> So beautiful the lungs
> are breathless. The hand remembers:
> I was a wing.
> Blue. The peaks in ruddy
> gold. Women of that land—
> small olives. On a spacious saucer
> wisps of smoke, houses, pastures, roads.
> Interlacing of roads, O holy diligence
> of man. How hot it is! The miracle
> of shade returns. A shepherd, sheep, a dog, a ram,
> all in gilded bells. Olive trees
> in twisted benevolence. A cypress—their lone shepherd. A village
> on a Cabris cliff, protected
> by its tile roofs. And a church, its cypress and shepherd.
> Young day, young times, young world.
> Birds listen, intently silent. Only a rooster crowing
> from below in the hamlet of Spéracèdes. How
> hot it is. It's bitter to die on foreign soil.
> It's sweet to live in France.

> —from "Songs of a Wanderer"
> [Translated by C.M. and Leonard Nathan]

To live is sweet. *I* am dying, but the world's youth remains. I, too, walking down a Paris street, stop for a moment to look at the pictures of a painter in which the invisible but present has been captured ("At the Exhibit"):

> Our world. So small
> that one guitar
> is enough

to populate it with sounds—
if played by Love.

Love is not seen
though it is present.

Beside the guitar a patera with apples
—a mark of royalty
known from the tarot;
the realization of evil-good;
the fruit of the Hesperides
but not made of gold,
on the contrary—of colors
from our world
which is so small
that one guitar
is enough
etc.

All this is seen
except Love
which is not seen
though it is present
in a small exhibit
of a picture dealer
on Faubourg Saint-Honoré.

[Translated by C.M. and Leonard Nathan]

Young poets think that simplicity is a lack of originality, that a line of poetry in which the words "are not astonished by each other" must be bland. That's not surprising. In order to have the kind of lightness of touch that Wat had, the gift of spontaneous *circumstantial* sketching (and Goethe insisted that there is no poetry that is not circumstantial), one must have experienced many things and be capable of many things; only then do the most ordinary words do the job. But let me get on with my argument; I cite the following in order to demonstrate that Wat's Muse is a maiden:

So your world is pure once again, like the breast of a young
    mother?
the traces of treason, blood and terror all erased?
Timorous, I stand before it, I touch its knocker,
but I dare not knock. I am like the poor guest.—

He was invited here to highlight the splendor of this house,
but he recognizes no one, and no one knows him.

The garden blazed in the sunlight as on the first days of Creation
and at this gate even I—like a specter—have no shadow.

Some may prefer the poems in which his style is "impoverished"; others, those in which it is "rich." Up till now I have selected only the former in order to refute the opinion that his poetry is a tropical thicket of baroque ornamentation (though Wat used to speak warmly of the Baroque). If the latter seem difficult on first reading, it is worth remembering that real places and real events appear in them, transformed, elevated, frequently made more dignified by humor. One could write a commentary on Wat's poems, relating each of them to what transpired on a particular day, in a particular year. Thus, "Return Home" ("There was so little in this poor head!: a bowl of cream of wheat / which the cafeteria had run out of by the time it was my turn") is a transposition of nighttime floundering through the muck and standing water of a square in Alma Ata. The "three good buddies, around a samovar with vodka and cucumbers" from *Mediterranean Songs* are Stalin, Voroshilov, and Kaganovich signing General Yakir's death sentence. A stroll through Oxford with his wife turns into an incredible burlesque after they encounter a turtle which, though reluctant to talk, nevertheless deigns to share with them a few selected stories of his forebears (for he himself is only 293 years old) before he falls into a rage because Wat (I am deliberately not saying "the lyric I"!) used to eat his relatives in Ili, in the Kazakhstan desert. A hunter wearing his cap at a jaunty angle, encountered on a street in a Provençal town, gradually changes into the Hunter, who symbolizes death. And even a minor incident in Warsaw returns (guilty conscience) in disguise; the deer is Wat himself:

> *I remember,*
> *a braggart stag, proud of his necklace,*
> *a changing rainbow in sunny dew,*
> *walked through Waliców, and in a window open to summer*
> *fragrance, to an array of lilacs and of chestnut trees in bloom*
> *a boy was sitting. He wore a skullcap,*
> *his black eyes stared nowhere. I remember,*
> *the stag mocked, he said something so mocking*

that the child withdrew into the room,
                                    offended.

—*"Dreams from the Shore of the Mediterranean"*
[Translated by C.M. and Leonard Nathan]

My task now is not to supply a key, which everyone can choose
for himself, after all, and one key will be as good as another; that's
not the point. I just want to emphasize that Wat's imagination is
always anchored in dramatic action and (fortunately) not "liberated"; that is, it does not turn back on itself. It is appropriate, then,
when approaching it, to avoid using terms that are too convoluted
or grandiloquent. Do the poems I have selected represent him adequately? Not necessarily. I might perhaps have even preferred others, the ones with longer phrases, spoken in a slow voice, or those
that have a strong beat, as in the opening lines of this "Song of a
Wanderer":

Disgusted by everything alive I withdrew into the stone world:
  here
I thought, liberated, I would observe from above, but
                                    without pride, those things
tangled in chaos.

[Translated by C.M. and Leonard Nathan]

The aim of this article was to explain why a small coterie of friends
made such a fuss over Wat—aside from ordinary human considerations, we knew with *whom* we were dealing. This coterie was very
small; two volumes of Wat's poems had appeared in Poland (*Poems*,
1957; *Mediterranean Poems*, 1962); for émigré readers Wat the poet
simply did not exist, they had never heard of him. The issue of
Oficyna Poetów and the volume of collected poems just published
by Libella in Paris will perhaps introduce a change. But a long journey through time awaits Wat's poetry; it is not worth worrying about
ephemeral tastes. Since I do not want to end with a rhetorical flourish,
I shall open *Mediterranean Poems* at random:

So I squat under the bougainvillea, the
                    one from the quarries
where naked Artemises in topsail hairdos, laden with jewels,
shot at us with golden bows, looking at our agony
                            from above. At agony—

always from above. When not seen from above, what is agony?
                              One cloud curiously white
floats away.

—*"Dreams from the Shore of the Mediterranean"*
[Translated by C.M. and Leonard Nathan]

Berkeley, 1967

WHO IS GOMBROWICZ?

THE BARD

A picturesque though bitter image appeared before our eyes after the death of Gombrowicz. Omnipotent customary Form lifted his incorporeal remains, twirled them around, and transported them into that distant land inhabited by the geniuses of bygone days. Since I, too, have contributed to this by writing a rather lyrical obituary about him, I must hasten to counteract the slavery of Form. For our native traditions have scored a much too flagrant triumph here. In life he was a buffoon; after his death, he became a king-spirit, since there is an enormous demand for king-spirits. In life he was a nut, a fop, a snob, an arrogant man; but since his death we have heard the voice of Professor Pimko, conducting the choir: "Why should we love Witold Gombrowicz?"

And the choral response: "Because he was a bard."

This game of bards, ridiculed by Gombrowicz in the past, imposes its immutable, long-established laws. You would think that if someone left behind an exceptional work, that would be enough. Not so! A bard has to be a luminous, magnificent, heroic figure; if he had a hump on his back, it will be deftly concealed when the monument is erected. And vice versa: those who try to cast doubt on his position as a bard are not interested in his work but in the details of his biography. Boy-Żeleński once led a campaign against "the bronzers," which was instructive in that it was a complete failure. Had he lived longer, he would have found that bronzing activity has increased in strength, if not in beauty, now that state governments have joined up. A few years ago, a just published book was pulped in Poland because it contained a certain unheroic document about Bard Adam. The next edition appeared minus that document, which no doubt will remain a professional secret, handed down from old to young Mickiewicz scholars when the former are on their deathbeds. Bearing in mind the power of this custom, need we be surprised that those who want to belittle the unworthy writer Witold would peer into his private letters?

Respect for Gombrowicz, for the great daring of his spirit, demands that we extricate him from these truly lamentable posthumous entanglements. This can be done only by recalling how very disturbing, provocative, enigmatic his writing was, how many insoluble puzzles it contained, how little bronze there was in it for a monument to the author who, after all, stated openly on many occasions that he built upon his own weakness. Who knows, perhaps at times it will be necessary to side with those who always admitted that they did not understand Gombrowicz, rather than with the clever folk who insist that everything in his work is clear. For Gombrowicz dealt with questions that are incomprehensible to us in this century, or perhaps at all times.

DIGRESSION

It is not popular today to judge literary works in terms of whether they are beneficial or harmful to the soul. And yet, responsibility for the current trend in Polish literature, which is, one must admit, exceptionally poisonous, has been weighing on me. After all, reading the works of Witkiewicz, Gombrowicz, Mrożek, Borowski, Andrzejewski, Różewicz cannot incline young people to view the world in a favorable light. That is why, when I walked into my class at Berkeley one March morning in 1970, I told the students before I handed out their exam questions that as an antidote they should read *Man's Search for Meaning*, by the Viennese psychiatrist Viktor Frankl. I also explained to them briefly that in the first part they would find a description of the author's experiences as a prisoner in Auschwitz, which would confirm what they knew from Borowski; in the second part, they would find an exposition of the principles of "logotherapy." Afterward, the students wrote for three hours, mainly about Gombrowicz. These young Americans, who read him only in translation (they were almost exclusively English or comparative literature students), are highly intelligent. The California spring sun shone outside the window. The huge bare feet of a young man in the front row looked black, the skin trampled and calloused. Long-haired girls wearing pants scratched their backsides and heels while they wrote. People conceive of the study of literature in many ways. But Dostoevsky, toward the end of his life, cared about one thing only:

whether "the truth is on my side." After all, sessions with students should be nothing other than logotherapy sessions or searches for meaning. This meaning cannot be ordered or forced; it must be discovered by each individual for his own benefit, in accordance with his own fate; and the person who is leading the discussion must exercise a great deal of restraint, taking as much as he gives. "Gombrowicz was my greatest discovery since reading Henry Miller and Anaïs Nin," writes a female student; good, it doesn't mean that I have to be an admirer of Miller. A nineteen-year-old writes about "the political implications of Gombrowicz's *Cosmos*," seeing, especially in the character of Leon, the insanity of the imagination to which the structural rigidity of technical societies condemns the individual today. "I dread the task of laying bare the intellectual contents of a work that is a dance," writes another. I have encountered such differing interpretations for a long time. In an Egyptian dreambook once sold at church fairs, under the entry "Dreaming about School," were the words: "deathly boredom and loss of health." But sometimes, very rarely (through the intersection of favorable circumstances), the classroom is also a place where the instructor and the student (the one who imposes form and the one who is being formed) can influence each other, where a presence is revealed, where the rites of the "interhuman church" are freely accepted. This digression about a California morning will not be unproductive. The name of the Viennese Dr. Frankl will also reappear.

AT THE MANOR

Gombrowicz was the young master of a Polish manorial estate during a historic period when the "normality" of that institution was turning into a joke and a disgrace. As a matter of fact, it is amazing how long the manor maintained its venerable melancholic aura in Poland as the social grouping most deeply rooted in native traditions. Sienkiewicz wrote *The Połaniecki Family* on the threshold of the twentieth century; the novels of Weyssenhoff and other extollers of the gentry nest were written in the twentieth century. The left's attacks on the landowning class, the proprietors of estates, fell wide of the mark. The fact that these agrarian factories (which had been in existence for centuries, ever since the rise of the plantation system) derived their profits from human labor was not the only concern. The exploitation of man, the dependence of the weak on the strong have had a stubborn existence and it is not our task today to make speeches in the name of a just society. However, on a daily basis the manorial estate celebrated the division of people into those who gather in dining rooms or drawing rooms, with a view of the lawn, and subhumans, Calibans moving about in the fields and the kitchens, and this division was veiled by the bucolic sentimentality of Polish culture. It is true that the spirit of history has treated this system very kindly for a long time. To this day we give no thought to the individuals whose labor made possible the enchanting feasts at Soplicowo. There was also a particular reason, I think, for this veil, which was expressed symbolically by the lawn, the orchard, the vegetable garden, beyond which the servants' quarters were concealed. The manor re-created on the lowest rung the general pattern that was in force on all the rungs. For the servants were not only required to work for the masters; their dependency also forced upon them the doffing of caps, the baring of teeth in a show of goodwill, and, for the girls, eager giggling in response to the master's pinches. Somewhat higher up, the petty squire doffed his cap and ingratiated himself with the large landowner, and the landowner strove through flattery to gain the attention of the magnate. This pattern is apparently indestructible; it was passed on to the bureaucracy, as any petitioner in a Polish office, both before and after the war, could easily ascertain: ingratiating behavior before those whom we depend on; indifference to the fate of those who depend on us.

In sum, Gombrowicz's experience looked like this: I, Witold Gombrowicz, am a man and my own self, but I am not allowed to be a man and my own self because I have been classified. I am Master Witold, I belong to those who are superior, and the inferior ranks treat me not as myself but as a young master. The key to Gombrowicz's entire philosophy can be found in his confessions about the games he played with the children of the farmhands and his fascination with the servants' quarters. He was not alone, of course, in taking from his childhood a feeling of shame at the dress, gestures, and customs that had been imposed on him. Others, however, simply chose to flee the manor and erase its traces. Gombrowicz had an independent mind and he soon arrived at the conclusion that when one is hunchbacked it is useless to pretend that one does not have a hump; on the contrary, speaking about oneself as hunchbacked is the way to regain one's unhunchbacked humanity. Later, he adopted this method in dealing with the different (or is it the identical?) hump of Polishness. All his books revolve around the axis that links inferiority and superiority in a mutually defined whole. The peasants standing in the rain with bared heads in front of the manor-house porch "pump up" the superiority of the master, who addresses them with a hat on his head, protected by an umbrella. A master is a master as long as a physical distance separates him from a churl. Touched by a churl, he loses his masterhood, his blue blood, which suddenly flows out of him. Gombrowicz later enriched his system of opposition with other contrasting pairs: maturity-immaturity, or the ugliness of old age and the beauty of youth; fatherland-sonland, or the duel between them. The superior, oppressed by its own falseness, the falseness of Form, yearns for the inferior, just as the inferior wants to become the superior; the mature dreams of being renewed by immaturity, just as the immature unconsciously yearns to submit to the mature; the youth imitates the gestures of the adult, but the adult, conscious of his wrinkles, idolizes the youth. The young master in the drawing room among ugly, mature adults who represent the fatherland thinks about the boys from the servants' hall and the farmhands' quarters, about inferiority, about sonland. And even the artist, conscious that Form is making him rigid and disinheriting him from indefinite possibility (because it is a choice), yearns for trash, for sleaze, for everything that is "unartistic," inane, but alive.

The action of Gombrowicz's philosophical parables (and that is what his entire body of creative work is) takes place in the manor house and the tavern, or in a manor house threatened by a tavern-brothel that exposes and verifies it. A brief survey will demonstrate this.

Ferdydurke: The school and the Youthfuls' apartment are like an introduction to the flight into real Poland, with its division into oppressed countryside and arrogant city, also with the manor house, or the division into masters and servants.

Ivona, Princess of Burgundy: The manor in the form of a fairy-tale royal court.

The Marriage: In a dream, Henryk sees his family manor transformed into a tavern, his fiancée into a slut of all trades. Is this a metaphor for Poland in general? Either a manor or a tavern?

Trans-Atlantic: The embassy as a manor. Pyckal, Baron, Ciumkała as characters from a tavern. Estancia of Gonzalez as an exact counterpart of a Polish manor. A carnival ride.

Pornografia: The Polish manor during the German occupation. Those who insist that the setting is "unrealistic" (I am not speaking of the threads of the plot; they have a different purpose) only demonstrate that they were never in the countryside during the war years.

Cosmos: A boardinghouse in Zakopane, but the picnic, which couldn't resemble an outing of manor-house society more closely, is of fundamental significance.

Operetta: The Himalay palace on the eve of and during a revolution, but this is a revolution of lackeys. That is to say, a revolution as seen by the masters in the manor house, i.e., a rebellion of servants, of churls. In the first act the lackeys lick (not figuratively!) the masters' boots.

To this must be added the short stories, above all "The Feast at Countess Kotłubaj's," where the elegant company dines on the body of Cauliflower, the child of landless peasants.

THE INTERHUMAN

Gombrowicz lived in an era that neither quantitatively nor qualitatively recalls any previous eras and is distinguished by the universality of incidents of "contagion," of individual and mass insanity. His Polish inheritance might have been a great burden, as it was for many people; however, because he focused his attention on it, rather than accepting it unconsciously, this inheritance became his most valuable asset. A comparison of Gombrowicz with Western authors, for example with Sartre, would reveal the poverty of those authors' historical-cultural experiences, a poverty which was compensated for with theory. The Polish squire was better prepared in this regard. Gombrowicz's energies were aimed at healing himself, and that is more successful as a rule than healing a world which is an abstraction. His writing, compared with practically all the books of his rivals in the West, is striking in its dispassionateness, its classical restraint, the harmoniousness of its language. That same Sartre, after all, in an interview in *The New Left Review*, expressed the supposition that the "naïve" novel is no longer possible (we know that) and that Gombrowicz has given us the model of the future "analytical" novel, shaping his novels like self-destructing "infernal machines."

Aesthetic values need not concern us too much. Obviously, an artist-craftsman has to know how to mix his paints correctly, but something else determines what he is himself: whether "the truth is with him." Certainly, a reduction of Gombrowicz's works to their conceptual skeleton would be improper, since his mind, like the mind of every true writer, both controlled and was controlled by whatever created itself under his pen. Nevertheless, his work offers his contemporaries a number of propositions, some of which can be clearly discerned, although we must always keep in mind that our "understanding" of many of the elements of this work, which were also not particularly clear for their author, will always be incomplete.

I, who was born although I did not ask to be, who was flung into the world, have no basis for proclaiming that anything outside my "I" exists. Only the data of my own intellect are accessible to me. (Gombrowicz always stubbornly repeated: Descartes, Kant, Husserl.) I also have no basis for proclaiming the existence of any objective principle of the cosmos, any "laws," not even the law of causality. But that which, it would seem, is truly mine, is not mine, because I am entangled with people, continually being constructed by them; the only reality is an interhuman reality, people are always mutually creating each other, only man can be a god to man. I, Gombrowicz, a son of the gentry and a Polish man of letters, try to be "myself" against the masks that my gentryhood and the Polish historical tradition impose on me, but by doing so, by overcoming existing Form, I am also not completely "myself," because every act of rebellion gives birth to a new Form.

Of all his works, Gombrowicz valued *The Marriage* most highly. In this new version of *Hamlet*, everything takes place in a dream, and what, after all, is more "inside the mind" than a dream? Henryk is always conscious of the fact that he is dreaming, but his consciousness is completely powerless, it cannot avert anything; Henryk participates in the action or, rather, he is acted upon by others, and whatever is supposed to happen, happens. The awareness that whatever I do is nonsense and yet I cannot act otherwise because the interhuman reality in which I find myself (even worse, which resides in my own head) forces me to do so—this is the very essence of twentieth-century schizophrenia, a feature common to daily life in technological civilization, to participation in mass movements, and to the establishment of terror. For the number of sadists among prison guards and concentration-camp guards is limited; the majority are simply bureaucrats. *Cosmos*, too, can be interpreted as a progressive descent into dream. The mind defends itself, clinging to a waking state: how absurd to build a system based on circumstantial evidence just because one has seen a sparrow hanging on a wire. But it is sufficient to take the first step in this direction and the evidence multiplies and forms itself into a system that is replete with its own logic and that generates tangible results. Thus, for example, once attention has been directed to Jews or Trotskyists, a large amount of circumstantial evidence will turn up to suggest that they are the cause of all evil. The mind's "circumstantial" tendency transforms the law of cause and effect into a mockery and imposes a dream state from which there is no awakening.

Gombrowicz's propositions, therefore, are proportional to the present record-breaking population density, the constant pressure of people upon people, a pressure that we might call incest inasmuch as that term signifies the impossibility of any relations other than with close relatives. Where on earth, then, can there be a one-on-one relationship with an extra-human world, or even with oneself? In religion? But a man who does not believe in God does not believe *out of opposition* to those who do believe in Him; on the other hand, a man who does believe in God does so *out of opposition* to those who do not believe in Him. The dying Catholic matron in *Pornografia* looks not at the cross but at Frederick the atheist, wanting to prove to *him* that it is possible to have faith; *he* is her God. For when we turn to a "reality" that is inaccessible to us, all we carry in our heads are images of human faces.

One of my students correctly noted that Gombrowicz went beyond Witkiewicz in his pessimism. In Witkiewicz there are at least Particular Existences, monads who are overwhelmed by astonishment at the very fact of how the verb *to exist* is defined, and each of these monads contains an inviolable "I." The social leveling that Witkiewicz feared (he apparently borrowed that fear from Leontiev, although he preferred to cite the much later Spengler) represented a menace that was, at least to some degree, external; for Gombrowicz, in contrast, the very nature of social intercourse causes man to dig his claws into man, so that the "I" becomes unattainable and illusory.

The twentieth century corroborates Gombrowicz. Nothing is more depressing than the sight of people who believe that they are following collective manias of their own free will, that they have been visited by their own personal, most personal revelation, while in fact their complete ape-like dependence on propaganda and advertisements could be calculated with the help of enhanced computers. The concentration camp that compresses humanity is both a model and a template of our beautiful era. That is where the game of mutual dependence between master and slave that recurs repeatedly in Gombrowicz finds its extreme and ultimate form. But though the twentieth century corroborates the author of *The Marriage*, it does not do so completely. Dr. Viktor Frankl, the psychiatrist who experienced Auschwitz, does not by any means ignore the horrifying ritual to which both executioners and victims submitted, apparently without exception. For him, a psychiatrist, the turning point occurred when he was given the striped uniform of a fellow prisoner who had vanished up the chimney and he found in its pocket a page torn out of a Hebrew prayer book with the *Sh'ma Yisroel* on it. This is a prayer of complete acceptance of everything that is received from the hand of God. What meaning is there in this? As already happened with Job, he is transported: I do not know the meaning because I cannot understand God's judgments, but this meaning does exist *beyond* my consciousness. Here the question arises: Was this prisoner's mind so controlled by people until the very end that he kept the Hebrew page *against* them, or did a genuine one-on-one relationship occur here? Dr. Frankl is convinced that the latter supposition is correct. If, however, we accept Gombrowicz's assumption and force it to its ultimate consequences, Gombrowicz the creator himself ceases to be intelligible because his striving for authenticity, his struggle with Form, will be revealed as "nothing more than" the outcome of the pressures of people upon people. Gombrowicz confesses to this contradiction in *A Kind of Testament*, saying emphatically at the same time, "Art is born out of contradiction."

NO TOUCHING

Gombrowicz's work is unique in the twentieth century, for there is not a single description of copulation in it. This must be ascribed to his refined, classical tastes and to his contempt for fashion. We should note, however, that there is also no *touching* in it. People touch other people solely in order to pump themselves up with power, to degrade the one who is touched ("*dutknięcie*" ["touching"] with a finger, "*wrzepienie*" ["pounding"] with a spur, placing a finger into the mouth of a hanged man, a blow with a knife). Albertynka in *Operetta* dreams of "life as a touched woman," but it is a petty thief who touches her by grabbing at her purse. Forever in a crowd, forever exposed to one another, people are deprived, then, of any contact with each other aside from the contact of domination. This applies to their bodies as well as to their souls. Thus, Gombrowicz, while casting doubt on the existence of anything other than the data of our consciousness, had no doubt about one thing: pain, and this pain *of the other* returned reality to the world. But what joy can be felt by a man who is locked inside his own pain if his fellow man either dominates him or is dominated by him and a *meeting* never ensues? Neither between the characters in a novel or a play nor between the characters and the author. By a "meeting" I mean the way in which, for example, Solzhenitsyn relates to the old woman in "Matryona's

House." Reading some of Solzhenitsyn's pages (and without over-estimating his role, for he represents a minuscule, powerless minority in his country), I compared him with the French writers of today. I don't know what made me recall a Soviet soldier's saying: "*Frantsuzy w shelkakh, no voinu proigrali*" ("The French wear silk, but they lost the war"). For if the dehumanization of literature is the object of a competition today, the French, wearing the silks of style (preoc-cupied, that is to say, with how one speaks, not what one says), are not far from receiving the gold medal. This is a pitiful gold medal and the appearance of even one writer like Solzhenitsyn covers them with shame. Gombrowicz stands apart from them; he used to ascribe his distinctness to his sensitivity to pain, which protected him from the folly of writing conceived out of structuralist theory. However, this was a negative advantage, in a sense, because, aside from a few pages in his *Diary*, he was unable to make anything artistic out of his sensitivity. In Dostoevsky, Stavrogin's curse and his torment is his complete isolation, and as a matter of fact, Witkiewicz must have had something of Stavrogin in him, since all the characters in his novels and plays are windowless monads. They butt horns furiously, but their pansexuality lacks both Eros and *agape*. In this regard, Gombrowicz is similar to Witkiewicz, with the difference that sex, loaded with cosmic menace in Witkiewicz, is in Gombrowicz a met-aphor for the bonds of feudal mastery and submission that destroy the autonomy of the human monad. Perhaps we deserve nothing but deformed writers. But deformity must always be called deformity.

IT'S ALL IN YOUR MIND*

Gombrowicz is not all that hard to explain to young Americans, because one of their most frequently uttered sayings is "It's all in your mind." This is the form in which the centuries-long struggle of philosophers to prove that we cannot speak of the existence of an objective world has penetrated beneath their thick heads of hair or, rather, their bushy manes. Here, then, is the reason for the contem-porary successes of Hinduism and Buddhism, a-theistic religions which lack a Creator-universe opposition or a subject-object oppo-sition. For there *are* links between that philosophy, which Gom-browicz also subscribed to, and susceptibility to the influence of the East, although stubborn as he was in his attachment to Western

* In English in the original.

Europe, Gombrowicz would have resented this greatly. I am sorry to have to philosophize, but unfortunately C. G. Jung must be quoted here, even though his language is scholarly and therefore not graceful: "Psychic existence is the only category of existence about which we have *immediate* knowledge, since nothing can be known unless it first appears as a psychic image. Only psychic existence is immediately verifiable. To the extent that the world does not assume the form of a psychic image, it is virtually nonexistent. This is a fact which, with few exceptions—as for instance in Schopenhauer's philosophy—the West has not yet fully realized. But Schopenhauer was influenced by Buddhism and by the Upanishads."*

I confess that the wisdom of the East is inaccessible to me, but in my defense I can cite this same Jung, who asserts that the Western mind encounters insurmountable difficulties when it attempts to grasp the essence of that wisdom, and if it thinks that it has grasped it, it is mistaken. That is why so many young Americans are falling victim to a fuzzy syncretism. It is appropriate to inject the East into this discussion because its continuous presence, especially in California, brings into relief, by means of contrast, a number of characteristic features of Gombrowicz's thought.

The interior of the mind . . . It is a well-known fact that people who suffer from a persecution mania interpret the most innocent gestures, words, looks as proof of a conspiracy against them. We refer colloquially to a disturbance in their sense of reality, assuming that there is a reality which their minds interpret incorrectly. But if the suspicion arises that the difference between the "normal" man and the paranoiac is a difference of degree or orientation, that the mind is always left only to its own devices (this is the essence of *Cosmos*), then what? The medicine that Gombrowicz used was the greatest possible honing of consciousness and strengthening of the ego. "*I* think, therefore I am." His mind is as Western as can be. A Buddhist, starting from similar assumptions—for him, both "reality" and the gods are projections of the mind—will declare that whoever wishes to save himself by honing his consciousness and strengthening his ego is a madman, for he condemns himself to delusions fabricated by the ego and entangles himself in a circle of anguish. The liberation a Buddhist strives for has nothing in common with finely honed consciousness, and it is precisely the "other dimension," which he

* *The Collected Works of C. G. Jung*, 2nd ed., eds. Sir Herbert Read, Michael Fordham, Gerhard Adler, William McGuire—exec. ed.; trans. R.F.C. Hull (Princeton: Princeton University Press, 1969), vol. 11, 480–81.

enters by getting rid of the ego, and that is quite simply forbidden to us who have been raised in another tradition—unless we feign knowledge about that which we do not understand.

There are so many threads here that I must impose some limits on myself, because I am not writing a specialized treatise that demands dry terminology and long sentences; they are useful only if one is paid by the line. I only want to draw attention to the complexity concealed beneath Gombrowicz's seemingly straightforward parables.

In the Judaeo-Christian tradition, the "thinking I" has found the means to turn against itself and to pronounce a verdict of distrust against itself. The concept of sin is identical with the concept of *self-love*; that love for oneself is our nature, whence the opposition between Nature and Grace is derived. Contemporary literature continues this tradition on occasion; see, for example, Camus's *The Fall*. In addition to the concept of sin, another means has been to pull the ground out from under our feet by an attack on the presumed independence of the "thinking I." I am under the impression that what I feel and think is mine, but in fact it is not mine at all, because I am directed, determined (by the subconscious, by the class to which I belong, etc.). Gombrowicz's strategy is similar to the Freudians' and the Marxists'; he differs from them in that they establish causal ties that reach into the past (the history of illness, the history of societies), whereas he specializes in the *now*, which is to say, in the phantasmagoria created in the mind by its exposure to the interhuman, by constant role-playing. Here, I am afraid, is the point at which I cease to understand Gombrowicz. He who fights fire with fire, or employs consciousness to discover what defines consciousness, is seeking "salvation" of a sort. But what kind of "salvation" (truth, authenticity) is there if, as in Gombrowicz, phantasmagoria is inescapable and Form breeds Form without letup? Who, for example, is demonic Frederick in *Pornografia*? A disembodied spirit, we might say, were it not for the fact that his ugliness as a mature man, his suffering from his *lack of a body* bestow upon him the role of a perpetrator, a procurer, who (with the help of circumstantial evidence) unites the teenage couple, Karol and Henia, organizes an entire spectacle in his imagination, and that spectacle, engendered by the lust of an impotent man, the lust for feudal power over others as a substitute for sex, becomes independent, dictates its own laws, going so far as to add corpses "for flavor," for symmetry, like the corpse of the young Skuziak.

It is not literature's task to provide answers; it is sufficient if it poses questions. No doubt. But the author seeks answers, for if he were not seeking, he would not pose the questions; the reader is also seeking. The book lies between them like a piece of evidence. The derisive moralizing fervor of Gombrowicz, who often spoke out as a teacher with important truths to impart, emboldens us to take him at his word. The writers he cited most frequently were probably Shakespeare and Dostoevsky. I deeply regret that I never discussed Dostoevsky with him, and now I will never know how he would have behaved upon hearing that there are many points of convergence between his technique as a writer, especially his central problem, and *Notes from the Underground*. Dostoevsky's hero-narrator rebels against his subjugation to "rational" human activities and goals, which contradict his free will. He chooses his misery as a downtrodden creature—only let it be a completely conscious misery. And he hones his consciousness, but it only reveals his hopeless dependence on people, precisely what he had rebelled against—a dependence even on the reader, whom he reviles, whom he flirts with, for whom he puts on airs. *Notes from the Underground* depicts an ego gone mad; it is a negative proof by means of *reductio ad absurdum*. For Dostoevsky, it was a stage on the road to the characters of Alyosha Karamazov and the monk Zosima.

Another resolution is possible, however: the creative act. Gombrowicz the creator emerges as consciousness elevated to the second power, as a sort of super-Frederick organizing the spectacles of his own creations, his "infernal machines." And there is no doubt but that he succeeded. The work constructed by him served as his guiding star, it constructed him, and he ended his life as master of his own estate. But we are not very far here from Przybyszewski's manifesto and "the priesthood of art." I shall not presume to declare if art can "save." Many arguments speak against it, especially now, when the very concept of art seems to be disintegrating. In any event, the redemptive power of art appears only when art is not sufficient unto itself, as Gombrowicz was perfectly well aware. "In literature, which, fortunately, is not pure art, but is more than art . . ." he says in *A Kind of Testament*.

The aphorism "It's all in your mind" seems dubious to me. The objective world most likely has its own weight and laws, among which is the law of the co-creation of people through Form. Even if Form always reaches us from the inside, kindling phantasmagoria in our minds. Gombrowicz offered some positive recommendations and we ought to ponder them.

Nakedness

I reject every order, every concept
I distrust every abstraction, every doctrine
I don't believe in God or in Reason!
Enough of these gods! Give me man!
May he be like me, troubled and immature
Confused and incomplete, dark and obscure
So I can dance with him! Play with him! Fight with him!
Pretend to him! Ingratiate myself with him!
And rape him, love him and forge myself
Anew from him, so I can grow through him, and in that way
Celebrate my marriage in the sacred human church!

—The Marriage
[Translated by Louis Iribarne]

Hail, eternally youthful nakedness!
Hail, eternally naked youth!

—*Operetta*

Every act of faith meets with a warm response within us, because we want to have faith. When, however, at the end of Krasiński's *Un-divine Comedy* the atheist and revolutionary, Pankracy, seeing the cross in the sky, cries out, "*Galilaee, vicisti!*" and dies, this seems to be not so much a dialectic as a quite desperate literary device intended to atone for the thoroughly pessimistic contents of the play. The quotations from Gombrowicz are grounded in the energy that radiates from his work. The celebration of naked, youthful man is, after all, no doubt the most accessible aspect of his work today, since Rousseau's noble savage has become fashionable once again. Presumably, that celebration would also have met with approbation from the Los Angeles psychiatrist who puts a group of naked men and women into a heated swimming pool and advises them to stroke, touch, and embrace one another, and to address each other in baby talk, so that they may regain their innocence (and sexual potency). In Gombrowicz's works, however, it is impossible to find any data from which one might derive an optimistic inference about the triumph of eternally naked youth. The descent into immaturity, into which the thirty-year-old hero is compelled by Professor Pimko in *Ferdydurke*, amounts to a discovery that youngsters are totally manipulated by adults, in their obedience and their rebelliousness alike. The two parties in the school, that of the idealist Syfon and the lewd Miętus, fulfill a rule of adolescent conduct that appears to have been dictated from above. The perfectly groomed paragons of virtue are the rude slobs' *raison d'être*, and vice versa, just as in the story about the philosophers, the synthetist Filidor and the analyst anti-Filidor are inseparably linked and could not exist on their own, and just as in general in Gombrowicz people who believe in something require non-believers, and non-believers would be suspended in a void were it not for the believers. Youth are as imprisoned by the law of Form as are adults, and the one thing that can be cited in their favor is their softness, their malleability, so that, in contrast to their elders, they are always a promise—but it is precisely their innocent incompleteness that seduces their elders, who want to exercise power over them, just as Henia and Karol seduce Frederick in *Pornografia*.

What, then, is Man, liberated from abstractions, doctrines, ideas, young, immature, open to everything? It just occurred to me that I myself, a long time ago, to be sure, in the spring of 1956, wrote *A Treatise on Poetry*, in which there is a rather peculiar idea. The City, Society, the Capital are defeated in it by the sight of a girl in a window of a gloomy tenement house (I can still see her from the train window, in the smoky air near the Gare Saint-Lazare, as she sits in front of a mirror, putting her hair up in curlers)—defeated, that is, by a specific human being. And from this comes a conclusion:

> *From walls and mirrors, windows and paintings,*
> *Ripping apart curtains of cotton and silver,*
> *Man emerges, naked and mortal,*
> *Ready for truth, for speech, and for wings.*
>
> *Weep, Republic! Cry out: "On your knees!"*
> *Test your spells with megaphones.*
> *Listen—in the ticking of the clocks*
> *Your death is coming, dealt from his hand.*

Unfortunately, perhaps a grain of irony is hidden in those curlers (the apish dependency on fashion)? Man liberated from all bonds is either a never-realized project or nothing, an anti-man. Dr. Henryk Skolimowski, in his essay "The Antinomies of Form in Contemporary Art," develops an analogy between the (liberating) figure of the jester in Gombrowicz and the (liberating) figure of the jester in Leszek Kołakowski. Let us note, however, that Kołakowski's jester is no less intertwined with the priest than is Gombrowicz's Filidor with anti-Filidor. Were there no priest, there would be no jester. In just the same way, in his monumental tome on seventeenth-century Christianity, Kołakowski opposes religious consciousness to the bond of the Church, but this consciousness is somehow nourished, negatively, by the bond of the Church and becomes, in turn, frozen inside it in order, once again, to turn against it.

Albertynka in *Operetta* (a girl-boy; compare Albertine in Marcel Proust) dreams of nakedness, while Szarm and Firulet (adults, society) frenziedly cover her body with costly garments. After the revolution, when everything has turned into chaos and the donning of shabby remnants of old costumes, Albertynka, who had apparently died, emerges radiant, triumphant, from her coffin. "Hail eternally naked youth!" "Tee hee," says the Devil, as he leafs through Gombrowicz's other books. From the look on his face we have to conclude that they will dress her immediately, oh my, will they dress her, and much more effectively than those two idiots, Count Szarm and Baron Firulet, could manage.

We may hazard a guess that the fame of several Polish authors in the West is the result of misunderstanding. This does not mean that their fame is undeserved but that they are appreciated for something other than what they ought to be appreciated for. Only a person who is dressed can be undressed; one can be a jester only in relation to a priest. But the Western world has shed God, fatherland, Victorian morality, reason, even the ordinary principles of decency. It is the Stomil family from Mrożek's *Tango*. When this lovely operation is over, however, all that remains is life's nakedness, which is definitely not lovely to look at, because its name is nothing, *nada*. And that is why the West is feeling nostalgic now for robes, for ritual, for a new priesthood; that is, for principles that would empower them to murder others in the conviction that what they are doing is good. As for the French intellectuals whom Gombrowicz came in contact with, they are in a much more favorable situation because they have had practice for generations in undressing without getting undressed: a Jacobin-gourmet ritual. Doesn't Gombrowicz note in his *Diary* that once, when he started to remove his trousers at a Paris *dîner*, people fled through the doors and the windows?

What determined Gombrowicz's work, however, was not his clash with those people. What determined it was his resistance to Polish custom, to tradition, and to the absolutes that that tradition has sanctified. Their power, their rootedness in history, their ability to be reborn in doctrines and abstractions cannot be comprehended by the foreigner. But there goes Gombrowicz loosening those bonds, an anti-Filidor whose *raison d'être* is the Polish Filidor, and he approaches his foreign reader, who is suffering from a lack of bonds and is ready to idolize that which has already tormented us excessively. That reader, I suspect, in his attempt to find a label for Gombrowicz, will see in him only a "further development" of the unraveling and destruction of all robes, a "further development" that is so new and still so exciting that Gombrowicz is intellectually sharper, more complex and well-ordered than his Western rivals. But this is probably a mistake: Gombrowicz is not a further development in general but only in relation to Polish literature, through resistance and opposition. Even through celebrating the rustic squire and the rustic squire within himself. He wanted to be an anti-rustic squire, but not an intellectual, not Brzozowski thundering against squires. He needed the rustic squire. Gombrowicz relishes nothing so much as his sermonizing jousting contests with his Polish readers.

IN CONCLUSION

My internal argument with Gombrowicz lasted for a long time, and now my apparent disloyalty troubles me, because here I am writing about it and yet I could still have discussed it with him not so long ago. In the final analysis, this quarrel came down to a difference in temperaments. To put it as concisely as possible: what fascinates me is the apple—the essential principle of the apple, the rules of the apple, appleness in and of itself. In Gombrowicz, on the other hand, what is emphasized is the apple as a "psychological fact," the reflection of the apple in consciousness. These two temperaments probably delimit a fundamental divide in the history of human thought. But in Gombrowicz there was also a constant striving to break through beyond consciousness, beyond the automatic trap. His energy ("let new tones resound") condemned the contemporary literature of apocalyptic-demonic despair, and he accused the French *nouveau roman* of *disloyalty to reality*. In fact, his most invigorating, most impassioned pages, about the pain of animals and humans that serves to verify reality, appear to restore the existence of the objective principle—of the apple and the world.

This is the only way I can be loyal: by showing how much there is in Gombrowicz that remains to be understood. May the critics occupy themselves with this, rather than digging into the details of his biography. You have a writer; rejoice! Reserve your noble biographies for authors whose rachitic works need propping up with a legend.

Berkeley, 1970

ON CREATORS

Creative is a term of praise much affected by the critics. It is presumably intended to mean original, or something like that, but is preferred because it is more vague and less usual (cf. "seminal"). It has been aptly called "a luscious, round, meaningless word," and said to be "so much in honour that it is the clinching term of approval from the schoolroom to the advertiser's studio."

—H. W. FOWLER, *A Dictionary of Modern English Usage*

Sometimes the career of a single word can lead us to the very crux of the problems of the century or period when that word became widespread. The English word *creative* means gifted with the property that is called "creativity" (creative ability). It is highly likely that, until quite recently, even the concept of such a human quality did not exist. We cannot find it on any list of virtues. Let us also direct our attention to the ways in which it differs from all the qualities that once were demanded of artisans and artists. Talent, cleverness, skillfulness always meant that a person was able to carry out what he intended to do; that is, emphasis was placed on aspiring to a particular goal through the application of means appropriate to that goal. A goldsmith who prided himself on his creations did not think of them as the fruit of some general *creativity* that dwelt within him, but only as the result of good workmanship. And a poet, no doubt, did not ascribe to himself a more general creative power than a gift for composing verses. True, the career of the words *creative* and *creativity* should be traced back to the time of the Romantic crisis, especially among the poets. They were helped in this by the noun *poiesis*, making; the Greek *poiein* is a noble verb. The Old Testament in the Greek version, the Septuagint, begins: *En arche epoiesen ho theos ton ouranon kai ten gen*—In the beginning God made (*epoiesen*) the heaven and the earth.

The development of the concept "creative" (and "creativity") can probably be studied most easily in English. The French language, proficient at utilizing words of Latin origin, has not coined such compound monstrosities as *creative arts* and *creative writing*. Nonetheless, an increase in the prestige of this concept can be seen there, too; one eloquent sign of this is the title *Evolution créatrice*—in English, *Creative Evolution; Ewolucja twórcza* in Polish. As for Polish, let us note that the word *twórczość* (creativity) cannot be found in Linde's dictionary. Yet not quite one hundred and fifty years later, lo and behold, the chief literary journal in Poland is the monthly magazine *Twórczość*.

After these introductory remarks, let us go backward in time and focus on a European society from before the Industrial Revolution. A child born at that time, even if he was a male, would have been more dependent for his future fate on the position of his family than on the orientation of the stars, especially in regard to his choice of a profession. Without assuming too great a risk, one could have predicted that a peasant's son would plow the soil and a squire's son would take up soldiering and supervise the labor of his peasants. A certain number of professions were open to a child from the merchant class, because the trades and commerce did not have to be inherited; furthermore, the arts were practiced in conjunction with the trades. With rare exceptions, wood carvers, architects, painters, musicians were born in urban households, not in peasant huts, nor in palaces. Nevertheless, whether a boy was apprenticed to a baker or a shoemaker, a painter or an organist, depended to a significant degree on the bonds of kinship or friendship within an area of neighboring streets. The clerical estate provided an important outlet for assorted talents, especially in the monasteries, where the monks were required to specialize in gardening, in music, in the copying and illumination of manuscripts. A general social mobility, both vertical and horizontal (i.e., from profession to profession), was not, however, widespread; thus, the adjective *creative* as a positive evaluation establishing the ability to choose one's occupation could not appear, nor would it have been understood.

The changes that came later can be demonstrated by the example of the nineteenth-century city street, which some of us may know from experience. Two rows of apartment houses, with gates opening on courtyards around a well, supplied an extraordinarily large number of people with shelter, for a large number of cramped apartments crowded around every stairwell, especially on the upper stories. The majority of the tenants earned their living by selling their labor in factories, stores, or offices, or by working at home in cottage industries. A questionnaire would also inform us that they, or their parents, most likely had migrated from the countryside or from small towns. An insignificant minority of the tenants, located on the lower floors, was composed of merchants who invested money, owners of small factories or restaurants, and also representatives of the "educated" professions: doctors, dentists, lawyers. It is highly likely that not a single person would be found on this street who would qualify for the title of artist. The only candidates for such a title would be the violinist, who earned his living by playing in a tavern, and the wife of a certain lawyer, who would perform on occasion as a singer at charity concerts. It's not worth quarreling about whether and to what extent this schematic street has by now been relegated to the past. It is characteristic of the history of human communities that various formations exist simultaneously, and therefore nothing is truly exotic. Anyway, regardless of this or that particular modification, we need only focus on a couple of characters in one of the apartment houses on that street and consider their fate in order to discover that we have not strayed very far from nineteenth-century models. Doesn't the tailor on the fifth floor, by virtue of his very existence, pose the question of what it means to be a tailor? If someone has become a tailor, is this a choice for eternity, since the very essence of tailoring, which at first implanted itself in him quite timidly, has gradually eroded all his individuality so that he has been changed into an ideal tailor? And the laborer from the public works, one floor above him, was he ever and can he ever become someone other than the sullen hulk in a workingman's cap who regularly gets drunk every payday and beats up his wife? Such questions, which are very difficult to pose, as is usual when we are disarmed by apparent obviousness, were formulated in the last century and were the impetus for all of Marx's work; however, to this day they are still awaiting an unequivocal answer. The goal of socialism was supposed to be to save people from "freezing" in their social role; that is, everyone would develop his human qualities and would perform his professional functions only supplementally. From this point of view, in search of still tentative foreshadowings of the type of the future citizen, Marx spoke approvingly of Americans, for while in Europe caste and class distinctions drew a line between mental and physical labor, only Americans were free of such prejudices, taking up a wide variety of jobs in the course of their lives, depending on circumstances.

That's right, go ahead and turn people's heads, said the nineteenth-century reactionaries. Teach everyone to read and convince them that everyone is equal; you'll see what whims and caprices you'll have to deal with. But you will have given them nothing but extravagant longings, for they shall earn their daily bread by the sweat of their brows, and will be even more unhappy than when each of them knew he had to be content with very little and not aspire to anything higher.

> . . . The development of industry and technology, the transition to pure technology in government administration as well as in war, the substitution of technology for art and the installation everywhere of bizarre machines to which millions have been handcuffed by necessity, as if to a wheelbarrow in a penal colony. These millions, who once marveled at God's world and rejoiced in it, adorning it with poetry's dreams and with legends, now work, eat, and, cursing their past and loathing the present, wait for a new life as for the morning star, wait for that moment when uncounted millions of the rest of the human race will be added to their numbers, already many millions strong, so that all of mankind, without exception, will hold the thread correctly and turn the wheel correctly, and for this they will receive an additional pound of meat for dinner as well as a mattress for the night and a quilt under which, at long last, they will not be cold. And among this multitude of millions are people who glide like shadows with armloads of books and pamphlets that speak to them of the happiness of their labor, teach them to adore these machines, and whisper to them about the coming dawn when the remaining nations who still live meaningless lives will join with them to share that happiness and that rapture. They tell them about how someday they will overturn the official hierarchies, how they will build comfortable bunks for them, and how they will feed them—and that the day when each man will be employed and none will be hungry, will be a day of joy when all longings will be assuaged.

—VASSILY ROZANOV, "The Theory of Historical Progress,"
Russkie Vesti (1892)

Since Rozanov did not expect any good from the future, he had an irritating answer to the political passions of the Russian intelligentsia. "What is to be done?" the impatient Petersburg youth would ask. "What do you mean, what is to be done? If it's *summer*, pick berries and make jam; if it's *winter*, drink tea with that jam." Rozanov's prophecy quoted above was fulfilled, but, as usually happens with prophecies, not completely. It is true that the laboring millions curse the past and either do not like or actually loathe the present. Regardless, however, of what shape industrialization has taken, one sees everywhere the awakened aspirations of the individual, which should be taken as a plus, although no one knows what the consequences of this will be.

For a long time labor was considered a necessity, the curse of Adam, and if those who worked dreamed at all, they dreamed only about better and better-paid work and not about completely free time. Imagination did not even come up with any reasonable ideas of what to do in case the burden of elemental necessity should suddenly vanish, as is demonstrated by the story of the peasant who, when asked what he would do if he became king, replied that he would eat millet porridge with cracklings all day long and crack his whip. Throughout the twentieth century, the idea of time "for oneself"—obtained either by shortening the hours of paid labor or by devoting oneself to "creative" occupations—has progressively gained in significance.

The following observations come to mind in the final quarter of our century. A growing number of people are completing high school, and this has become the norm (in America, for example), not a privilege for the few. The level of high school is declining in direct relation to the increase in the number of students and teachers. Irrespective, however, of what the youth are receiving there, during their school years they have a sense of at least a theoretical freedom to choose their occupation; they also organize the various occupations into a table whose lower slots are filled by boring, monotonous jobs that result in a kind of slavery from a given hour in the morning to a given hour in the evening. Various necessities, both internal, e.g., lack of ability, and external, then force the majority of these young people to lower their demands. Some of them will find compensatory satisfactions and will make their peace with fate; some, going to work in factories, stores, or offices, will nurture a stronger or weaker resentment against the "system" (whatever that may be). The most curious observations, however, are suggested by the minority that does not lower its demands and considers "creative" occupations to be its calling.

The insurance company bureaucrat Franz Kafka did not think of the hours spent behind his firm's desk as his "true" occupation; he should be mentioned here as one of the great patrons of a still quite widespread duality. Modern literature (let us take it as our model; it can appear here as the representative of painting, music, etc.) owes its triumphs chiefly to such authors who write "on the side," while appearing in their public role as bureaucrats, teachers, people of independent means, etc. This particular group of individuals with a dual occupation will be the most numerous among "creators"; if we place them in the center and color them dark blue, for example, we can plot a graph of diminishing frequency on either side. On the right, the color will be diluted to the point of almost total whiteness as we approach the borderline cases: literati who lived entirely on the honoraria for their books. For example, among the members of the Professional Union of Polish Writers prior to 1939 only a negligible percentage supported themselves by the pen, and those who did were more likely to be journalists than writers of *belles lettres*. On the left side, the color will fade because the number of persons who are self-confident enough to consider their second occupation as their "true" occupation will decline—all the way down to cases that are difficult to classify, such as when someone shamefacedly keeps hidden in a drawer a couple of poems or stories written ten years earlier.

In a free-market economy the chances of supporting oneself by writing books are practically nil. The few exceptions (best-sellers) prove the rule; after all, the initiated know that even widespread acclaim brings profits that are primarily incidental, in the form of fellowships, invitations to give readings, lectures, film versions, etc. Thus, in many countries the right side of our graph will hardly be light blue, and will even grow whiter and whiter. On the other hand, as a result of the increase in the number of individuals who lead a dual, two-occupation life, we will achieve an almost black center and this dark color will be spreading sideways toward the left; in other words, more and more people consider that their salaried work deserves the expenditure of only a part of the energy that ought to be used for more lofty ends.

Kafka spent his nights toiling away at a sheet of paper. Among his successors we meet a large number of devotees of all the arts who call themselves artists. They don't limit themselves to a single specialty; they'll write a poem, then do a metal sculpture, paint, or throw pots on a potter's wheel. This would seem to indicate that opinions about so-called art are susceptible to change and that the emphasis is shifting from the final result (the work) to the activity itself: do what you like, as long as you do it creatively.

Whom, then, should we count as creators? This is quite a bewildering question. Are virtuoso pianists creators? Actors? Members of symphony orchestras? Of jazz ensembles? Architects? Is the high opinion that theater and film directors have of themselves justified? And what about ballet masters? Or dancers? Even were we to limit ourselves to the most traditional definitions and include under this concept *belles lettres*, the plastic arts, and composed music, it would turn out that in each of the industrialized countries creators form quite an army—and that they are conscious of their rights in relation to the rest of society.

Several years ago a certain Paris literary journal circulated a questionnaire among writers, asking them how they envision changes in the organization of the publishing market that would be most conducive to pursuing a literary profession. The results of this questionnaire were not at all unexpected and would have turned out the same in many other capitals. The complaints and yearnings that were expressed in the answers could be translated into an absolutely unequivocal program. We write, the respondents to the questionnaire said, but no one wants to read us. Why is this happening? Because the publishers cater to the public's low tastes, and even if they publish us they don't bother about advertising our works. Everything would change if the publishers weren't guided by financial considerations. Then both difficult poetry and experimental prose would come out in huge printings. And if this suggests that the publishing houses ought to be subsidized by or become the property of the state, then why not? We can add to this that we deserve society's total protection and that society ought to pay us because we are the creators of its culture.

Considering the situation of publishing houses in a free-market economy (their directors, as one of my acquaintances put it, are "bestialized by failure"), this was a rather reasonable program, with only one weak point that did not bear witness to a sober evaluation of their own possibilities by the participants in the questionnaire. Obligatory distribution of their poems and novels, which under socialism is usually taken care of by a network of public libraries, might well increase the size of printings; however, no governmental advertising will convince the public to consume products that are as inedible as cutlets made from minced paper. On the other hand, one cannot find fault with the demand that society should support creators, unless one questions their fundamental convictions.

Thus, a professional cohort is growing into the hundreds of thousands, wishing to be paid for its services, but under the condition that those services will not be subject to evaluation based on the fluctuations of supply and demand. Who, then, is to determine whether these services are needed? Obviously, the creators themselves. Taking this to an extreme but logical conclusion, we arrive at a rationally organized state in which the personnel of the Creative Forces, whether or not they wear uniforms and epaulets like the personnel of the Armed Forces, receive, most importantly, a salary, and a pension upon completing their term of service. But who will decide on admission into the ranks of this army? Will it be those who are obedient to their inner voice and are called in this way?

Many noble customs dull our sensitivity to new, previously unnamed phenomena if they appear under old names. We spend all our time in an immense museum of the imagination (*Le Musée Imaginaire*, as Malraux called it), in the company of famous works from the past that have been bequeathed to us by various civilizations and finding out many details about the conditions under which these works arose. Most often, they are stories of sacrifices made to one goal that was acknowledged to be the highest, of renunciations, humiliations, slander, starvation; truly, the authors of those triumphs of the human spirit nourished their progeny with their own blood, like the legendary pelican. Just think, what a disproportion: the names of a few are remembered with respect, while not a trace is left of the millions who disdained them, humiliated them, or simply were unaware of their existence. Who cares about the insurance company where Kafka worked? Who would remember the name of the commander of the Peter and Paul Fortress (General Nabokov) if one of his prisoners had not been Dostoevsky? Does it matter if Stendhal fulfilled his duties well or badly when he was consul in Civitavecchia? An artist's power over his contemporaries, as was understood very well in the Renaissance, is truly terrifying, because in comparison with him they are like poor shadows and with a single motion of the pen or brush he can rescue them from or condemn them to oblivion. A stroll through the museum of the imagination is sufficiently instructive, and nowadays administrators know that creators should be paid to maintain the honor of the house.

If someone belongs to this caste, a healthy self-defensive reflex usually prevents him from cutting off the branch on which he is sitting by expressing doubt about the occupations defined by the adjective *creative*. In Europe people used to subsume them all under a word imposed by German teachers: *Kultur*, and this word itself, which at one time was used among the receptive Slavic tribe even for the custom of brushing one's teeth, is capable of curbing skeptics. For it is ugly to oppose the blessings of culture. It is possible that someone who lives in Europe has a harder time ridding himself of a variety of silently accepted assumptions. One, for example, is the conviction that literary and artistic works have educational value. From there it's no great distance to administrators' demands on creators—if the latter want to be worthy of money and honors. The situation in places like America, where there is simply no tradition of the educational influence of literature and art, and where truly significant amounts of public funds (since the market turns out to be the worst patron of the arts) go to support creativity as such, that is, without the slightest directives as to its contents and form, is much clearer, almost clinically pure. When one stops for a moment in front of the splendidly furnished buildings of theaters and museums, which are often marvels of modern architecture, it is not easy to banish thoughts about what they are serving, that is, what theatrical arts, what exhibitions of painting, what music, what poetry evenings.

Some old words that refer to human activities continue to be used although their meaning has long since changed. *Hunting*, for example. Hard necessity, the need to put in a supply of meat, the dangers associated with this, adventures, rituals, magic incantations lent hunting a solemnity that is not to be found in ordinary sports and games. Some of this was still present when the hunter set out with a spear to hunt down a wild boar or a bear, even though he was no longer compelled to do so by necessity. But gentlemen armed with semiautomatic rifles who came to the woods for a couple of days were much less hunters than a poacher from a neighboring village—because in the latter, passion and the need to obtain meat happily coincided. And what of that *cacciatore*, whose image I cannot get out of my mind, even though I would like to? He was sauntering down the road that leads to Assisi from the hermitage where St. Francis once lived by himself, talking with the birds. It was autumn, the height of the hunting season, the time of bird migrations. The *cacciatore* was returning from a hunt, victorious, and, if I may risk using this expression even though I am not a woman, radiating a repulsive masculinity. He had a cartridge pouch and a belt around his belly, and from the belt, hanging by their necks, dangled the corpses of a dozen or so tiny song birds. Ultimately, this, too, is hunting. Although more or less as in Daudet's novel, which is worth mentioning, about the adventures of Tartarin of Tarascon. The hunters from the little town of Tarascon would go out in a group every Sunday, even though they knew very well that there was only a single hare in the vicinity and it had already been thoroughly shot up by them. But the activity itself—composed of cleaning the double-barreled shotguns, getting dressed up in the prescribed clothing, assembling, staying alert as they slipped through the stubble fields in single file, etc.—was more important than any trophy, although in theory the possibility of a trophy ought not to have been excluded, and the last hare was in a silent compact with them. A bitter secret may be concealed behind the unusually rapid increase in the number of creators of all sorts, so that their ranks are equal to the thousands of hunting clubs of Tarascon, for what would happen if it turned out that the hare is no longer alive?

"That is unfair," I hear someone saying. If the number of people devoted to creative occupations is increasing, then, considering the rarity of true talents, we will of necessity stumble across unsuccessful attempts at every step, which is why we are inclined to make such harsh judgments. But after all, there are neither more nor fewer extremely interesting, often marvelous poems, paintings, sculptures, novels today than in the past. Besides which, does this comparison of creativity and hunting hit the mark? And what do we suppose are the animals hunted by writers and artists?

Unfortunately, after lengthy consideration one has to reject these arguments and propose the following theses:

Thesis number one. The hare no longer exists. He died a natural death. This metaphor is appropriate everywhere, at all longitudes and in every system. Which does not in the least suggest that it foretells the decline of the hunting ritual. On the contrary, the more widespread the awareness that this is all for show, the more frequently do people put their fingers to their lips, signaling to each other, "Psst, shh, don't reveal the secret," the more ceremony and passion and even frenzy there is.

Thesis number two. There will be more creators with every passing year and their victory as a social group ("the creative intelligentsia") cannot be doubted, which means that their chief source of support will be state or municipal contributions.

Thesis number three. The means of recruiting them will depend on the tactics chosen by the administrators of public funds, those who hold power, that is. Basically, two tactics and their numerous permutations and combinations are possible. Either pent-up energy will be made use of in letting loose a mechanical hare (political-educational aims), and that will guarantee profits for a certain period, because everyone who chases after it will be convinced of the importance of his own role. Or, in order to have peace, creators will be neutralized by permitting them "free experimentation," which, since the hare no longer exists, will lead them to complete incommunicativeness, standing on their heads, pretending that they are lizards, chairs, and so forth.

An attempt at establishing a theoretical grounding for these theses would lead us too far astray, into an argument about some fundamental principles, and would probably not be successful. If, on the other hand, we appeal to what we see (a horse is what everyone sees it as), we meet with the complication that time is speeding up geometrically, so that what existed ten years ago loses importance. Let us limit ourselves, then, to a few observations.

The game that devotees of the Muses always used to hunt was, if I may use a rather arbitrarily chosen phrase, *man's substance* or, if you will, *substantiality*; that is, it was a question of confirming a specific faith, but not too consciously, since what faith is can be determined only when it is lacking. Some understanding of what this is is proffered by the ongoing struggle within people between form and chaos, harmony and disharmony, the defined and the indefinite —in the final analysis, nothing more than the struggle against the pressure of nothingness which undermines confidence in man's place on earth and in the universe. One can understand both the Homeric rhapsodies and Dutch still lifes as acts of bestowing a blessing, so that Hölderlin's words may be fulfilled: *Dichterisch wohnet der Mensch auf dieser Erde* [Man lives poetically on this earth]. The ability to perform such acts does not depend on any postulates or efforts of will. What has happened in the domain of the Muses during the last few decades (and is still happening) comes to light indirectly, through a lack of interest in artistic fiction on the part of readers. If a creator does not bestow a blessing, does not affirm, because he does not believe in the reality, the substantiality of himself and of what he is presenting, doesn't the reader, the viewer, the listener notice such an essential deficiency? To be sure, quite a few technically distinguished works come into being, but their very technique, for example the way the narrative is structured, is symptomatic: it is the transformation of consciousness into dream (usually a nightmare); in other words, three-dimensional objects dissolve, lose their contours. Works with a clear political tendency still preserve some degree of harmony and substantiality; however, as their short life span indicates, we are dealing with substitute game in this instance.

There has always been something miraculous about the birth of outstanding works, and a Ministry of Culture and Art could just as well be called a Ministry of Miracles. No less fantastic is the linking of "production" with "literature," since when we speak of "literary production" we imply that masterpieces can be mass-produced. There is a reason, however, why this and similar terms have come into use; they can be seen as an identifying emblem of the transformation of quality into quantity. Creators act as a group and proclaim their entitlement to a portion of society's income. There have been attempts to define similar groups as "the proletariat," "the lumpenproletariat," "the petite bourgeoisie"; there is no reason to shut one's eyes to certain features that distinguish this particular caste or stratum.

The most distinctive feature is the limited degree of its independence, which has a historical explanation. Poets, musicians, painters, sculptors have always depended on those who wield power, and it could not be otherwise, since aspiring to power or striving to maintain it demands the expenditure of all one's time and strength. As a rule, people with artistic temperaments do not have either the sword or money inscribed in their stars. But even in relation to control over minds, they would be assigned an executory role, whereas the priest, the theologian, and later the scientist had at their disposal an ample store of injunctions and prohibitions. True, we know of examples of a rapprochement between art and theology or art and science in its early phase, for example, when Leonardo was both a painter and an observer of nature; however, these were rarely alliances of equals.

Insufficient independence need not be equated with dependence on individuals or institutions, for there is also another kind of dependency: whoever employs the style of his own epoch and achieves perfection only within the limits of this style will not soar beyond his time and place. Although purely intellectual inquiry (theology, philosophy, science) is also marked by a certain style (language), it is not as obviously dated; we can demonstrate this by comparing the syllogisms or mathematical models of, let us say, the year 1650 with the paintings or poetry produced at that time, whose beauty, alleged to be timeless, seems also to benefit from the fact that it hints at the year of their birth. We refer to turning points in the history of civilization by the names of thinkers, whether it be Augustine of Hippo or Copernicus, and not by the names of even the most renowned artists. They will not build the house, that's not their job; the foundations and walls are erected by others.

Dependent for their ideas on the society in which they grew up, creators have rebelled time and again, but since first-rate minds are rarely encountered among them, each of them was more like a medium for contending forces on the same generally accepted level. The craftsman's attitude toward the artistic professions was actually conducive to good workmanship, and the later cult of Art with a capital A was a sign of serious disturbances.

The substantiality of man, to which I referred earlier, was fostered by the absolutely extraordinary amalgam of Christianity and Greek civilization. This lasted for centuries, right up to the first hours of our day, that is, until the eighteenth century. We were taught in school that Romanticism was sensibility's reaction to the coldness of eighteenth-century Reason. This is too simplistic, though it is not the worst possible formulation, provided that the opponents are identified more precisely. Simultaneously with the establishment of physics and mechanics as the foundations of the so-called scientific worldview (in 1769 Watt patented the piston for the steam engine), there was a gigantic surge of Promethean hope whose causes remain poorly understood even today. "Move from your foundations, you lump of the world!" This surge (could it have been a prophecy of spiritual salvation through steam and electricity?) was not simply a function of the scientific revolution but, rather, continued to exist in a confrontational, although incredibly complex, relationship with it, which is why, although it was given a form in literature and art and the name of Romanticism, it cannot be distinguished from the Enlightenment and its heritage by any elegant definitions. It appeared at that time that "the dawn of freedom" would bring victory to the "Divine Arts of Imagination" (Blake), that poets would be "the institutors of laws and the founders of civil society" (Shelley). Casting about for a definition, one might say that Romanticism was a movement that for the first time in history granted creators an independent position as leaders and thinkers. Their high opinion about themselves did not, alas, accord fully with the truth. In the triumphal imagination of these creators, Romanticism was actually a defensive movement: all of Greco-Christian civilization was defending itself against something conceived in its womb that would eventually destroy it. The other Enlightenment, competing with this better-known scientific one, and hostile to it, supplied the Romantics with their intellectual weapons. Neo-Platonists, members of the "mystical lodges," Swedenborg, Saint-Martin, the commentators on Jakob Boehme—people, that is, who were known as philosophers, theologians, not poets and artists—were the first to challenge the language of the sciences (and of classicism) by holding up the older language of symbols and myths in opposition to it.

Thus, the Romantics' enchantment with the Middle Ages and the Renaissance (Shakespeare, the alchemists) had hidden, deeper causes; namely, a yearning to return home, although not necessarily to a picturesque past. But this did not come to pass and the "scientific worldview" emerged victorious from their duel. Creators, under the pressure of their surroundings, gradually relinquished their Christian-Platonic assets, and after a splendid if short-lived explosion Romanticism settled in to perfecting only various shades of irony and sarcasm, and this has continued to the present time. The genius of the Romantics and post-Romantics was indisputable; their independence and resistance turned out to be minimal and their aspirations to a regime of souls rarely well-founded. A small number, who were sufficiently powerful to be unnerving, were interpreted in such a way as to avoid offending progressive people and so that their names could be mentioned in polite society. How this was accomplished would furnish enough material for more than one study. Mickiewicz, for example, who owed his greatest poetry and his very ability to write *Forefathers' Eve*, that medieval morality play, to the "coarse superstitions" of his province; Mickiewicz, with his spirits, his cabalistics, and his philosophy borrowed from Saint-Martin, was turned into a leader of the people after the universal amnesty. The prophesying gnostic, Blake, has been so cleaned up that the most perceptive books about him are omitted from bibliographies; he has been turned inside out and a meaning read into him that is the opposite of his intentions, so that now he can be the ally of liberal and leftist professors. Everyone knows what happened to poor Gogol: ahead of his time, because he was already tormented by the devil of nothingness—namely, the decline of substance, he had to watch himself be transformed, for that was what the others wanted, into a satirist advocating social ideals.

The above observations are simply intended to demonstrate that creators are like the intellectual structure of the world in which they live, and that the triumph of the "scientific worldview" presaged the swift extinction of their longed-for game. Let us loyally note that this situation strikes a blow at the devotees of a particular initiation that is achieved only through art. Obviously, the pride of creators that was awakened by Romanticism did not admit defeat. In the age of steam and electricity they were already straining to create a new justification for their rights. If the universe is devoid of any transcendental meaning, they reasoned, if man is an unexplained accident who confronts the indifferent limitless expanses in absolute isolation, for even his intellect turns against him and sides with the inexorable laws of nature or history, our only support is in the creations of our hands and of our imagination. The creative act became independent, detached from all discourses that had been monopolized by the rational order of progress, and closer to the dark visions revealed by the *dérèglement* of the five senses (Rimbaud), hashish, or, above all, by the play of the infinite combinations potentially contained in syntax, *melopeia*, the sounds of music, and colors.

Some fifty years ago anyone who took a stand against ritual in praise of ritual, observing that, after all, it would lead only to sterility, to intellectual chaos, would have been labeled a reactionary, a defender of old-fashioned "content." Alas, today one can prove to oneself experimentally what happens to the language of symbols and myths when it is deprived of its deepest reason for being and yet is honored as if nothing had gone wrong. The pursuit of a truth that is otherwise impossible to express used to be its *raison d'être*, and whatever names that truth might have borne, however much it may have been valued, a language that speaks to itself, with symbols and myths that mean nothing outside a particular closed system (a poem, a painting), gradually loses all its charm and receives its just deserts: indifference. The indifference of others—let us assume not of the creator himself. Thus, the result of the activity ceases to be its goal (for a result is in some sense objective and thus destined for others); the goal becomes the activity itself. It, too, is supposed to be rewarded by society.

"What then must we do?"
  "Rethink everything from the beginning."

1975

Part 4

TWO
PORTRAITS

ZYGMUNT HERTZ

Zygmunt, a buzzing bee in search of the sweetness of life, and the demonism of great historic events: it is difficult to reconcile the one with the other. He grew up in Poland in the 1920s, when virtually nothing of what was to happen later seemed possible. He came from a respectable family and I assume that those who knew him before the war could see in him many character traits that were common to the spoiled only sons of patrician families. A handsome man, reasonably well-to-do, who ordered his clothing from fine tailors; an habitué of cafés and dance halls, sociable, popular, he probably had a reputation as a typical gilded youth, although his enlightened, well-educated father, a social worker in Łódź and also a bit of a littérateur, had infected him with a love of books. After completing his studies and his military service in an artillery academy, Zygmunt became an office worker in the Solvay firm, which sold caustic soda. He made a decent salary, bought automobiles, traveled, lived. He met a young woman who had recently completed her law studies and was already making a name for herself in a law firm, and he married her. Zosia was lovely and her beauty went hand in hand with exceptional virtues of character, which Zygmunt probably noticed immediately. He was quick-witted, impressionable, and, I think, had a thoroughly cheerful temperament, and thus he was free of any pangs of conscience because he had so many earthly goods and so much happiness and others did not. His skepticism and, as it were, innate liberalism, protected him from both the profound soul-searching and the ideologies of our century. A private man by temperament and predilection, he shied away from politics.

When the two totalitarian states concluded the Ribbentrop–Molotov pact, replete with a clause about the division of the spoils, and unleashed the Second World War, Zygmunt was thirty-one years old. The division was carried out and as a result of the official slogan—*Nikakoi Pol'shi nikogda ne budet* [There will never again by any kind of a Poland]—roughly one and a half million Polish citizens were deported into the depths of Russia. Among them were Zygmunt and his wife, who were sent to fell timber in the Mari Autonomous Republic. His life as a lumberjack was to surface repeatedly in Zygmunt's conversation. The convoy of citizens of a state that had ceased to exist, sent off to the northern forests, came upon piles of wood that had been lying there for years due to lack of transportation and by now were rotted, like the already rotted remains of the Kuban Cossacks, the people who had chopped down that wood—which did not put the newcomers in too joyous a mood.

When I met Zygmunt in 1951, he had already lived through the exodus of Anders's army, Iran, Iraq, and the Italian campaign, after which the demobilized artillery lieutenant Hertz had attached himself to the three-man cooperative in Rome that founded the publishing house which was officially called the Instytut Literacki [Literary Institute] but was popularly known by the title of its journal, *Kultura* [*Culture*], and which was shortly afterward transferred to Maisons-Laffitte on the outskirts of Paris. Obviously, I have no intention of writing the history of *Kultura* here, but a few observations seem to be unavoidable.

Time is the enemy of our attempts at preserving reality, for it keeps piling new layers upon already existing layers, so that it is inevitable that we keep on projecting into the past. The great terror in Poland in 1951 already escapes our imagination, but it is easier to understand its causes than the phase through which the West European, or at least Parisian, spirit was then passing. This spirit, if we are to believe its pen-wielding spokesmen, was wallowing in existential melancholy because of its lost chance, that is, because the western part of the continent had been liberated by the wrong, read "capitalist," army. The few people who stammered out that maybe this was actually for the good were condemned as American agents, socially ostracized, and also dragged into the courts. The trial of David Rousset, a former prisoner of Hitler's concentration camps and author of the book *L'Univers concentrationnaire*, was being held at that time. He had had the audacity to write somewhere that there are concentration camps in Russia, too; hence the trial for libel (I don't recall on what acrobatic legal foundation it was mounted) brought against him by *L'Humanité*. Under these conditions, the émigré journal *Kultura* was absolutely isolated; in other words, the situation bore no resemblance at all to the position of the émigrés after 1831, when the European spirit welcomed them as the defenders of freedom—which frequently counted for far more than the disapprobation of governments. In our century, only at the end of the fifties or, for good measure, only in the sixties, was there a lifting of the taboo, that is, a grudging admission that émigré journals are not necessarily the hangouts of scoundrels, fascists, and agents, and that one might even invite their contributors to one's home.

So there was Zygmunt in an unavoidably heroic situation simply because, despite his inclinations, he had done some instructive traveling and now could only shrug his shoulders at the buffoonery and disgrace of the European mind strolling along Boulevard Saint-Germain. Also because while other old hands like him quietly busied themselves with making money in this West that wasn't, after all, the worst of all places, he had become a member of a cooperative that couldn't have been more obviously dedicated to impractical goals. Worse yet, he, such a private person, who so loved his own belongings and his own ways, had stumbled into a commune. This word has acquired so many meanings that perhaps it would be better to replace it with another word: *phalanstery*. This will not change the fact that *Kultura* was an insane undertaking that, for want of money, could exist only if its cooperative lived together, ate together, and worked together, giving to each according to his modest needs, no more. Zygmunt, I suspect, must have felt tempted to leave many a time. And considering his talent for getting along with people, his knowledge of languages, his energy, industriousness, he would have succeeded anywhere, in whatever he undertook to do. But he had made an emotional investment. Wonder of wonders, that commune or phalanstery or kolkhoz, the *Kultura* community, was to endure for decades.

The beginnings of our friendship. That first *Kultura* house, a rented *pavillon*, immensely ugly and inconvenient, on the avenue Corneille; the cold of winter in the outskirts of Paris, with scant heat from the potbellied *chaudières*, loaded with coal; and that district of chestnut-tree-lined avenues that went on for kilometers, piles of dry leaves, and also something reminiscent of the nineteenth century in Tver or Sarajevo. It was there that Zygmunt became the witness of my by no means imaginary sufferings. And though someone may remark that it is his own fault if a humiliated man suffers, since he deserves punishment for his pride, still, the pain is not any the less.

I started writing *The Captive Mind* on avenue Corneille, but the simplest questions were missing from it, for I truly had no one whom I could ask them of. If, as long as I remained on the Communist side, I benefited not only from material but also from moral privileges, on what incomprehensible magic grounds had I, escaping from there, been transformed into an individual whom everyone considered suspect? After all, over there it was sufficient not to be with them one hundred percent, to publish a "Moral [or dissident, as we would now say] Treatise" and be engaged in translating Shakespeare, to be considered a decent man. And a second, or maybe the same, question: Does an animal have the right to escape from a forest that has changed ownership? The European spirit had a ready-made opinion on this and it stood guard with a double-barreled shotgun, that European spirit incarnated in my Paris of Eluard, Aragon, Neruda, with whom I used to share a drink not so long ago. Because Zygmunt also knew about my miserable financial situation and visa complications, which caused me to be separated from my family for three years, he considered my situation to be dreadful. He watched over me tenderly, took care of me, and whenever I went to the city he made sure that I had a couple of francs for lunch and cigarettes. When I accepted his offerings, I was too preoccupied with my own troubles to value those gifts at the time, but I did not forget about them, and for years afterward there was a good deal of ordinary gratitude in my affection for him.

Zygmunt was already a fatty at that time, but vigorous, with a thickset body, healthy. A glutton, a gourmand, a tippler, and above all a talker, the personification of jovial humor and a passion for sociability. I say "passion" because he seemed to have a built-in radar that directed him unerringly to warm relations with others, to laughter, gossip, anecdotes, stories. He could not have borne isolation. And he himself radiated such warmth that in the gloomy house on the avenue Corneille he would take the chill out of whatever the stoves could not warm up. He often irritated me with his excesses: he would keep popping into the study, its air thick with the smoke from my cigarettes, for I lived and wrote there, and just sit down and begin a conversation; his desire to do so was stronger than his decision not to get in the way.

"Czesiu, don't talk, you'll say something stupid. Write." Zygmunt's advice, which I often repeated to myself later on, was very apt, and it referred to my bad habit of pronouncing extreme, offensive opinions out of spite. His advice was directed especially at my relations with *Kultura*, which at that time were not particularly harmonious. After all, we were creatures who were neither made nor molded in the same ways, and our meeting, at the intersection of different orbits, did not take place without friction, for which my provocations were chiefly responsible. Zygmunt, as his advice indicates, did not let himself be taken in, because he distinguished between my spoken and my written speech. He tolerated the former; the latter, he trusted.

I didn't treat Zygmunt as a friend at that time, as someone whom one chooses and with whom one is supposed to have an intellectual understanding. He was more like a classmate, assigned to us without our participation. I sought other partners for my talmudic hair-splitting. In my eyes Zygmunt was a preserved specimen of the pre-war intelligentsia, who had been formed by *Wiadomości Literackie* [*The Literary News*], *Cyrulik* [*The Barber*], *Szpilki* [*Pins*], with a philosophy transmitted by Boy and Słonimski of "The Weekly Chronicles," while I was bent on breaking away from prewar Poland in both its manifestations—the liberal and the "national." And yet, as it turned out once again, intellectual friendships and loves often take a dramatic turn, while those other ones, founded on sympathies that are harder to grasp, are often more enduring. We were not standing still, after all; we were changing, Zygmunt and I, in a way that, I think, brought us closer.

Identity crises are thresholds in everyone's life on which we can smash ourselves to pieces. To know who one is, what role to adopt and in relation to which group of people, even a small group, how one is viewed by others: in all of this, one's profession plays a prom-inent, if not key, role. That is also why I have never advised indi-viduals who were already immersed in certain professions to emigrate from Poland—especially not writers and actors. I myself, after all, had to change my profession and accept the fact that in the eyes of those who surrounded me I would be only a university professor. Before that came to pass, I had accumulated a good many interesting experiences. The obstacles aren't what's important here, although I was certainly hurt when a young Parisian author, who had been recommended to me as a translator, said outright that he would love to translate me, but if he did, he could publish nothing of his own because "they" control the literary journals. Some years later I was overcome with hollow laughter when I learned that a famous Parisian publishing house had given my new book (*Native Realm*) to a Party writer from Warsaw to referee—which is better, to be sure, than the French police of the nineteenth century gathering information about émigrés in the tsarist embassy. But let me not exaggerate the obsta-cles. In 1953 I represented France in the Prix Européen in Geneva, although the French jury surely knew that my manuscript was a translation from the Polish. It was success that terrified me, because that's when I realized that in writing for foreigners I did not know and could not know who I am, and that it was necessary to end my

French career. These adventures could not but lower my aspirations. I chose my language, unknown in the world at large; that is, I chose the role of a poet of Vistulania, as Zygmunt called it.

In light of these adventures of mine, I can summarize Zygmunt's great internal battles as I observed them; I came to feel more and more respect for him because of them. Those who have held in their hands the *Kultura* annuals and the books published by the Literary Institute, and those who will hold them in their hands in the future, ought to think for a moment about the kitchen pots, the preparation of breakfast, dinner, and supper by those same three or four individuals who were also responsible for editing, proofreading, and distribution, for washing up, for doing the shopping, fortunately an easy task in France, and should multiply the number of these and similar domestic tasks by the number of days, months, and years. And also think about string, about wrapping paper, about dragging, carrying, handing over the parcels at the post office. Zygmunt's identity crisis was not unrelated to his former self-indulgence; that is, to his unenthusiastic purging of his self-will. Had he had a taste for renunciation, were he an ideological fanatic, he could have entered more easily into the skin of a manager, a cook's assistant, a shipping clerk, and a porter. But his relations with ideas were always less than cordial. Absolutely polite, loyal, he opened up only to people, not to far-reaching intentions which were abstractions for him. Who should he have been, how did his acquaintances, and perhaps he himself, view him? The director of a large, smoothly functioning enterprise, several telephones on his desk, secretaries, conferences, and, at home in his villa, an infinitely generous, genial host, a patron of artists, a collector of *objets d'art*, a benefactor of orphanages and hospitals. Undoubtedly all this was within his grasp, only under the condition that he get started in good time. But in the meantime, year after year slipped away in packing, transporting the packages in a handcart to the Maisons-Laffitte station, loading them into the train, unloading them at the Gare Saint-Lazare, shopping, cooking, etc.

Only if a collective lasts long enough will it appear *ex post* as an idyll, on the strength of its very survival. As a matter of fact, its daily life is full of tensions between individuals, and since Zygmunt was sensitive to individuals, he often suffered greatly. For it is not easy to accept the modest place that somebody has to occupy in a collective, and although it is clear that somebody has to take on the jobs for the physically strongest, this demands no small amount of self-discipline. Zygmunt's struggles with himself, his search for solutions, and finally his acceptance of the identity of an almost anonymous worker—that is the substance of his mature years.

Again I must turn to the distortions introduced by time. If one were to believe the Warsaw press of the 1950s, *Kultura* was a powerful institution that was equipped by the Americans, almost the equivalent of Free Europe, with the same number of personnel (everyone judges by his own situation) as is necessary in Poland to publish a journal and books. Visitors from Poland were astonished to discover that this picture had nothing in common with reality and was one more example of the fabrication of legends in which the creators of those legends themselves eventually begin to believe. But today, when *Kultura* has passed its thirtieth anniversary, the significance if not the image ascribed to *Kultura* at that time no longer looks like an exaggeration. For *Kultura* undoubtedly has exceeded in longevity and in influence everything that the Great Emigration achieved after 1831, and has its chapter in the history of Polish writing, or, quite simply, in the history of Poland. Lo and behold, Zygmunt the bee, buzzing today above otherworldly meadows, is a historical personage. Only, when he made his choice, he did not know he would become one. The whole undertaking could have fallen to pieces and vanished without a trace, or the uncertain, unpredictable political conditions in Europe could have put an end to such experiments.

Can fat people experience deep emotions? Zygmunt was a combination of delicacy and gluttony, emotional circumspection and hooting laughter. His abdomen continued to grow larger and he came to resemble Zagłoba. Marek Hłasko addressed him as "Uncle." But Zagłoba's mouth probably wasn't shaped like his: very sensual and somehow infantile, prepared to accept a pacifier or a swig of aqua vitae, capricious and nervous. He was born a hedonist and he was governed by the pleasure principle. And he found an abundance of pleasure in this world. Thanks chiefly to him, the necessity of a communal kitchen at *Kultura* turned into delights of the table, into feasts, revelries, because there was no stinting on food at least. Guests—non-stop, from everywhere, from European countries, from Poland, from America—assuaged his passion for company, his enormous curiosity about faces, characters, biographies. The trips to Paris with the packages gave him the opportunity to meet with one person or another over a glass of wine, to talk and gossip and watch the crowd. So it was that by following his natural inclinations Zygmunt discovered his true calling and his talent. And when he discovered it, everything began to fall into a discernible pattern, the individual scattered pieces of the puzzle of predestination now fit together, and what at first had seemed resignation turned out to be the most ambitious of choices.

In brief, Zygmunt was a *philanthropos* by calling, a friend of people, and his ability to do good for people could have found no better application anywhere than in that peculiar zone "between Poland and abroad." Zygmunt lived and breathed Vistulania; he empathized, flew into a fury, rejoiced, felt ashamed because of what was going on over there, treated his involvement with it as an illness, but an incurable one, one that he had stopped struggling against. As was his wont, this constant worry over Poland always took on a concrete form: the level of earnings, prices, labor conditions, personal freedom or lack thereof; that is, the fate of real people whom he knew through their names or through a detailed, though imagined, knowledge of their daily life. An idea would suddenly pop into his head about active participation, about offering assistance. The list of people who owe their fellowships to Zygmunt, their foothold in Paris, their invitations abroad, would be enormous. He thrived on his intrigues, deliberated over his moves, whom to set in motion, whom to target through someone else—just as he tormented me for the longest time until I agreed to go see Jean Cassou, the director at that time of the Muśee d'Art Moderne, with a certain young female artist, who immediately seated herself on the Parisian potentate's desk (and was victorious). How many similar intrigues there were, telephone calls, urgings, reminders! It looked as if Zygmunt had said to himself one day: "Here I am, no greater future awaits me, so let's do as much good as possible." If I have not emphasized his participation in the political formation of *Kultura*'s profile, it is because he was ruled by his sympathy, anger, pity, his wonder at the noble and revulsion at the base—that is to say, in him everything had its beginnings in an ethical reflex. And as he grew ethically, enlarging his personal field of activity, his role as inspirer, intermediary, superb public-relations man in the service of independent thought grew apace, and in this way, it can be said without exaggeration, his presence transformed and humanized the house of *Kultura*.

A skeptic. He responded with disbelief to the possibility of reforming a system guarded by its neighbor's tanks. As for those whom he helped, he had few illusions and noticed the mark of pettiness on them, of habits acquired in the struggle of all against all for mere pennies. He did not doubt, however, that he would have been just like them and, who knows, would probably have done some swinish

things like many of them if he lived there. Zygmunt was always
delighted that he was living in France, but also that he was not
dependent on anyone in that West from which he expected so little.
The house of *Kultura* on the avenue de Poissy, already an institution,
already affluent, with its large library and paintings by Polish artists,
was like an island that had emerged from the swirling seas, between
one cataclysm and the next, and Zygmunt the skeptic would often
express the hope that he would not live to see the next cataclysm.

I weep for Zygmunt for extremely egotistical reasons. Is there
anything one can have on this earth that is better than a few friends
holding each other by the hand, who together create a circuit and
feel the current running through it? For me, after my emigration
from there to America in 1960, Paris was just such a little circle of
friends, but it was Zygmunt above all who held us together, it was
his current we felt most powerfully, and now, as in a dream, our
hands reach toward each other's but cannot connect. So my point
of reference eastward from California has lost its distinctness. One
might also give a different interpretation to the feeling of emptiness
that has suddenly descended on me. For two decades Zygmunt was
my faithful correspondent. He lovingly practiced an art that has been
virtually forgotten today; his letters were charming, brilliant, intelligent, sometimes so amusing that they set off spasms of laughter,
although his macabre Warsaw humor was dominant. And from those
letters I learned not only what was going on among our Paris friends
but also all sorts of Warsaw gossip through which the daily life of
Poland was revealed, because Zygmunt's ambition was to know
everything—and if throughout such a long period of exile I somehow
did not feel that I had ever left Poland, it was thanks to him most
of all.

Very likely, we were linked by being mired in Vistulania, he
through his passion to know, I through language, in ways that were
as complicated in him as in me, *odi et amo*. I never noticed any
snobbery in his eager socializing with artists and writers; he was, if
I may say so, a natural kibitzer and guardian of the arts, which
stemmed from his curiosity about this particular species of animal.
He knew this species and good-naturedly observed the parade of
hunchbacks as, with more or less grace, they toted their variously
shaped humps around, usually tormented with grief that they were
who they were and not somebody else. Zygmunt had an aphorism
for this: every woman of easy virtue dreams about being a nun, every
nun about being a woman of easy virtue; a tragic actor wants to
make people laugh and a comedian wants to play Hamlet. If I com-

plained, he would remind me of this as consolation. In any event, in his opinion I was good-looking for a hunchback, which is to say, he saw certain manifestations of normalcy in me. As a matter of fact, our friendship was consolidated outside literature, as it were. His grumbling about "philosophizing"—in which he included my essays—didn't bother me in the slightest. I have written various things out of inner necessity, but not without an awareness of the merely relative significance of intellectual edifices, so that Zygmunt's voice, the voice of the average reader, no doubt alerted me to something there.

"Czesiu, write for people!" But what did Zygmunt mean by writing "for people"? He thought *The Issa Valley* was my best book. Many of his letters exhorted me: "When are you going to write about the Dukhobors?" Once, when I came to Maisons-Laffitte from America, as we sat around the table I talked about a Dukhobor ceremony that I had seen with my own eyes in the woods of British Columbia, and Zygmunt's love of comically unbelievable sights found this almost too satisfying. Instead of accommodating myself to Zygmunt's request, I again wrote some "philosophizing," *The Land of Ulro*, only to hear again, "Why don't you write for people?" This was already the summer of 1979, after Zygmunt's operation, when he was growing weaker by the day. I didn't cite my poetry (perhaps too difficult?) in my defense, but asked him: "What about my translation of the Psalms? Isn't that for people?" He thought for a moment. "Yes," he said, "that is for people."

What good are our triumphs and defeats if there is no one for them to warm or chill? Zygmunt was upset when things went badly for his friends and rejoiced when they went well. One of his last letters is exultant because Czapski's paintings had finally "caught on" in the market, and in his old age he had begun to sell a lot of pictures. And now I can't help thinking that Zygmunt, who witnessed my triumphs and my miseries, was the first person I wanted to please with a report of some piece of good luck, as if I owed him this for worrying about me when I was down. Living as we do in a fluid, hurried civilization, in which titles, names, fames change with great rapidity, we learn to value personal ties, and when someone like Zygmunt passes away, it is immediately apparent that nothing counts if we have no one in whose presence we can weep or boast.

Zygmunt was never ill, and having made it to seventy in good health, he considered that an achievement in itself. I have to mention here a fairly recent dinner party at Jeleński's, at which Zygmunt, in contrast to the rest of the company who were drinking wine, drained a bottle of vodka all by himself. I took him to the Gare Saint-Lazare by taxi and he started up the steps, unsteady but in control. The next day I asked him why he'd done that. "To test. If I can." At the same time, however, he was stoically pondering the briefness of time and grieving, but not for himself. He was also thinking about what would happen to his collection of abominations for, incorrigible scoffer and perverse tease that he was, he had amassed a large collection of decorations for distinguished service, from various epochs, like the tsarist medal *"Za usmirenie polskogo miatezha"* ["For pacification of the Polish rebellion"]. What Polish museum would be pleased by such a bequest?

He was balancing his accounts, then, when there was still no hint of illness. So I was not surprised by his letter from the hospital after he learned that he had a tumor and was awaiting surgery. I have no intention of exploiting his correspondence; it is private. I will only permit myself to quote from this particular hospital letter, dated July 22, 1979.

Affairs in our fatherland are *non existing.** For the time being, calm. Very little is happening. From the perspective of the operation somehow in the course of a few days everything has assumed the size of dwarfs. Mentally, I feel terrific. I have lived for 71 years, up till 1939 in luxury considering conditions in Poland—before I was 31 years old I had managed to own 3 automobiles, then that *drôle de guerre*, what can I say, you know those times that have continued to this day.

True: from 1939, the kolkhoz. At my uncle's in Stanisławów, in the Mari Autonomous Soviet Socialist Republic, in the army, then *Kultura* for the last 32 years. I have met hundreds of interesting people, whom I would never have known even had I been not a bureaucrat but the director of Solvay. I have never done anything truly swinish to anyone, I have been quite useful, I have rendered crucial service to a couple of people, there is a small group of people whom I can count on. So what's the problem? I will not go down in the history of literature as you will. So what? I have no qualifications. You will go down, but so what?

I'm holding up as well as before and I hope that I will remain in good shape until the end. I'm even amazed, because it turns out that I have "character"; that's blatant nonsense, I don't. Most likely in painful situations like this some kind of whalebones materialize to keep a man stiff, or else the whalebones disappear and a man is turned into jelly. I am fortunate that the former eventuality came into play.

Not everything had lost importance for him: "the most essential thing" was his thoughts about his wife. Opposed to all melancholy,

*"Non existing" in English in the original.

he comforted himself immediately: "But then, why should I kick the bucket? After all, it's not inevitable."

And just think, in his hospital bed, as always, he was planning his jolly prankster's tricks: "Should worse come to worst, a bit of mischief. I shall request, not I, but it's already been arranged for here in Paris, that Paweł Hertz will place an obituary notice in *Życie Warszawy* [*Warsaw Life*] and order a Mass at St. Martin's. I won't learn who 'was sick,' 'was out of town,' 'had business obligations.' It will be a riot."

There is something terribly upsetting in writing about dead friends: one subject used to associate with another subject, and although his understanding of the secret of the other's personality was incomplete, and frequently replaced by an "objectifying" glance, still, it was an exchange, every judgment remained open to correction. But then all of a sudden: an object. And the embarrassing incompleteness of a description of an individual human being from the outside, the usurpation of divine vision, or, quite simply, a totalitarian intervention as this unique being is subsumed under "the universal," "the typical." That's where the falsity of literature lies, literature that supposedly depicts man "from the center" but actually constructs him so that a whole will be pieced together, subject to the law of form. There is nothing to hide. I have Zygmunt's portrait in front of me instead of Zygmunt, and I am piecing together details that are supposed to represent him, leaving room for only an insignificant number of contradictory details. A rare thing: to live one's life as a good and honorable man. Because I understand that this is a rarity, the demands of construction guide my pen. But the most important thing for me is what remains of Zygmunt's subjectivity, of his appetite, the greed with which he would toss back a glass of whiskey, his jokes, intrigues, pranks: all the motion, the incompleteness, the change through which, imperceptibly for him and for others, his destiny was being fulfilled—for who among us ever expected that from a distance Zygmunt would begin to look like a statue?

1980

FATHER JÓZEF SADZIK

Once again I must write an obituary. I shall at least try to give as much information as possible and in this way avoid a certain ritualistic quality that frequently intrudes into this form. Everything will unfold, of course, around a few dates, beginning with the final one.

Father Józef Sadzik, the director of the publishing house of the Pallotini Fathers in Paris, Les Editions du Dialogue, died suddenly on August 26, 1980, at the age of forty-seven, on the twenty-eighth anniversary of his vows in the Association of the Catholic Apostolate (the Pallotini). On that very day, in the morning according to Paris time, I placed a telephone call to him from California, disturbed by his silence since our farewell at Charles de Gaulle Airport on July 18. He told me that he had extended his vacation in Switzerland, where he had not touched a pen, that a letter was en route, that he felt marvelous and was getting ready to leave for work. Asked if he had the new German medicine for his arrhythmia, he said yes. After that we discussed our printing and publishing plans. As a matter of fact, he was intending to go to Osny, to the Pallotini Fathers' printing plant, to deliver the proofs of *The Book of Job* in my translation and with his foreword. He died a couple of hours later, in Osny. His letter dated August 20 arrived just as I received the telephoned news about this; it was cheerful, praising the Swiss countryside: "Alas, no one wants to hire me anymore as a professional shepherd. I'm too old."

For a long time I scarcely knew Sadzik, and what I knew was mainly hearsay, because the couple of meetings we'd had in the sixties were just social occasions. This would undoubtedly not have been the case had I continued to live in Montgeron instead of moving to California. Since I wasn't there I missed the initial phase of the Pallotini Fathers' house on rue Surcouf, which, thanks to Józef Sadzik, gradually was transformed into what it is now—and long may it endure: an institution of Polish Paris, theoretically impossible but brought into being, primarily by lectures and authors' evenings in the chapel, which is transformed into an auditorium on these occasions. So I was not a witness to the initiatives of this host, who commissioned artists: an apocalyptic stained-glass window by Jan Lebenstein covers an entire wall of the chapel, made of glass; on the front wall hangs a sculpture by Alina Szapocznikow, the face of Christ. I also know very little about the beginnings of the weekly evenings that ignored the division into people from Poland and the émigrés, as concerns both the lecturers and the public. I discovered that public—overwhelmingly young, composed of students from Poland—with joy and amazement when I read my poems before it during the 1970s. Our collaboration and friendship dates from those years, a collaboration that grew closer and closer, a friendship that grew more and more intense, leading to confidences such as we rarely share in life, so that for me the sudden disappearance of this man is the painful interruption in mid-word of a lengthy conversation that had only just begun.

I take the facts about his life from that period, the hours spent together over revisions of my translations from the Bible and, in our breaks, conversation about many things. Józef Sadzik was born in Cracow. He served his novitiate with the Pallotini in Wadowice. He studied theology in Cracow and then was sent to Switzerland to attend the university in Freiburg, where he wrote his doctoral dissertation on Heidegger, which was published soon afterward in Paris: *Esthétique de Martin Heidegger* (Paris: Editions Universitaires, 1963). My copy bears an inscription dated Christmas of that year: "With thoughts of a great friendship"—which came to pass, but only in the following decade. After his studies he was assigned to organize a center for the Pallotini Fathers in Paris. Here begins one of his inner conflicts, and his incredibly intense presence may, perhaps, be explained by the fact that his life was a constant struggle, a constant wrestling with himself. He became an organizer against his will. Cost estimates, purchases, contracts, correspondence were not for him, as they are for many people, an outlet for his energies, but a burden. His superiors had made a good choice, for the house on rue Surcouf flourished beyond all expectation, but this was achieved at no small cost for Sadzik. He accepted his superiors' orders, did what he had to do the best he knew how; nonetheless, looking back at those years when he had set everything into motion, he discovered that they had devoure⅃ and depleted him. I myself could appreciate, through experience, his accuracy, diligence, rare gift for attentiveness, but these qualities increased the daily number of hours of labor, and who knows if that overload of duties didn't contribute to his heart ailment. He dreamt of time for himself and felt that he was smothering his philosophical calling. Editions du Dialogue, despite its French name, serves the Polish word, publishing liturgical texts, encyclicals, and papal pronouncements as well as books about religion, mainly translated from other languages. Sadzik had a philosophical mind, which is not at all the same as having a knowledge of philosophy, and it is not common among people who make their university careers in that field. This attribute had a positive influence on the quality of the books that he published, but it did not mesh very well with his role as editor; hence his quiet rebellions against this yoke.

For us, his friends, Sadzik was a rather exotic type of priest, before we grew accustomed to accepting him as he was, without transforming him to accord with a lay model. Obviously, the figure of the priest, the Polish priest as well, has been changing throughout history. Once upon a time, in the eighteenth century, he was an elegant *labuś* [*l'abbé*] who read Voltaire. At the beginning of the following century, too, as we learn from *Forefathers' Eve*, more than one Greek-Catholic priest kept "brigands' books" in his dwelling. In later years, the identification of Catholicism with Polishness pushed the clergy farther and farther away from worldly innovations that were hostile to religion. During my youth the separation of the Church, if not from the state then from intellectual circles, was an accomplished and almost political fact, if one excludes the small Laski circle and the journal *Verbum*. It would never have entered my mind, nor the minds of my colleagues at that time, that one could become friendly with a man in a cassock as if he were just one of us. Quite simply, it was a different social class, and also a different camp, for which few literati, artists, or intellectuals felt any sympathy, and which benefited from the prestige of the political right. The enormous transformation that took place during the postwar decades received what was probably its first definition in Adam Michnik's book *The Church—the Left—a Dialogue*. But political realignments are only one aspect of this transformation. The change in the social status of the clergy is certainly more important.

There have always been and there still are clergy devoted to the sciences or the arts who maintain a strict separation between these occupations and their priestly function. This sort of balancing act on two parallel lines has an old tradition. Since Józef Sadzik would appear at our Paris dinner parties as "one of us," and his otherness could not be sensed at all, people might have the impression that this was more or less how he resolved the problem—as a polarization.

That impression was erroneous, however. Just because, following the new custom, he did not wear a cassock, that does not mean that he wanted to resemble everyone in everything and submit to the world. During the period of great changes following the Vatican Council he was searching for a formula for associating with lay people and finding it was not at all easy. Sadzik never tried to appear to be someone else. Superbly natural, he also had no need of defensive behaviors, such as when someone speaks ironically about his own position or profession. However, he did conceal his shyness, which was not so much a personal characteristic as a consequence of his understanding the distance, still not completely overcome, between a cleric and "society."

This shyness was definitely not my invention. I related to him not only as to a friend, someone whose weaknesses are known and forgiven. My response to him included another nuance: reverence, bowing to authority, because what he said and did was absolutely honorable, because of the innate integrity of his nature. In other words, it would be no exaggeration to say that I idolized him. Thus, I was almost horrified, but amused, too, when he confessed that there was a time when he was afraid of me. "How is it possible?" I asked. "Were you thinking, Here's an ignorant priest but that's somebody from the intellectual or literary clan? Is that it?" He didn't contradict me. Here, perhaps, I put my finger on the secret of our harmonious collaboration. I had been growing more and more skeptical in my attitude toward literature, and of all the possible theories of creation I believed only one, the most banal, but one that was proven to be true: inspiration. It assigns the creator the role of a medium, of an instrument, and it is difficult to understand why a pencil, a brush, or a hammer, or, to put it more sublimely, a lyre should demand homage. And there are higher and lower inspirations. Not having very much respect for inspirations born of the twentieth century, and wishing to be useful, I had turned to translating biblical texts. Perhaps it is better when someone is able to feel at home in literature and locates his scale of values in it. For me, however, human greatness has little in common with the writer's craft. I was susceptible to Józef's approval (who isn't susceptible to approval?), but I would push it aside somewhat, so that I could believe that he liked me as a man, not as a servant of the Muses. For him, in turn, I was the person who was pulling him toward self-realization. Sadzik did not in the least resemble those authors who fill their drawers with manuscripts and silently dream of fame. The thought that he would not leave a trace of himself in anything and would disappear without a trace was painful for him, but he wrote only when forced to by suggestions and requests or, what worked most effectively, the need of the publishing house. My requests forced on him the introduction to *The Land of Ulro*, while a series of translations from the Bible, starting with *The Book of Psalms*, begun on his initiative and commissioned by him, imposed the writing of introductions as part of his publishing obligations: the best means for shyness in search of subterfuges. That summer we also taped a couple of conversations as an experiment and came to the conclusion that we ought to think about recording a larger number, which would turn into a book. In our final telephone conversation he returned to that enthusiastically and I learned that he had been giving a great deal of thought to the project.

What could people who barely knew him guess from his physical appearance? He was one of those dark-haired, dark-eyed types that are quite common, especially in southern Poland, not tall and thin, but rather sturdy and of medium height, short-tempered; thus, hot-blooded with a dash of melancholy. An attentive observer had to notice the alternating currents that would pass across his face, the inner tension, perhaps some long-standing anguish. Sadzik was uncommunicative and did not like to draw other people's attention to himself, so only a few people knew how much he suffered. I don't know all the causes of his susceptibility to recurrent bouts of depression and even despair, which were not easy for him to overcome. One cause was a lack of time "for himself," but I think the main one, which encompassed all the others, was the contradiction between his fervently accepted calling and his recalcitrant energies. The military discipline demanded by the Church comes effortlessly to some people; others struggle with it constantly. At the same time, Sadzik could not imagine himself apart from his priestly state and did not seek any compromise solutions: "I am devoted to the priesthood like a dog," he wrote in one of his letters. He bore his cross, but that is also why he placed suffering at the very center of Christian thought. His introduction to *The Book of Job* also addresses this.

I am writing this most of all for those who never met him and now never will, so I shall add a few details about his daily life to make it easier to picture him. The house of the Pallotini Fathers on rue Surcouf is a monastic community, small in numbers and oriented toward active participation in the world, so that each of its members has another assigned function. The center administers its estate in Osny northwest of Paris, which includes a print shop and a French-language high school; it publishes *Nasza Rodzina* [*Our Family*], a

268 · · · BEGINNING WITH MY STREETS

journal for Polish émigrés; it runs a publishing house, as I've said;
it organizes lectures and authors' evenings. There are two chapels
in the building, offices, private apartments, and a dining hall where
the monks gather three times a day. But not only the monks: guests
come from Poland, so that there is almost always someone from the
Pallotini in Poland or some lay persons, mainly professors or students. The hospitality of the house and its contacts, especially with
the Catholic University of Lublin (KUL), turn Surcouf into a virtual
mountain hostel during the summer, and people run into each other
there, too, just as in hostels; when I sat down to dinner a couple of
years ago, it was as if I had returned to the Mensa in Wilno's Stefan
Batory University, for my former classmates were seated beside me:
Irena Sławińska, professor of literature at KUL, and Leokadia Mał-
únowicz, professor of classical philology, also at KUL, now no longer
among the living. That was the place where Józef Sadzik spent entire
days, rising early and, especially in his last years, because of his heart
disease, trying not to sit up late into the night. Lest someone should
picture the publishing firm of Editions du Dialogue on the model of
huge enterprises, which would reduce the credibility of what I said
about his overload of duties, I should add that for a long time it was
a one-man firm. I don't pretend to a chronicler's knowledge of how
functions were divvied up in the commune on rue Surcouf. The last
years brought changes for the better, because Sadzik received help
in the person of the efficient Danuta Szumska, a graduate (could it
be otherwise?) of the Department of Classical Philology at KUL.

No matter what one's inner loneliness is like, it is good to have a
family. Sadzik found it in the community of the Pallotini Fathers;
he was loved, and people cared for him. And there were also us,
that is, a group of friends among whom he filled the role of confidant
and hospitaler, while Zygmunt Hertz, whom Sadzik bade farewell
last autumn in the cemetery in Mesnil-le-Roi, fulfilled the honorable
function of Master of Revels. Seasoned by his hidden suffering, Sadzik was open to the troubles of others, and—what's there to hide?
—in a circle composed of people of the pen and brush it's not hard
to find serious cases. His active attentiveness and delicacy enabled
him to have a positive effect on more than one occasion. Zygmunt,
who masked his tendency to passionate emotions with his apparent
coarseness, and who loved Sadzik dearly, enjoyed scheming with
him about how to cure someone's misery. He would telephone his
friend every morning and pour out his harvest of news, gossip, and
anecdotes from the past twenty-four hours, and they would meet a
welcoming ear, because the listener was gifted with a sense of humor.

After his first heart attack, Sadzik became the object of Zygmunt's concern. Zygmunt would rail against him for his lack of attentiveness to his health, for his excessive industriousness, his idiotic diligence, which made him even drag heavy suitcases by himself. Until finally, genuinely apprehensive, he started using as his ultimate argument the teaching of Christian ethics that forbids suicide: "Should *I* have to teach this to you, Father?" It is possible that had Zygmunt lived he would have forbidden Sadzik to vacation in Switzerland, recalling the lamentable results of his previous stay there and the deleterious effect of changes in air pressure.

His friendships and acquaintances with lay people contributed to the success of the Paris center of the Pallotini Fathers, but Józef hadn't planned them ahead of time; they happened of themselves. I used to joke that he hadn't even noticed that he'd solved the problem of the modern, non-territorial parish and that he had his own parish, tiny but by no means of the worst quality. True, it was composed of people who held a wide variety of positions on religion, including declared atheists; our pastor, however, himself a man of strong faith, was not a fisher of souls and did not act like a missionary. I thought about his silences a lot. After all, life in a monastic community since boyhood, among all sorts of people (for the criteria for selection cannot have been only intellectual), must have subjected his refinement to considerable trials, and perhaps it was then that he learned to be silent. His silences were not only a form of tolerance, which avoids sermonizing out of respect for differing opinions. They simply rendered unimportant, transferred into another dimension much that might have been a source of differences and altercations. Along with the division into the chosen and the rejected, the pure and the sinful. For him, the secret of salvation was the truth of pain: how much someone had suffered.

Born in 1932, he belonged to the generation that came of age in the new Poland, and a pessimist expatiating on universal brutalization would find the contradiction of his thesis in him. Associating with Sadzik, one was inclined to believe that Polish popular culture is characterized by a particular aristocratic quality that is suppressed by circumstances but surfaces every now and then, perhaps even by a certain aristocratic humanism which is a significantly stronger force at present than it was in the past, when the owners of crests and titles claimed the right to preserve it. And every so often, from the subsoil of the people, from Cracow in Sadzik's case, great personalities sprout.

Writing about a dead friend brings relief. By focusing my attention on his person I can feel his presence intensely. I hope, however, that when I lay down my pen he will continue to keep me company. We will not put together a book of philosophical conversations, but I promise him that I will continue to work on the translations from the Bible that were so dear to his heart.

Berkeley, 1980

Part 5

THE
NOBEL
LECTURE

THE NOBEL LECTURE

I

My presence here, on this tribune, should be an argument for all those who praise life's God-given, marvelously complex unpredictability. In my school years I used to read volumes of a series then published in Poland—"The Library of the Nobel Laureates." I remember the shape of the letters and the color of the paper. I imagined then that Nobel laureates were writers, namely persons who write thick works in prose, and even when I learned that there were also poets among them, for a long time I could not get rid of that notion. And certainly, when, in 1930, I published my first poems in our university review, *Alma Mater Vilnensis*, I did not aspire to the title of writer. Also, much later, by choosing solitude and giving myself to a strange occupation—that is, to writing poems in Polish, while living in France or America—I tried to maintain a certain ideal image of a poet who, if he wants fame, wants to be famous only in the village or the town of his birth.

One of the Nobel laureates whom I read in childhood influenced to a large extent, I believe, my notions of poetry. That was Selma Lagerlöf. Her *Wonderful Adventures of Nils*, a book I loved, places the hero in a double role. He is the one who flies above the earth and looks at it *from above* but at the same time sees it in every detail. This double vision may be a metaphor of the poet's vocation. I found a similar metaphor in a Latin ode of a seventeenth-century poet, Maciej Sarbiewski, who was once known all over Europe under the pen name of Casimire. He taught poetics at my university. In that ode he describes his voyage—on the back of Pegasus—from Wilno to Antwerp, where he is going to visit his poet friends. Like Nils Holgersson, he beholds under him rivers, lakes, forests; that is, a map, both distant and yet concrete. Hence, two attributes of the poet: avidity of the eye and the desire to describe that which he sees.

Yet whoever considers writing poetry as "to see and describe" should be aware that he engages in a quarrel with modernity, fascinated as it is with innumerable theories of a specific poetic language.

Every poet depends upon generations who wrote in his native tongue; he inherits styles and forms elaborated by those who lived before him. At the same time, though, he feels that those old means of expression are not adequate to his own experience. When adapting himself, he hears an internal voice that warns him against mask and disguise. But when rebelling, he falls in turn into dependence on his contemporaries, various movements of the avant-garde. Alas, it is enough for him to publish his first volume of poems to find himself entrapped. For hardly has the print dried when that work, which seemed to him the most personal, appears to be enmeshed in the style of another. The only way to counter an obscure remorse is to continue searching and to publish a new book, but then everything repeats itself, so there is no end to that chase. And it may happen that leaving behind books as if they were dry snake skins, in a constant escape forward from what has been done in the past, he receives the Nobel Prize.

What is this enigmatic impulse that does not allow one to settle down in the achieved, the finished? I think it is a quest for reality. I give to this word its naïve and solemn meaning, a meaning having nothing to do with philosophical debates of the last few centuries. It is the Earth as seen by Nils from the back of the gander and by the author of the Latin ode from the back of Pegasus. Undoubtedly, that Earth *is* and her riches cannot be exhausted by any description. To make such an assertion means to reject in advance a question we often hear today: "What is reality?," for it is the same as the question of Pontius Pilate: "What is truth?" If among pairs of opposites which we use every day the opposition of life and death has such an importance, no less importance should be ascribed to the oppositions of truth and falsehood, of reality and illusion.

2

Simone Weil, to whose writings I am profoundly indebted, says: "Distance is the soul of beauty." Yet sometimes keeping distance is nearly impossible. I am "a child of Europe," as the title of one of my poems admits, but that is a bitter, sarcastic admission. I am also the author of an autobiographical book which in the French translation bears the title *Une autre Europe*. Undoubtedly, there exist two Europes, and it happens that we, inhabitants of the second one, were destined to descend into the "heart of darkness" of the twentieth century. I wouldn't know how to speak about poetry in general. I must speak of poetry in its encounter with peculiar circumstances of time and place. Today, from a perspective, we are able to distinguish outlines of the events which by their death-bearing range surpassed all natural disasters known to us, but poetry, mine and my contemporaries', whether of inherited or avant-garde style, was not prepared to cope with those catastrophes. Like blind men we groped our way and were exposed to all the temptations the mind deluded itself with in our time.

It is not easy to distinguish reality from illusion, especially when one lives in a period of the great upheaval that began a couple of centuries ago on a small western peninsula of the Euro-Asiatic continent, only to encompass the whole planet during one man's lifetime with the uniform worship of science and technology. And it was particularly difficult to oppose multiple intellectual temptations in those areas of Europe where degenerate ideas of dominion over men, akin to the ideas of dominion over Nature, led to paroxysms of revolution and war at the expense of millions of human beings destroyed physically or spiritually. And yet perhaps our most precious acquisition is not an understanding of those ideas, which we touched in their most tangible shape, but respect and gratitude for certain things which protect people from internal disintegration and from yielding to tyranny.

Precisely for that reason, some ways of life, some institutions became a target for the fury of evil forces—above all, the bonds between people that exist organically, as if by themselves, sustained by family, religion, neighborhood, common heritage. In other words, all that disorderly, illogical humanity, so often branded as ridiculous because of its parochial attachments and loyalties. In many countries, traditional bonds of *civitas* have been subject to a gradual erosion, and their inhabitants become disinherited without realizing it. It is not the same, however, in those areas where suddenly, in a situation of utter peril, a protective, life-giving value of such bonds reveals itself. That is the case of my native land. And I feel this is a proper place to mention gifts received by myself and by my friends in our part of Europe and to pronounce words of blessing.

· · ·

It is good to be born in a small country where nature was on a human scale, where various languages and religions cohabited for centuries. I have in mind Lithuania, a country of myths and of poetry. My family in the sixteenth century already spoke Polish, just as many families in Finland spoke Swedish and in Ireland English; so I am a Polish, not a Lithuanian, poet. But the landscapes and perhaps the spirits of Lithuania have never abandoned me. It is good in childhood to hear words of Latin liturgy, to translate Ovid in high school, to receive a good training in Roman Catholic dogmatics and apologetics. It is a blessing if one receives from fate school and university studies in such a city as Wilno. A bizarre city of Baroque architecture transplanted to northern forests and of history fixed in every stone, a city of forty Roman Catholic churches and of numerous synagogues. In those days the Jews called it a Jerusalem of the North. Only when teaching in America did I fully realize how much I had absorbed from the thick walls of our ancient university, from formulas of Roman law learned by heart, from the history and literature of old Poland, both of which surprise young Americans by their specific features: an indulgent anarchy, a humor disarming fierce quarrels, a sense of organic community, a mistrust of any centralized authority.

A poet who grew up in such a world should have been a seeker for reality through contemplation. A patriarchal order should have been dear to him, a sound of bells, an isolation from pressures and the persistent demands of his fellow men, the silence of a cloister cell. If books were to linger on a table, then they should be those which deal with the most incomprehensible quality of God-created things; namely, being, the *esse*. But suddenly all this is negated by the demoniac doings of history, which acquires the traits of a bloodthirsty deity.

The Earth, which the poet viewed in his flight, calls with a cry, indeed, out of the abyss and doesn't allow itself to be viewed *from above*. An insoluble contradiction appears, a terribly real one, giving no peace of mind either day or night, whatever we call it: it is the contradiction between being and action, or, on another level, a contradiction between art and solidarity with one's fellow men. Reality calls for a name, for words, but it is unbearable, and if it is touched, if it draws very close, the poet's mouth cannot even utter a complaint of Job: all art proves to be nothing compared with action. Yet to embrace reality in such a manner that it is preserved in all its old tangle of good and evil, of despair and hope, is possible only thanks to a distance, only by soaring *above* it—but this in turn seems then a moral treason.

Such was the contradiction at the very core of conflicts engendered by the twentieth century and discovered by poets of an earth polluted by the crime of genocide. What are the thoughts of one of them, who wrote a certain number of poems that remain as a memorial, as a testimony? He thinks that they were born out of a painful contradiction and that he would prefer to have been able to resolve it while leaving them unwritten.

3

A patron saint of all poets in exile, who visit their towns and provinces only in remembrance, is always Dante. But how the number of Florences increased! The exile of a poet is today a simple function of a relatively recent discovery: that whoever wields power is also able to control language and not only with the prohibitions of censorship but also by changing the meaning of words. A peculiar phenomenon makes its appearance: the language of a captive community acquires certain durable habits; whole zones of reality cease to exist simply because they have no name. There is, it seems, a hidden link between theories of literature as *écriture*, of speech feeding on itself, and the growth of the totalitarian state. In any case, there is no reason why the state should not tolerate an activity that consists of creating "experimental" poems and prose, if these are conceived as autonomous systems of reference, enclosed within their own boundaries. Only if we assume that a poet constantly strives to liberate himself from borrowed styles in search of reality is he dangerous. In a room where people unanimously maintain a conspiracy of silence, one word of truth sounds like a pistol shot. And, alas, a temptation to pronounce it, similar to an acute itching, becomes an obsession which doesn't allow one to think of anything else. That is why a poet chooses internal or external exile. It is not certain, however, that he is motivated exclusively by his concern with actuality. He may also desire to free himself from it and elsewhere, in other countries, on other shores, to recover, at least for short moments, his true vocation—which is to contemplate Being.

That hope is illusory, for those who come from the "other Europe," wherever they find themselves, notice to what extent their experiences isolate them from their new milieu—and this may become the source of a new obsession. Our planet, which gets smaller every year, with its fantastic proliferation of mass media, is witnessing a process that escapes definition, characterized by a refusal to remember. Certainly, the illiterates of past centuries, then an enormous majority of mankind, knew little of the history of their respective countries and of their civilization. In the minds of modern illiterates, however, who know how to read and write and even teach in schools and at universities, history is present but blurred, in a state of strange confusion. Molière becomes a contemporary of Napoleon, Voltaire a contemporary of Lenin.

Moreover, events of the last decades, of such primary importance that knowledge or ignorance of them will be decisive for the future of mankind, move away, grow pale, lose all consistency, as if Friedrich Nietzsche's prediction of European nihilism found a literal fulfillment. "The eye of a nihilist," he wrote in 1887, "is unfaithful to his memories: it allows them to drop, to lose their leaves . . . And what he does not do for himself, he also does not do for the whole past of mankind: he lets it drop."

We are surrounded today by fictions about the past, contrary to common sense and to an elementary perception of good and evil. As the *Los Angeles Times* recently stated, the number of books in various languages which deny that the Holocaust ever took place, and claim that it was invented by Jewish propaganda, has exceeded one hundred. If such an insanity is possible, is a complete loss of memory as a permanent state of mind improbable? And would it not present a danger more grave than genetic engineering or poisoning of the natural environment?

For the poet of the "other Europe," the events embraced by the name Holocaust are a reality, so close in time that he cannot hope to liberate himself from their remembrance unless perhaps by translating the Psalms of David. He feels anxiety, though, when the meaning of the word Holocaust undergoes gradual modifications, so that the word begins to belong to the history of the Jews exclusively, as if among the victims there were not also millions of Poles, Russians, Ukrainians, and prisoners of other nationalities. He feels anxiety, for he senses in this a foreboding of a not distant future when history will be reduced to what appears on television, while the truth, because it is too complicated, will be buried in the archives, if not totally annihilated. Other facts as well, facts for him quite close but distant for the West, add in his mind to the credibility of H. G. Wells's vision in *The Time Machine*: the earth inhabited by a tribe of children of the day, carefree, deprived of memory and, by the same token, of history, without defense when confronted with dwellers of subterranean caves, cannibalistic children of the night.

Carried forward as we are by the movement of technological change, we realize that the unification of our planet is in the making, and we attach importance to the notion of international community. The days when the League of Nations and the United Nations were founded deserve to be remembered. Unfortunately, those dates lose their significance in comparison with another date, which should be invoked every year as a day of mourning, although it is hardly known to younger generations. It is August 23, 1939. Two dictators then concluded an agreement provided with a secret clause by virtue of which they divided between themselves neighboring countries that possessed their own capitals, governments, and parliaments. That pact not only unleashed a terrible war; it reestablished a colonial principle according to which nations are no more than cattle, bought, sold, completely dependent upon the will of their instant masters. Their borders, their right to self-determination, their passports ceased to exist. And it should be a source of wonder that today people speak in a whisper, with a finger to their lips, about how that principle was applied by the dictators forty years ago.

Crimes against human rights, never confessed and never publicly denounced, are a poison which destroys the possibility of a friendship between nations. Anthologies of Polish poetry publish poems of my late friends Władysław Sebyla and Lech Piwowar, and give the date of their deaths: 1940. It is absurd not to be able to write how they perished, though everybody in Poland knows the truth: they shared the fate of several thousand Polish officers disarmed and interned by the then accomplice of Hitler, and they repose in a mass grave. And should not the young generations of the West, if they study History at all, hear about 200,000 people killed in 1944 in Warsaw, a city sentenced to annihilation by those two accomplices?

The two genocidal dictators are no more, and yet who knows whether they did not gain a victory more durable than those of their armies? In spite of the Atlantic Charter, the principle that nations are objects of trade, if not chips in games of cards or dice, has been confirmed by the division of Europe into two zones. The absence of the three Baltic states from the United Nations is a permanent reminder of the two dictators' legacy. Before the war, those states belonged to the League of Nations, but they disappeared from the map of Europe as a result of the secret clauses in the agreement of 1939.

I hope you will forgive my laying bare a memory like a wound. This subject is not unconnected with my meditation on the word *reality*, so often misused but always deserving esteem. Complaints of peoples, pacts more treacherous than those we read about in Thucydides, the shape of a maple leaf, sunrises and sunsets over the ocean, the whole fabric of causes and effects, whether we call it Nature or History, points toward, I believe, another, hidden reality, impenetrable, though exerting a powerful attraction that is the central driving force of all art and science. There are moments when it seems to me that I decipher the meaning of afflictions which befell the nations of the "other Europe," and that meaning is to make them the bearers of memory—at the time when Europe, without an adjective, and America possess it less and less with every generation.

It is possible that there is no other memory than the memory of wounds. At least we are so taught by the Bible, a book of the tribulations of Israel. That book for a long time enabled European nations to preserve a sense of continuity—a word not to be mistaken for the fashionable term *historicity*.

During the thirty years I have spent abroad, I have felt I was more privileged than my Western colleagues, whether writers or teachers of literature, for events both recent and long past took in my mind a sharply delineated, precise form. Western audiences confronted with poems or novels written in Poland, Czechoslovakia, or Hungary, or with films produced there, possibly intuit a similarly sharpened consciousness, in a constant struggle against limitations imposed by censorship. Memory thus is our force; it protects us against a speech entwining upon itself like the ivy when it does not find a support on a tree or a wall.

A few minutes ago I expressed my longing for the end of a contradiction which opposes the poet's need of distance to his feeling of solidarity with his fellow men. And yet, if we take a flight *above* the earth as a metaphor of the poet's vocation, it is not difficult to notice that a kind of contradiction is implied, even in those epochs when the poet is relatively free from the snares of history. For how to be *above* and simultaneously to see the earth in every detail? And yet, in a precarious balance of opposites, a certain equilibrium can be achieved thanks to a distance introduced by the flow of time. "To see" means not only to have before one's eyes. It may mean also to preserve in memory. "To see and to describe" may also mean to reconstruct in imagination. A distance achieved thanks to the mystery of time must not change events, landscapes, human figures into a tangle of shadows growing paler and paler. On the contrary, it can show them in full light, so that every event, every date becomes expressive and persists as an eternal reminder of human depravity and human greatness. Those who are alive receive a mandate from those who are silent forever. They can fulfill their duties only by trying to reconstruct precisely things as they were and by wresting the past from fictions and legends.

Thus, both—the earth seen from above in an eternal now and the earth that endures in a recovered time—may serve as material for poetry.

4

I would not like to create the impression that my mind is turned toward the past, for that would not be true. Like all my contemporaries, I have felt the pull of despair, of impending doom, and reproached myself for succumbing to a nihilistic temptation. Yet, on a deeper level, I believe, my poetry remained sane and in a dark age expressed a longing for the Kingdom of Peace and Justice. The name of a man who taught me not to despair should be invoked here. We receive gifts not only from our native land, its lakes and rivers, its traditions, but also from people, especially if we meet a powerful personality in our early youth. It was my good fortune to be treated nearly as a son by my relative Oscar Milosz, a Parisian recluse and visionary. Why he was a French poet could be elucidated by the intricate story of a family as well as of a country once called the Grand Duchy of Lithuania. Be that as it may, it was possible to read recently in the Parisian press words of regret that the highest international distinction had not been awarded half a century earlier to a poet bearing the same family name as my own.

I learned much from him. He gave me a deeper insight into the religion of the Old and New Testaments and inculcated a need for a strict, ascetic hierarchy in all matters of mind, including everything that pertains to art, where as a major sin he considered putting the second-rate on the same level with the first-rate. Primarily, though, I listened to him as a prophet who loved people, as he says, "with old love worn out by pity, loneliness and anger" and for that reason tried to address a warning to a crazy world rushing toward a catastrophe. That a catastrophe was imminent I heard from him, but also I heard from him that the great conflagration he predicted would be merely a part of a larger drama to be played to the end.

He saw deeper causes in an erroneous direction taken by science in the eighteenth century, a direction which provoked landslide effects. Not unlike William Blake before him, he announced a New Age, a second Renaissance of imagination now polluted by a certain type of scientific knowledge, but, as he believed, not by all scientific knowledge, least of all by the science that would be discovered by men of the future. And it does not matter to what extent I took his predictions literally: a general orientation was enough.

Oscar Milosz, like William Blake, drew inspiration from the writings of Emanuel Swedenborg, a scientist who earlier than anyone else foresaw the defeat of man, hidden in the Newtonian model of the universe. When, thanks to my relative, I became an attentive reader of Swedenborg, interpreting him not, it is true, as was common in the Romantic era, I did not imagine I would visit his country for the first time on such an occasion as the present one.

Our century draws to its close, and largely thanks to those influences, I would not dare to curse it, for it has also been a century of faith and hope. A profound transformation of which we are hardly aware, because we are a part of it, has been taking place, coming to the surface from time to time in phenomena that provoke general astonishment. That transformation has to do, and I use here words of Oscar Milosz, with "the deepest secret of toiling masses, more than ever alive, vibrant and tormented." Their secret, an unavowed need of true values, finds no language to express itself, and here not only the mass media but also intellectuals bear a heavy responsibility.

But transformation has been going on, defying short-term predictions, and it is probable that in spite of all horrors and perils, our time will be judged as a necessary phase of travail before mankind ascends to a new awareness. Then a new hierarchy of merits will emerge, and I am convinced that Simone Weil and Oscar Milosz, writers in whose school I obediently studied, will receive their due. I feel we should publicly confess our attachment to certain names because in that way we define our position more forcefully than by pronouncing the names of those to whom we would like to address a violent no. My hope is that in this lecture, in spite of my meandering thought, which is a professional bad habit of poets, my yes and no are clearly stated, at least as to choice of succession. For we all who are here, both the speaker and you who listen, are no more than links between the past and the future.

[Translated by C.M.]

NOTES

PAGE 7 Zbigniew Pronaszko (1885–1958), painter, sculptor, graphic artist, and, for a time, a member of the art faculty at the University of Wilno.

10 *With Fire and Sword (Ogniem i mieczem*, 1884), a novel by Henryk Sienkiewicz (1846–1916). An immensely popular book, the first of a trilogy of historical novels about the seventeenth-century Polish *Respublica*.

11 The "green border" divided Soviet-occupied Poland from German-occupied Poland.

15 Leon Petrażycki (1867–1931), a famous Polish scholar (philosophy and sociology of law), was a professor at Petersburg University and, after 1917, at Warsaw University. Dr. Lande taught at Stefan Batory University in Wilno, then at Jagiellonian University in Cracow. He was a follower of the "Petrażycki School."

15 *Defense of the West*, trans. F. S. Flint (New York: Harcourt, Brace & Co., 1928).

18 Zygmunt Sierakowski (1827–63): A Polish officer based in St. Petersburg, he was one of the leaders of the 1863 Uprising.

22 *Ashes* [*Popioły*, 1904] by Stefan Żeromski—a huge, neo-Romantic historical novel about the Napoleonic era.

The story was adapted from *Les Chouans*, a novel by Honoré de Balzac.

24 Adam Mickiewicz (1798–1855): Poland's national poet; in *Pan Tadeusz*, *Forefathers' Eve*, and other poems, plays, and treatises, he expressed a vision of Polishness and Polish destiny that remains an integral part of Polish consciousness today.

The Philomaths were a secret student literary club in Wilno in the 1820s; Adam Mickiewicz was a member.

Juliusz Słowacki (1809–49): Romantic poet and playwright whose later mystical works foreshadow the achievements of *fin-de-siècle* Symbolism; he is one of Poland's "Three Bards" of the Romantic era—the others being Zygmunt Krasiński (1812–59) and, *primus inter pares*, Adam Mickiewicz.

Józef Piłsudski (1867–1935): Patriot, socialist, and military commander, with a broad vision of Poland as a multiethnic state. He seized power in 1926 and remained in office until his death.

24   Mickiewicz, Słowacki, and Piłsudski all spent at least their formative years in Wilno and elsewhere in Lithuania.

     Endecja: The National Democratic Party; a right-wing, fervently nationalist political movement of the interwar period.

28   "Lithuania, my fatherland" are the first words of *Pan Tadeusz* by Adam Mickiewicz.

29   Roman Dmowski (1864–1939): One of the founders of the National Democratic Movement. Even before independence, Dmowski opposed Piłsudski's vision of a confederative, multiethnic Poland; his political posture grew increasingly xenophobic during the two interwar decades.

31   Jeronimas Plečkaitis (1887–1963): Lithuanian political activist.

40   Gediminas (c. 1275–1341): Grand Duke of Lithuania; he forged an alliance with Poland in order to fight against the Teutonic Knights.

41   Aušros Vartai [Ostra Brama]: A noted religious shrine in Vilnius.

42   Tadeusz Zieliński (1859–1944): Classical philologist; professor at the Universities of Petersburg and Warsaw; author of a number of books on ancient Greece.

46   Selma Lagerlöf (1858–1940): Swedish novelist, short-story writer, author of a famous children's book, *The Wonderful Adventures of Nils* (1907). She received the Nobel Prize for Literature in 1909.

     Jurgis Baltrušaitis (1873–1944) began his literary career as a Russian Symbolist poet; he started publishing in Lithuanian in his fifties.

48   Stefan Jędrychowski (1910–   ): A Communist with strong Moscow ties, he eventually rose through the Party ranks to become a member of the Central Committee of the Polish Politburo and also held important government posts in the 1960s and 1970s.

50   Dionizas Poška (Dionizy Paszkiewicz) (1757–1830): Lithuanian poet and historian, compiler of an unfinished Lithuanian-Polish-Latin dictionary, and author of a study of the Lithuanian peasantry.

     Simonas Daukantas (Dowkont) (1793–1864): Lithuanian writer, historian, folklorist; one of the founders of the Lithuanian revival.

     Kristijonas Donelaitis (1714–80): Author of an idyllic narrative poem in classical hexameters, *Metai* (*The Seasons*), which is considered one of the greatest achievements of Lithuanian poetry.

52   The Union of Lublin (1569), orchestrated by King Sigismund August, merged the crown lands of Poland with the Grand Duchy of Lithuania into a single body politic—the *Respublica* or Commonwealth, formed in part as a defensive measure against the growing power of Muscovy.

     Jogaila (c. 1350–1434): Grand Duke of Lithuania, who became King of Poland in 1386 and established a union of both countries.

     Janusz Radziwiłł (1612–55): Grand hetman of Lithuania, who took the side of Sweden. Considered a traitor by the Poles.

54   The unforgivable "Żeligowski Episode" was the creation by armed might of a new political entity—Central Lithuania—in October 1920. Lucjan Żeligowski (1865–1947) commanded the Polish forces that occupied Wilno and carried out Piłsudski's secret orders in this matter. "Central Lithuania" was eventually annexed by Poland.

55 Władysław Syrokomla (1823–63): A Lithuanian-born poet who wrote about the life of the petty gentry in the eastern provinces and also about the misery of Belorussian peasant life. Some of his poems were written in peasant dialect.

100 Gustaw: The protagonist of Mickiewicz's multi-part poetic drama, *Dziady* (*Forefathers' Eve*).

108 Marian Zdziechowski: Professor, philosopher, religious writer. Stanisław Ignacy Witkiewicz (Witkacy) (1885–1939): Playwright, novelist, painter, philosopher, one of the most important figures in twentieth-century Polish literature.

110 Jerzy Zagórski (1907–86): Poet, essayist, and literary translator; he was connected with the Żagary group of poets during the 1930s.

172 Locke and Raków: H. J. McLachlan pointed this out in his book, *Socinianism in Seventeenth Century England*.

199 Cyprian Kamil Norwid (1821–83): Neglected during his lifetime, a precursor of modern Polish poetry and a supremely intellectual writer devoted to exploring the philosophy of history through his art.

203 Aleksander Wat (1900–67): Co-founder in his youth of the Polish futurist movement in poetry and author of fantastic tales, he was also an active fellow-traveler, deeply involved in leftist politics. His experiences over many years in prewar Poland and in the Soviet gulag are chronicled in *Mój wiek* [*My Century: The Odyssey of a Polish Intellectual*], the transcript of tape-recorded conversations C.M. held with Wat in the mid-1960s, when Wat was struggling with an incapacitating neurological affliction marked by excruciating chronic pain. Wat returned to poetry in the last decade of his life, making it a vehicle for all the bitter wisdom he had accumulated in his life's journey.

206 "About Fridrusz . . .": An often-anthologized poem by the sixteenth-century poet Mikołaj Sęp-Szarzyński (ca. 1550–81). An English translation of this poem can be found in *Monumenta Polonica: The First Four Centuries of Polish Poetry*, ed. and trans. Bogdana Carpenter (Ann Arbor: Michigan Slavic Publications, 1989), 203–9.

210 "one walks, one lives": The reference is to the impersonal reflexive forms denigrated by Heidegger.

216 King-spirit (*Król-duch*): A reference to the unfinished metaphysical poem of the same name by Juliusz Słowacki (1809–49), which traces the incarnation of the historic Spirit in European (especially Polish) leaders throughout the ages.

Tadeusz Boy-Żeleński (1874–1941): An extraordinarily prolific (and successful) translator and popularizer of French literature, including major works by such different authors as Rabelais, Racine, Balzac, Proust.

219 Soplicowo: The manorial estate that is the setting for Adam Mickiewicz's *Pan Tadeusz* and the model for the sentimental view of the manor house as the locus of the noble culture of the Polish gentry.

228 Stanisław Przybyszewski (1868–1927) issued his manifesto, "Confiteor" (1899), to assert the primacy of Art as "the highest religion," and of the artist as its priest.

241 Alphonse Daudet (1840–97) wrote a series of novels about a small-town braggart who constantly was in search of adventures that would live up to the stories he told. The first of these, *Tartarin de Tarascon*, was published in 1872.

257 Zagłoba: The big-bellied, joke-telling, Falstaffian nobleman in Henryk Sienkiewicz's popular historical *Trilogy* (1884–88).

Marek Hłasko (1934–69): Author of violent short stories and novels expressing the author's profound alienation from society.

260 Józef Czapski (1896–) was trained in Paris in the 1920s. He and his fellow members of the Paris Committee grouping of Polish painters emphasized the use of color in their landscapes and portraits.

264 Jan Lebenstein (1930–): A painter whose early work depicted urban landscapes and who later moved on to fantastic explorations of human and animal figures.

Alina Szapocznikow (1926–73): A sculptor known for her abstract figures based on organic forms.